THE ETERNAL CITY

The

Eternal City

ROMAN IMAGES IN THE MODERN WORLD

BY PETER BONDANELLA

THE UNIVERSITY OF NORTH CAROLINA PRESS

CHAPEL HILL & LONDON

© 1987 The University of North Carolina Press

All rights reserved

Manufactured in the United States of America

Library of Congress Cataloging-in-Publication Data

Bondanella, Peter E., 1943–

   The Eternal City: Roman images in the modern world.

   Bibliography: p.

   Includes index.

   1. Civilization, Occidental—Roman influences.

2. Renaissance—Italy. 3. Italy—Intellectual life.

I. Title.

CB245.B64   1987   909'.09821   86-30847

ISBN 0-8078-1740-6

FOR M. M.

CONTENTS

ILLUSTRATIONS

On 8 October 1354 the citizens of Rome attacked the Capitoline Palace. They pushed past the guards and once inside the building, surrounded the ruler of the city, Cola di Rienzo. Only seven years earlier, this remarkable orator-charlatan, this demagogue whose rhetoric never failed to move his Roman audiences, had been swept to power in a coup d'état aimed, so Cola intended, at the reestablishment of the Roman republic as the capital of the world. Master showman that he was, Cola almost succeeded in eluding the angry mob by a clever disguise, but the splendor of the gold jewelry he wore belied his apparent lowly station. He was stabbed, his mangled body was dragged through the courtyard, hanged from a balcony, and eventually burned.

Six centuries later, another would-be dictator of a renascent Rome was warned by an old Socialist friend that his fate would be similar to Cola's. But Benito Mussolini displayed his short, stubby fingers and laughingly replied that he wore no such gaudy jewelry. And yet in the end, when the Fascist regime he founded collapsed in 1945, his death occurred in much the same horrible fashion.

Cola and Mussolini were both destroyed by a myth—the same myth that has shaped many, more benign, political philosophies. But the myths of ancient Rome, whether called forth in their republican or imperial guises, have shaped more than the outlines of political life for the last six hundred years. These myths have permeated our civilization as a whole, our art, music, drama, cinema, and even our notions of history itself.

The revival of classical antiquity began in Renaissance Italy, where for the first time in modern history, a people chose its own past—that of ancient Rome—as a guide for the future as well as the present. Through the ensuing centuries, in different eras and for different purposes, two diametrically opposed views of Roman antiquity were called forth: the virtuous republic of selfless citizen-soldiers and the corrupted empire of power-hungry and decadent tyrants. The power and sustained influence of these Roman images are second only to the images derived from Christianity in constructing our modern culture. From Petrarch in the fourteenth century to Fellini in the twentieth, by way of Machiavelli, Michelangelo, Titian, Shakespeare, Rembrandt, Mozart, George Washington, Napoleon, Garibaldi, Isaac Asimov, Robert Graves, and George Lucas, the enduring power of the Roman model has served as one of our civilization's greatest sources of inspiration.

To some classically minded viewers, the characters in *Star Wars* may seem familiar—the evil emperor, ruler of the corrupted galactic empire; Darth Vader, the leader of his Praetorian Guard; the Jedi Knights, defenders of moral values from the virtuous republic of old. If such heroes and villains recall a classical model, the resemblance is not coincidental. George Lucas's galactic empires are direct descendants of Isaac Asimov's *Foundation Trilogy*, which is, as Asimov himself admits, based upon Edward Gibbon's *Decline and Fall of the Roman Empire*. From Gibbon's work in the eighteenth century, the line of influence leads ever backward, to the fourteenth-century Renaissance rediscovery of the classical historians, and then backward once again to its origin in Livy, Tacitus, and their Latin contemporaries. The ancient world of the Romans is no mere dead history. It continues to live, as it has done for the past six hundred years, in our everyday, contemporary world.

Peter Bondanella
Florence-Rome-Bologna-Bloomington
1979–86

ACKNOWLEDGMENTS

The initial research for this book was carried out during 1980–81 in Italy with a Senior Fellowship from the National Endowment for the Humanities. Subsequent work was supported in part by the Office of Research and Graduate Development of Indiana University. Without the initial enthusiasm of Willis Barnstone and Nick Bakalar, I should never have tackled such an imposing topic. Any book of the scope of *The Eternal City* necessarily owes a great deal to scholars in a wide variety of fields, and I trust I have accurately reflected their influence upon my own ideas in the footnotes accompanying the text.

Special thanks must go to those friends and colleagues who bravely read the entire manuscript or parts of it at various stages of development during the last six years: Bruce Cole, Evelyn Ehrlich, Heidi Gealt, Harry Geduld, George Kennedy, Maureen Fennell Mazzaoui, Mark Musa, J. E. Rivers, and Denis Mack Smith. I trust they will find that I have taken their many suggestions and objections very seriously.

I must also acknowledge my sincere gratitude to Gino Cincotti of the Centro Sperimentale di Cinematografia (Rome) for assistance in obtaining hard-to-locate prints of a number of films. Numerous museum directors and superintendents of museums or art galleries around the world generously granted me permisson to reprint the photographs employed to illustrate the book.

It would be difficult to imagine a more supportive editor than Lewis Bateman of the University of North Carolina Press. I should also like to express my gratitude to Sandra Eisdorfer, Charles S. Feigenoff, and the staff at the University of North Carolina Press for their superb, professional editorial assistance.

THE ETERNAL CITY

INTRODUCTION

The Eternal City has for centuries fired the Western imagination. Its prestige is unmatched. Not even Greece, Rome's ancient rival for cultural hegemony in Western civilization, can boast such an extended, profound, and intense influence, largely because much of what we have inherited from the Greek or Christian traditions was bequeathed to us through Roman institutions or colored by Roman values. Surprisingly, this fundamental formative influence upon us has not derived primarily from a clear historical understanding of Rome itself. On the contrary, in literature, the arts, and social thought, the most original expressions of the myth of Rome have modified, changed, or even distorted historical fact. The power of this mythology has even at times changed the course of history. And the works of the great classical historians of the Eternal City ultimately furnish much of the mythical materials. It is their most profound expressions of this myth which modify history, and the Western tradition owes far more to this protean and inexhaustible myth of Rome than to sober scholarship, because Roman mythology and history is a vital, living part of our consciousness. The myth is not so much a relic to be venerated as it is a flexible and limitless source for self-expression, a common heritage which has met the needs of successive generations, influenced the styles of different periods, and inspired widely different forms of artistic expression. Something in the myth of Rome has helped us to understand our human condition, our world, and ourselves.

Of necessity, mythic expression, characterized by a willingness to suppress accuracy in order to explain higher truths, abbreviates history, compresses it, shapes it to diverse and sometimes contradictory purposes, and may even willfully distort it, as in the case of Nero's legendary musical performance. The popular expression "to fiddle while Rome burns," obvious evidence of Roman influence upon everyday language, may ultimately be traced back to The Twelve Caesars by Suetonius (A.D. 69–121) and the Annals by Tacitus (ca. A.D. 55–120). The fiddle, of course, had yet to be invented in the first century of the Christian era, and the two historians actually recount that as Nero gazed upon the burning city of Rome, he recited a tragedy, The Fall of Ilium. Suetonius is convinced that this anecdote is true and that Nero set the fire himself; Tacitus states only that the story was a rumor and proceeds to list a number of praiseworthy deeds Nero did on behalf of the victims of the conflagration. Nonetheless, the creation of this idiom and its importance to the mythology of Rome in the English-speaking world demonstrates how easily an episode in a historical narrative may take on a mythical life of its own.

While the myth of Rome has sometimes been shaped by developments in classical archaeology or scholarship, it has in turn affected the assumptions of these sober disciplines. This phenomenon can be traced at least to the dawn of Italian humanism, the fourteenth-century intellectual movement that prepared subsequent generations to welcome and to elaborate the myth of Rome. Both Francesco Petrarca (1304–74), or Petrarch as he is known in the English-speaking world—the most important Latinist of his day—and Flavio Biondo (1392–1463), Petrarch's disciple and a founder of modern archaeology, accepted a sepulchral inscription discovered in Padua between 1318 and 1324 as evidence that Livy (59 B.C.–A.D. 17), the greatest of Latin historians, was buried in that northern Italian city.[1] Yet both experts overlooked the complete inscription on the tomb, which made it clear that the "T. Livius" buried inside had an additional surname (Halys), that he was a freedman, and, therefore, that he could not possibly have been the same Livy who wrote the narrative to which we owe so much of our Roman mythology. Both Petrarch and Biondo committed this error not so much because they were unable to decipher the inscriptions correctly (the situation which had hindered early medieval antiquarians) but because they allowed their minds to be swayed by their hearts. So badly did they wish to believe their beloved Latin author was buried in Padua that they remained blind to whatever ran contrary to their hopes. Upon seeing two of the most able interpreters of Rome led astray by their enthusiasm, we can more easily comprehend how the myth of Rome has evolved.

Much that is accepted as historical fact about Rome in one generation has eventually been revised or even ignored by its successors. Despite six centuries of intensive classical scholarship, however, the myth of Rome has not only survived but prospered because the dialogue between history and the imagination seems destined never to be resolved. The myth of Rome naturally arises from the perspectives of various writers, but it is more supple, more adaptable, and more ambiguous than its complex historical reality. It is more flamboyant, more fascinating, and more attractive to the imagination of a sculptor, painter, poet, or film director. And it is more capable of providing artists and speculative thinkers with morally edifying models and negative exempla. Careful analysis of what we know of Roman history demonstrates conclusively that the Roman experience was dominated by economic, geographical, and political phenomena that rarely received adequate or accurate treatment by the great classical historians. This knowledge, however, would probably never have prevented generations of Europeans or Americans from finding in the myth of Rome a pattern for the noble life. This myth encouraged them to found cities such as Cincinnati in honor of Roman republicanism, erect buildings and monuments in the Roman style, organize institutions along Roman republican or imperial principles, portray themselves in art, literature, music, and film in Roman garb, and comprehend their world by viewing it first through the prism of the Roman past.

Before looking at how the myth of Rome evolved from the early Italian humanists' fascination with the classical historians and poets, artists and scientists whose spirit they had so recently rediscovered and whose achievements excited and motivated them, a brief definition of what I mean by the myth of Rome and an examination of why the myth of Rome enjoyed so momentous an appeal is in order. Mythmaking has characterized the Western mind since antiquity. And myths have always had a radical effect on our perception of ourselves and our understanding of our world. It is possible to dismiss the singularity of the myth or to refer to Rome as a mere pretext that could easily have been replaced by another myth had one been handy.[2] But to declare Rome's influence an accident of fortune belies the perennial preeminence of its image. Were the city but an occasion or pretext, should it have attracted so many and diverse followers, so many imitations and reelaborations that cross historical boundaries, period styles, and artistic media? Why has no other city and its history evoked such excitement? Too many writers, philosophers, and artists of genius unequivocally place Rome in a category by itself. Petrarch once asked, "What is history but the praise of Rome?"[3] It was a rhetorical question to which he expected no sensible reply. Niccolò Machiavelli (1469–1527) declared that he would never advise deviating, in any human undertaking, from the venerable model proved by "his" Romans in *The Art of War* (Book 1). In another private letter addressed to a friend, the Florentine political theorist reverently paid tribute to the ancient Romans in his description of an intellectual kinship with them that surpassed all other ties Machiavelli felt:

> When evening comes, I return to my home, and I go into my study; and on the threshold, I take off my everyday clothes, which are covered with mud and mire, and I put on regal and curial

robes; and dressed in a more appropriate manner I enter into the ancient courts of ancient men and am welcomed by them kindly, and there I taste the food that alone is mine, and for which I was born; and there I am not ashamed to speak to them, to ask them the reasons for their actions; and they, in their humanity, answer me; and for four hours I feel no boredom, I dismiss every affliction, I no longer fear poverty nor do I tremble at the thought of death: I become completely part of them.[4]

Niccolò Machiavelli obviously believed that a dialogue with the ancient Roman writers of the past was much easier than a conversation with his own contemporaries. Others have held equally strong sentiments. On his death bed, the Italian artist Giambattista Piranesi (1720–78) is said to have pushed aside a Bible proferred him by a friend and to have clasped a copy of Livy's history of republican Rome to his breast, as he declared, "I only have faith in this."[5] The point is simple, and other numerous examples of this attitude need not be recited. We cannot dismiss these sentiments or treat these gallant tributes to Rome as a mere occasion or pretext unless we label the statements of a great many major figures as insincere. To the men and women whose works have been shaped by the myth of Rome, the city very nearly represents a form of secular religion, a realm of superhuman affairs where ordinary street clothes are insufficiently elegant for this metropolis of the mind.

A definition of the basic issues embodied in what I have been calling the myth of Rome must begin by eliminating several elements of Roman history that I do not intend to discuss in this book. In the first place, my use of the term "myth of Rome" does not include a treatment of the place of Roman religious mythology (the various gods and deities) in Western culture. Nor is this book primarily concerned with the impact of Roman Christianity upon our tradition, even though Rome in its role as the capital of the Catholic Church has in countless and important ways influenced the course of modern history. I am primarily concerned, instead, with a secular political mythology. At the core of the myth of Rome are two diametrically opposed models of political and ethical behavior: a virtuous Roman republic defended by stalwart citizen-soldiers and ever vigilant guardians of public liberty, on the one hand; and a corrupted empire, on the other, whose citizens are occupied by an overriding lust for power, lust for wealth, or lust pure and simple. This stark contrast is at the heart of the myth of Rome as it influences Western culture and creates a dynamic tension in the Western imagination that has sustained it over six centuries. The basic materials that went into the construction of the myth (the subject of the first chapter) were first supplied by the major historians of classical Rome. However, during the long period from the gradual decline and eventual fall of the Roman empire until the dawn of the Italian Renaissance in the mid-fourteenth century, these mythic materials were largely disregarded or superceded by the religious beliefs and exempla of the Catholic Church. Only with the humanists' revival of interest in the essentially *secular* aspects of Roman history and culture did the myth of Rome in its various republican and imperial manifestations begin to play a crucial role in the evolution of Western culture.

More than any other civilization before or since, Rome has been inextricably connected to the historical, philosophical, and human problems of change, process, growth, evolution, revolution, decline, decay, corruption, and death. In every modern expression of the myth of Rome from Petrarch to Fellini, Rome endures as the symbol and victim of inevitable change rather than the chief earthly expression of stasis and unity that it represented for those medieval thinkers who so strongly believed in a divinely inspired Christian universe with Rome as the head of both a universal Catholic church and a temporal government based upon Christian political values.

The philosophical problems inherent in the contrast of stability and corruption that Rome embodies become quickly associated with the moral categories of vice and virtue, both public and private. The interplay of these two sets of values constitutes the essence of Roman myth, for great art and literature as well as influential ideas grow more readily from concrete embodiments of vice and virtue in the lives of striking individuals than they do from abstract visions of change and process. The mind of the scholar may be moved by logic and evidence, but this particular myth survives because of its appeal to our imagination. Within the Roman myth, the conflict of vice and virtue represents a crucial link between private conduct and historical process. Virtue embodies a heroic attempt to combat or delay temporal finitude, a dominant concern of Roman mythography. Virtue becomes a personal attribute, not simply an ethical or a philosophical category. It is possessed by larger-than-life figures from the Roman past, and its significance transcends the private moral realm. Because Roman mythology expresses itself through the exemplary deeds of particular individuals, the myth appeals to our sense of the dramatic and to our common human hopes and ambitions. Its fundamentally optimistic message is that we too can become the masters of our destinies or the creators of our destruction. Just as the pure, white marble facing of its classic buildings provided Rome's inhabitants with an almost inexhaustible quarry for ten centuries after the empire's fall, so too the classical Roman historians have provided us with an unending supply of stories, ideas, and images for every age of the modern world.

In *Civilization and Its Discontents*, Sigmund Freud selected the physical image of the Eternal City as a metaphor for the human psyche. Century upon century of Roman life lay in consecutive strata beneath the modern soil, just as an individual's past experiences remain buried in layers, masked by the most recent ones. Only occasionally do we glimpse underneath the surface:

> Now let us, by a flight of the imagination, suppose that Rome is not a human habitation but a psychical entity with a similarly long and copious past—an entity, that is to say, in which nothing that has once come into existence will have passed away and all the earlier phases of development continue to exist alongside the latest one. This would mean that in Rome the palaces of the Caesars and the Septizonium of Septimus Severus would still be rising to their old height on the Palatine and that the castle of S. Angelo would still be carrying on its battlements the beautiful statues which graced it until the siege by the Goths, and so on. But more than this. In the place occupied by the Palazzo Caffarelli would once more stand— without the Palazzo having to be removed—the Temple of Jupiter Capitolinus; and this not only in its latest shape, as the Romans of the Empire saw it, but also in its earliest one, when it still showed Etruscan forms and was ornamented with terracotta antefixes. Where the Colosseum now stands we could at the same time admire Nero's vanished Golden House. On the Piazza of the Pantheon we should find not only the Pantheon of today, as it was bequeathed to us by Hadrian, but, on the same site, the original edifice erected by Agrippa; indeed, the same piece of ground would be supporting the church of Santa Maria sopra Minerva and the ancient temple over which it was built.[6]

With this ingenious comparison, Freud has provided us with a conceptual model for our approach to the myth of Rome. While a modern tourist strolling through the Piazza Navona cannot simultaneously perceive both the Bernini fountain which presently dominates the piazza and the amphitheatre of Domitian upon which the piazza was built, the limitations imposed upon our physical senses do not extend to our imagination, where there exist no such spatial or historical obstacles and where all phases of the myth of Rome coexist for us in a contemporaneous present tense. Just as an individual's past experiences can often explain or at least illuminate his current behavior, so too a culture can learn much from a look at the history of its myths. The myth of Rome constitutes a fundamental psychical entity for Western civilization. It has served as both father and mother to us all.

Unhindered by building codes and preservation societies, postclassical architects and masons traditionally plundered ancient Roman buildings for marble, burning what they could not use to provide lime for their mortar. In this fashion, Rome provided the material for buildings in every corner of the Italian peninsula and even places as distant as Westminster and Constantinople.[1] Likewise, the eloquent Roman historians of the republic and the empire produced a series of fascinating, often shocking, and always entertaining narratives which became an integral part of humanistic education for centuries to come. However, the exportation of such mythic materials proved to be of greater moment than the quarrying of those tons of white, mute marble. They formed the basis for the myth of Rome.

Roman history is formidable in its scope and breadth. And since twentieth-century readers no longer have the extensive training in the classical tradition that was typical until the nineteenth century, the general reader may well feel the need for a brief sketch of the major events in the history of The Eternal City from its founding in 753 B.C. to the deposition of the last Roman emperor in A.D. 476. Across this period of over twelve centuries, Roman history reflected an infinite variety of governments. Kings ruled Rome from 753 B.C. until 509 B.C. When these tyrants were expelled in that year, a republic governed by two consuls (executive officers) and advised by an assembly of senators led the city until the rise to power in 27 B.C. of Octavian, known to posterity as the Emperor Augustus. While retaining the outer trappings of ancient Roman republicanism, Augustus created what is known as the Principate, a monarchy supported by an oligarchic circle of patrician aristocrats. After A.D. 285, beginning with the reign of the Emperor Diocletian, the trappings of republican government that masked the realities of imperial rule were gradually abandoned. They were replaced by an autocratic, sometimes despotic, form of government similar to that of the oriental states east of the Roman provinces in Asia Minor. This period, known as the Autocracy, lasted until the final Roman emperor, Romulus Augustulus, was deposed by Odoacer, the leader of a band of German mercenaries. By this point, as one recent summation of this long historical development has put it, "ancient Roman civilization simply became something else, which is called medieval."[2]

Roman history may thus be divided into three general periods. After kings controlled the city for some two-and-one-half centuries, a republican form of government lasted for almost five centuries, followed by some five additional centuries of imperial power. Such a mass of historical experience could never have been assimilated into a coherent set of political and ethical myths even by the indefatigable Roman chroniclers. Moreover, for some historical periods (particularly in Rome's late imperial phase), reliable documentation from primary sources is often either unavailable or suffers from serious lacunae. Thus, it is not surprising that Roman myth focuses upon a limited number of key narratives and only a brief portion of the vast historical expanse that constitutes Rome's history.

The republican aspect of the myth of Rome was virtually created by one of the most influential historians of all times, Titus Livius or Livy as he is usually known. Livy lived during the last days of the Roman republic, survived the reign of the Emperor Augustus, and died during the reign of Augustus's successor, Tiberius, in A.D. 17. His masterpiece, *From the Foundation of the City*, was a massive work originally in 142 books, of which only 35 are extant. Livy was also primarily responsible for the emphasis in Roman historiography upon exemplary history, focusing upon striking personalities and dramatic events rather than upon the minute analysis of socioeconomic conditions. For Livy, as well as for all the historians of ancient Rome whose narratives provide materials for the myth of Rome, history served a didactic purpose. As Livy himself declared in a preface, the study of history is "the best medicine for a sick mind; for in history you have a record of the infinite variety of human experience plainly set out for all to see; and in that record you can find yourself and your country both examples and warnings; fine things to take as models, base things, rotten through and through, to avoid."[3]

Livy's narrative covered the period stretching from Rome's foundation through the city's rise to preeminence in the Mediterranean world after its victorious triumph over rival Carthage in the Punic Wars. However, the most important of his republican figures occur in the first five surviving books of his narrative, which cover the heroic early period between Rome's founding in 753 B.C. and its temporary occupation by the Gauls in 386 B.C. In this extremely influential section of his history, Livy firmly established in the Western imagination the image of a virtuous, noble republic composed in its best moments of selfless citizen-soldiers who preferred even to execute their sons or to sacrifice their daughters rather than suffer an affront to their patriotism, their sense of honor, or to civic morality. Death before dishonor was the watchword for Livy's stalwart Roman republicans, and this was the essence of the republican ideal that Livy bequeathed to successive generations of fascinated readers.

Unlike the later imperial version of the myth of Rome, which of necessity concentrated upon the single, solitary, and often sinister figures of successive emperors, Livy's republican history presented a bewildering array of heroic personalities and memorable historical events. Like any skillful writer intent upon catching and holding the interest of his audience, Livy linked his opening account of Rome's founding to sexuality and violence. Romulus and Remus, twin brothers who created the city, were said to have been born as the result of the rape of their mother, a Vestal virgin. Livy also discussed the traditional tale that they were brought up by a she-wolf after being abandoned by their mother. The she-wolf nursing the two young brothers had become the symbol for the city of Rome. But Livy realized that the term she-wolf could also be the slang expression for "prostitute," and he suggested that the traditional story might well have arisen from the fact that a "common whore" rescued and sheltered the exposed twins. Thus even the historian whose work constituted the original source for much of what would eventually become the republican myth of Rome was aware of the important role fantasy and legend (as opposed to verifiable historical fact) could play in Roman historiography.

The walls of the city of Rome were cemented with the blood of Remus, murdered by Romulus in a moment of anger (Book 1). And the link of sexuality and violence in Roman history was continued in Livy's subsequent explanation of the legendary "rape of the Sabine women" around 750 B.C., when the male citizens of the fledgling city forcibly expanded their population by stealing wives from the nearby Sabine tribe (Book 1).

As Roman history became more complex, Livy's narrative presented more and more interesting political and moral exempla. Around 670 B.C., Rome came into conflict with a nearby city named Alba. Livy concentrated this struggle into a dramatic duel between two sets of triplets chosen by each city to decide its fate—the Horatii of Rome and the Curiatii of Alba. Once again passion clouded the picture, as Horatius, the sole survivor of the battle and therefore the conqueror of Alba, returned home victoriously. However, he was scorned by his sister, who was in love with one of the three Curiatii he had just slain. In a fit of anger and righteous patriotic indignation, Horatius killed his sister as well. Even though he was legally guilty of homicide, his father's eloquent defense and the public's admiration for his conquests won him acquittal (Book 1).

Perhaps the most memorable of all Livy's patriotic stories concerned the political revolution which resulted in the expulsion of the Tarquinian kings from Rome and the establishment of the Roman republic in 509 B.C. Once again, sex and violence, rather than social or political forces, are used by Livy to explain this crucial event. Tarquinius Sextus, the son of Tarquin the Proud, tyrant-king of Rome, fell in love with the beautiful but virtuous Lucretia, wife of Collatinus. Rejected in his suit, he raped Lucretia, warning her never to reveal his misdeed and threatening to tell her husband that she quite willingly submitted to his overtures. However, Lucretia denounced her rapist, declared her intention to kill herself to prove her innocence, and in spite of arguments that it is the mind not the body that commits a sin of lust, plunged a dagger into her breast before her horrified relatives could prevent her suicide (Book 1).

In Livy's account, this private tragedy became the seed for a momentous political upheaval. Seizing the bloody dagger from Lucretia's dead body, Lucius Junius Brutus aroused the entire population of Rome against Tarquin the Proud, and in this burst of patriotic fervor and moral outrage, the Roman republic was born. In the republican mythology of ancient Rome, Lucius Junius Brutus was usually known as the first Brutus in order to set him apart from the second Brutus (Marcus Junius Brutus, ca. 85–42 B.C.), who would figure so prominently in the assassination of Julius Caesar in 44 B.C., an attempt to preserve the Roman republic founded by the first Brutus. The first Brutus was to perform another amazing demonstration of love for country. As one of Rome's first two consuls, he executed his own two sons for treacherously negotiating with the exiled Tarquin kings during the abortive Tarquinian attempt to reestablish the monarchy (Book 2). Rarely had human history recorded a more startling or severe proof of elevating love of country over love of family.

In his accounts of the turmoil following the expulsion of the kings in 509 B.C. and the struggle of the young republic for its very survival, Livy provided his readers with ever more stirring examples of republican courage and self-sacrifice. The Tarquinian exiles obtained the support of Lars Porsenna, King of Clusium, in their attempts to return to power. Here, Livy's narrative offered superhuman heroes who rescue the republic in peril. A single man, Horatius Cocles ("Horatio at the bridge"), defended the bridge over the River Tiber against an entire army of invaders

(Book 2). Another hero, Mucius Scaevola, a Roman soldier, decided to assassinate Lars Porsenna in his camp during the siege of the city. However, he mistook another man for the Etruscan king and murdered him. Captured and brought before the king, he thrust his right arm into a burning fire to show his contempt for Lars Porsenna and the enemies of the republic, thus gaining the name Scaevola, which means "left-handed man" (Book 2). According to Livy's somewhat romantic account, when Lars Porsenna realized that the free citizens of Rome were all like this brave warrior and that they feared danger to their native city more than physical pain, he quickly withdrew from the military campaign, and the threat to the republic vanished. Modern scholarship has established, however, that Lars Porsenna actually did capture Rome, although republican institutions survived this defeat. But Livy ignored this historical fact in order to fashion a more edifying example of a republican hero in defense of the fatherland. As occurs so frequently in the development of the myth of Rome, historical accuracy yielded to the requirements of a good story and a didactic lesson.

Immediately following the establishment of the republic, internal struggles broke out in Rome between the privileged classes and the plebeians, the common people of the city. In the face of the arrogance and the presumption of their patrician masters, who controlled the republican government, the plebeians demanded in 494 B.C. that the office of tribune of the people be created. Two tribunes (the number was later expanded around 471 B.C.) were charged with protecting the rights of the plebeians against the upper classes. Now more sinister figures emerged in Livy's narrative. The specter of civil war, always lurking beneath Roman internal affairs, became a factor in his history. One aristocrat, Gaius Marcius Coriolanus, opposed the power of the tribunes and scorned the pretensions of the populace for political power. Forced into exile, he joined the nearby hill tribe of the Volsci against Rome. Coriolanus was a magnificent soldier, and under his brilliant leadership, the Volsci besieged Rome. When all Roman military efforts failed to dislodge the Volsci, Coriolanus's mother and wife, who had remained loyal to Rome, left the city with his two infant sons and went forth to confront their exiled relative. Their tears succeeded where the force of arms had not. Coriolanus lifted the siege, and once again, the city was saved by the personal intervention of brave individuals—this time women and children (Book 2).

An even more influential portrait of republican virtue was provided by Livy in his account of Lucius Quinctius Cincinnatus. Several times around 458 B.C., the republic, again surrounded by menacing enemies, named Cincinnatus dictator. The office of dictator was a temporary one, bestowed for periods of limited duration, usually six months, and only in extreme emergencies when the republican institutions of the consuls or the senate were considered too slow and cumbersome to meet a serious crisis. In response to these calls to duty, Cincinnatus left his humble three-acre farm to take the reins of power. Always victorious, he proceeded to give an even more exemplary proof of his love for country. In every instance he renounced power, rejecting the temptation to stage a coup d'état (Book 3). If Shakespeare would later immortalize Coriolanus in one of his tragedies as the prototypical aristocrat obsessed with pride of birth, subsequent generations of European and American republicans would recall the selfless devotion to duty of Cincinnatus and his generous retirement from a position of supreme power.

Rape and murder had accompanied the founding of Rome according to Livy's account of Romulus and Remus. The rape and suicide of Lucretia, followed by the expulsion of the Tarquinian tyrants under the leadership of the first Brutus, resulted in the overthrow of the kingship and the founding of the republic in 509 B.C. In 450 B.C., lust and violence again accompanied a major political upheaval. A year earlier, the Romans had appointed a board of ten, composed of ten *decemvirs*, to reduce the plethora of legislation to a unified written code, thereby reforming republican institutions. One of these *decemvirs*, an ambitious would-be tyrant named Appius Claudius, attempted to exploit his office to seize power and to curb the protection offered to the plebeians by the tribunate. Smitten with lust for the beautiful and virtuous Verginia, Appius Claudius had Verginia legally declared a slave in order to force his attentions upon her. But Verginia was rescued, after a fashion, by her enraged father Verginius, who stabbed her with a butcher knife rather than allow her honor and that of his family to be sullied. Once again, a political revolution arose from a sexual transgression. The results were similar to those which followed the suicide of Lucretia: the tribunate was restored by an outraged citizenry, and the tyrannical rule of the *decemvirs* and the usurpation of power by Appius Claudius were swept aside (Book 3). Livy certainly intended to draw a parallel between the death of Lucretia and Verginia, just as successive generations of republican thinkers would link the exploits of the first Brutus to those of his distant descendant, the second Brutus. Roman mythmaking in the Livian tradition not only modified or distorted historical facts when the requirements of an entertaining or didactic story demanded it. It also attempted, whenever possible, to detect recurrent patterns of human behavior within the confusing morass of historical information in order to highlight key events and crucial republican virtues.

The last part of Livy's first five books introduced Marcus Furius Camillus, a patrician general who eventually saved Rome in its darkest hour from invading Gauls after he had been banished from the city in disgrace. His nobility of spirit was underlined by one of Livy's most interesting anecdotes. While Camillus lay siege to the neighboring city of Falerii, a treacherous schoolmaster there, charged with the education of the sons of the city's aristocrats, attempted to deliver his students into the general's hands in return for his own safety. Incensed by such a cowardly and unrepublican means of gaining a military victory, Camillus sent the teacher back in chains to the enemy city. The inhabitants of Falerii were so moved by the nobility of Camillus that they decided to surrender to him to avoid further bloodshed (Book 5). Later in the same book, Livy reported the story of the married women of Rome who sacrificed their gold and jewelry to the Roman cause, a patriotic gesture which would later be imitated many times in European and American history.

The second five books of Livy's narrative described Rome's evolution from its apparent destruction by the Gauls in 386 B.C. to its development into a Mediterranean power just before the First Punic War, with Carthage, its most dangerous rival, in 264 B.C. Most of this section of the history was filled with an endless number of accounts of various peninsular wars fought between Rome and other Italian city-states, tribes, or kingdoms. Nevertheless, a few notable Livian models emerged from these years that would prove crucial in later manifestations of the republican myth of Rome. Livy contrasted the heroism and virtue of Camillus to the misdirected courage of Marcus Manlius, known as "Capitolinus" because of his heroic defense of the Roman Capitol during the invasion of the Gauls. After the war, this leader's demagoguery led to his trial as a potential usurper of republican institutions, and Capitolinus was eventually (in 384 B.C.) cast off the very rock of the Capitol, a spot known as the Tarpeian Rock, where he had once, in happier days, achieved his moment of greatest glory (Book 4). Except in the previously cited case of Horatius, virtuous Roman citizens rarely allowed the memory of one noble deed to cancel out the ignominy of another less edifying action.

Other figures from this period were more virtuous. In 362 B.C., an enormous chasm suddenly opened in the middle of the Roman Forum. Soothsayers consulted their auspices and concluded that the strange event was a portent from the gods. The Roman republic would not en-

dure unless the city sacrificed its "chief strength" to appease the earth-
quake. A brave young soldier named Marcus Curtius declared that Rome
possessed no greater strength than the military prowess and courage of
its young men. Donning full armor and mounting a magnificent charger,
Marcus Curtius leaped into the chasm (Book 7). Thus, the republic was
preserved by his suicide.

When compared to the stern example of severity and impartial discipline displayed by the consul Titus Manlius Torquatus, however, even the
self-sacrifice of this gallant warrior pales. In 361 B.C., this fearless military
leader gained fame and the title "Torquatus" by killing a gigantic Gaul in
single combat and despoiling him of his torque, a necklace or collar of
twisted metal worn by the Gauls in ancient times as a symbol of rank and
authority. Years later, as consul, perceiving that individual combat made
coordinated maneuvers difficult, he ordered Romans under his command to avoid just such self-seeking individual forays against an enemy.
Yet his own son, Titus Manlius, disobeyed his directive and repeated his
father's earlier feat. Unmoved by the boy's bravery and intent upon
maintaining discipline in the ranks of republican forces, Torquatus ordered his bodyguard of lictors to behead his own son. According to Livy,
as he gave this order, he pronounced the following words: "Titus Manlius, you have respected neither consular authority nor your father's dignity. . . . you have made it necessary for me to forget either the republic
or myself. We would therefore rather be punished for our own wrong-
doing than allow our country to expiate our sins at so great a cost to
itself; it is a harsh example we shall set but a salutary one for the young
men of the future."[4] Such draconian measures were forever after known
in Rome as "Manlian" commands, and they surely contributed to the
magnificent discipline that was the backbone of Roman armies and republican virtue.

Livy's concluding books of From the Foundation of the City revealed how
Roman values enabled the city to triumph over Rome's most formidable
enemy, the city of Carthage led by its brilliant general, Hannibal. Here,
more than anywhere else in his history, Livy aimed to convince his
reader that after the inconclusive First Punic War (264–241 B.C.), the
eventual Roman victory in the Second Punic War (218–202 B.C.) at the
epic battle of Zama (202 B.C.) was primarily due to Roman character rather
than to military superiority. As Livy's narrative moved Rome closer to
world domination, the virtue of its citizens eclipsed even their courage.
This is evident from Livy's praise for Quintus Fabius Maximus, the wise
Roman dictator whose policy during the Second Punic War of delaying

rather than offering Hannibal determining battles proved to be the ultimate salvation of the republic. The dictator's refusal to succumb to the
historic Roman proclivity for impetuousness and thirst for personal glory
was thereafter held in high esteem. In 1884 a society of English socialists
who preached a gradual move toward socialism rather than revolution
chose to be called Fabians.

In his narrative, Livy contrasted two superhuman military heroes: Hannibal, the almost invincible Carthaginian commander, who combined
superior military skills with inhuman cruelty, treachery, and guile; and
Publius Cornelius Scipio, later known as "Africanus," whose moral qualities seemed to Livy far more laudable and whose military skills were
equal to, if not greater than, Hannibal's. Livy remembered Scipio Africanus as much for his self-control and discipline as for his victory at
Zama. Nowhere is this admiration clearer than in an episode known as
the "Continence of Scipio" (Book 26), a relatively unimportant incident
that was nevertheless to become the subject of numerous paintings centuries later. After capturing the city of New Carthage in Spain (210 B.C.),
Scipio was brought a beautiful young girl as part of the spoils of victory.
Rather than satisfy his lust, as most conquering heroes were expected to
do, Scipio summoned the girl's parents and her fiancé. He then restored
the bride-to-be inviolate. This simple gesture not only was considered an
act of incomparable virtue but also had positive military effects. The
fiancé was so struck by Scipio's noble act that he later returned with
some 1,400 picked horsemen for Scipio's army, and the news of Scipio's
generosity helped the Roman general win allies in Spain from tribes allied to Carthage.

Scipio's life also allowed Livy to include in his history a touching love
story which modern manifestations of the myth of Rome would not
overlook. Masinissa, an ally of Scipio, fell desperately in love with Sophonisba, the wife of Syphax, an ally of Carthage, after Syphax was captured
and taken to Scipio's camp. But after a stern lecture by the Roman general to his young subordinate about the dangers of lust and its negative
effects upon Roman virtues, Masinissa repressed his passion and sent
Sophonisba a poisoned drink in order to spare her the disgrace of falling
into the hands of the Roman army. This stark contrast between duty and
passion recalls earlier episodes in the initial books of Livy's history.

Livy died in A.D. 17. His history of Rome represents for Western culture
the most important source of Roman political mythology, particularly
those stories which make up what I have labeled the "Livian model" of
republicanism. Livy was by no means, however, the only architect of this

imposing collection of republican narratives. Two Greek historians—
Polybius (ca. 200–ca. 117 B.C.) and Plutarch (ca. A.D. 46–ca. 120)—also
helped shape Roman mythology for future generations. They are also the
first important non-Romans to fall under the spell of Roman mythology,
and they in their turn did much to popularize it in Western culture. The
Histories of Polybius were actually Livy's source for the Punic Wars, and
Polybius's narrative of the rise of the Roman empire under the late republic contains the important theory of Rome's mixed constitution that
generations of republican thinkers in Europe and America would admire
and seek to put into practice. Polybius also included in his discussion of
the Second Punic War a comparison of the moral traits of Hannibal and
Scipio Africanus, a theme Livy continued. The taste for such comparisons found its greatest and most influential literary expression in a magnificent historical work based, in large measure, upon Livy: *The Lives of the
Noble Grecians and Romans,* by Plutarch. Plutarch arranged his biographical
sketches of major figures from Greek and Roman history so that the
diverse vices and virtues of comparable individuals could be studied.
Here we not only encounter the familiar tales of Livian heroes, but we
are also presented with a new gallery of characters who shaped Roman
history during the period from the end of the Third Punic War (146 B.C.)
to the birth of the empire after a series of internecine struggles for power
and disastrous civil wars. Plutarch, so important a source for future generations of dramatists (especially Shakespeare) and political theorists
mesmerized by the spell of Rome, offered the most detailed accounts of
the lives of Marcus Junius Brutus (the second Brutus), Mark Antony,
Marius, Sulla, Crassus, Pompey, Julius Caesar, and Cicero. Precisely because Plutarch's book was a collection of biographical sketches rather
than a traditional chronological narrative, there was more room for the
kinds of personal anecdotes and the exposition of specific moral attri-
butes which would guarantee the popularity of the work for centuries to
come. And thanks to the impact of Plutarch's work upon Shakespeare,
such Roman figures and their exploits have become extremely familiar to
most educated readers.

Two prominent Romans from the late republic—Julius Caesar and Cicero—also wrote a vast number of works, usually in some respects self-
serving. Cicero was responsible for the origin of at least one major myth
included in the Livian republican model, the story of the heroic Roman
republican general Marcus Atilius Regulus, which is contained in Cicero's
On Duties (Book 3). Victorious in Africa during the First Punic War, Regulus was later captured while consul in 255 B.C. He was sent back to Rome

by the Carthaginians to negotiate an exchange of prisoners, bound under sacred oath to return to Carthage to die if he failed. When in Rome, he urged the senate not to negotiate with their enemy, and in spite of the pleas of his friends and relatives, Regulus felt compelled to honor his oath even to his enemies. He chose a horrible death in Carthage rather than break his word.[5] Such a man, in Cicero's view, was worthy of Livy's heroes of an earlier and happier age.

Set against the largely positive portrait of the Roman republic of virtue primarily indebted to Livy's narrative was the more sinister picture of the empire that followed the struggle for power and the civil wars of the late republic. Plutarch, Tacitus, and Suetonius as well as Sallust, Herodian, and a host of minor writers provided the basis for the imperial aspect of the myth of Rome. Just as Livy represented the prototype for republican historiography, Tacitus clearly surpassed in influence all other historians of the empire. His narrative account of the empire in what remains of his *Histories* and his *Annals* did not encompass all of imperial history but focused only upon the reigns of Tiberius, Caligula, Claudius, Nero, and upon the eventful year A.D. 69, which saw the demise of three emperors (Galba, Otho, and Vitellius) before the Emperor Vespasian established the Flavian dynasty to replace the Claudian line founded by the Emperor Augustus. *The Twelve Caesars*, by Suetonius, more malicious gossip than true history, was perhaps the most shocking and scandalous account of the empire, containing biographical sketches of Julius Caesar, Augustus, Tiberius, Caligula, Claudius, Nero, Galba, Otho, Vitellius, Vespasian, Titus, and Domitian.

Most accounts of the Rome of the emperors evinced their authors' obsession with the corrupting influences of absolute power, a theme implicit in Livy's paean to republican virtue. After the reign of Augustus ended in A.D. 14, most accounts of the first century of Augustus's Principate abound with incidents of gratuitous violence, sexual perversion, moral corruption, and civil strife. The darkness of these early years (A.D. 14–69) seems to return between A.D. 180 and 285, an epoch characterized by a recent critic as the age of "barracks room emperors," when almost all of Rome's rulers were either victims of assassination or died by their own hands to escape certain execution.[6]

In the historical narratives covering these two phases of Roman imperial history, we encounter the proverbial rogue's gallery still exploited by the late-show potboiler or recreated in the recent popular British television production of the novelist Robert Graves's *I, Claudius*. The picture of the first years of the Christian era in Tacitus or Suetonius bears out Livy's worst fears about the malevolent influence of unbridled power, wealth, and license. Tiberius inherited a peaceful empire from Augustus but eventually squandered this rich legacy because of his suspicious fear of intrigues, his reign of terror against other patricians, and his reliance upon Sejanus, the ruthless leader of his Praetorian Guard. Although Tiberius eventually had Sejanus executed, his replacement, Macro, and Caligula, Tiberius's heir, probably murdered the aging and dissolute emperor, who had abandoned Rome and had given himself over to all forms of vice and perversion at his villa retreat on Capri.

When Tiberius was removed in A.D. 37, Caligula took his place and managed in only four years to surpass his predecessor's worst excesses. Although Tacitus's narrative of Caligula's reign has been lost, Suetonius's version (probably far less accurate) presents the reader with the horrifying portrait of a monster who slept with his sisters and proclaimed his favorite horse a senator of a decadent deliberative body that once had been characterized by its impassioned defense of republican liberties. Although much of what Suetonius says about Caligula is suspect, even a portion of what the historian described easily justifies Caligula's assassination by the officers of his Praetorian Guard.

Upon Caligula's death, Claudius, his uncle, was proclaimed emperor. A studious, erudite man who wrote numerous historical works, Claudius suffered from a facial tic and an embarrassing stammer—characteristics that would undercut the imperial demeanor of any man. Moreover, he had the misfortune to take as his third wife a woman named Messalina, a treacherous plotter whose lust for power almost equaled her sexual appetite. He was probably poisoned by his fourth wife, Agrippina the Younger, in order to ensure that her son Nero (adopted by Claudius) would ascend the imperial throne.

With Nero's reign (A.D. 54–68), the rule of terror begun by Tiberius was reinstituted after an initial period of calm. Almost no one was safe, and the victims numbered a large portion of the cream of Roman society, including Seneca, the Stoic philosopher, who had once served as Nero's tutor. It is easy to understand why Suetonius blamed Nero, given his character, for starting the fire which destroyed most of the city in A.D. 64. In an effort to find a scapegoat for the disaster, Nero blamed the Roman Christians, sentencing them to be tortured, crucified, or burned to death. Early Christian apologists, always eager to exaggerate the persecutions of Nero and other Roman emperors, would later find easy targets in them, adding their strictures to the already disgusting portraits painted by pagan historians.

Fortunately, not all aspects of the empire reflected moral decay, for the empire, too, enjoyed its interludes of moral restraint and tranquility. At times, the older and more stable virtues of republican Rome revived themselves in individual imperial rulers. Edward Gibbon, the master chronicler of the decline and fall of the Roman empire, nevertheless eulogized the successive reigns of Nerva, Trajan, Hadrian, Antoninus Pius, and Marcus Aurelius. He described this period (A.D. 96–185) in the most glowing of terms: "If a man were called to fix the period in the history of the world during which the condition of the human race was most happy and prosperous, he would, without hesitation, name that which elapsed from the death of Domitian to the accession of Commodus."[7]

It is not surprising that the qualities Gibbon admired in these happy rulers were the very ones Livy had praised in his republican heroes. Marcus Aurelius, almost out of his element in the empire, could most easily have figured in the early Livian mythology. Always within the image of imperial corruption and moral decay, there lay the republican potential for reform, renewal, and rebirth, just as conflict and corruption persisted beneath the calm surface of republican stability and virtue. The view Livy and others presented of the republic was, of course, not completely without blemish. Livy's enduring portrait of Roman history presented a dramatic conflict of virtue and vice, good and evil, patriotism and self-interest. The history of republican Rome, therefore, was never simply that of a single value system but reflected a continuous struggle for preeminence between contending values embodied in the lives and personalities of human figures who are larger than life. Its energy arose from the conflict of ideals, the colorful exploits of republican heroes or heroines, purposeful patriotism, and the intense excitement of molding a world in the Roman image. Its complexity ensured that the Livian model of the myth of Rome would have a greater influence than the less edifying but no less fascinating Tacitean model in the Western world from the Renaissance to the present. The dramatic contrast between the Livian model of the virtuous republic and the Tacitean model of the decadent empire lay at the core of the Roman myth. The theatrical potential of this vast morality play with all the known world as its stage could not but have appealed to early modern Europeans who viewed the Roman experience and the myth its history created as a normative source of artistic inspiration, philosophical contemplation, and practical counsel. With its centuries of worldly experiences, Rome furnished through its historians a full spectrum of examples for every new generation.

Although it may be impossible to overestimate the impact of such writers and the myths of their creation upon the Western imagination, scholars have only recently attempted to quantify this influence. Their findings are worth noting here. During the period between 1450 and 1700, from the advent of printing to the victory of the "moderns" over the "ancients" in the Battle of the Books, which, for the first time in Western culture, placed contemporary writers on an equal footing with the masters of classical antiquity, it is estimated that some twenty classical histories were circulating in approximately 2,355 editions for a total of 2,500,000 printed volumes. Surely this staggering figure is large enough to persuade the skeptic of the power that antiquity exercised upon the early modern reader. The figures confirm, furthermore, that the rebirth of interest in classical antiquity that the Italian Renaissance began and that spread over the rest of Europe was primarily a rebirth of Roman antiquity. The least popular of the Latin historians, Florus, enjoyed just over twice as many editions as the most popular Greek writer, Josephus. They corroborate the notion that Greece presented no serious challenge to the cultural hegemony of Rome in Western civilization until the eighteenth century.[8]

The fluctuation of a historian's reputation can be an important indication of cultural changes which accompany new adumbrations of the myth of Rome. The shifting preferences for Livy and Tacitus and their very different mythic models disclose much about the tastes of an era. Livy's popularity surpasses that of Tacitus in an age which values republican virtue and eloquence, such as the Florence of Machiavelli or the revolutionary periods in England, America, and pre-Napoleonic France. Tacitus, on the other hand, appeals most to artists and writers in an age of monarchs, where prudence pleases more than eloquence or heroic virtue, and in any culture with imperial designs abroad, such as post-Machiavellian Florence, most of seventeenth- and eighteenth-century Europe, Napoleonic France, or Fascist Italy.

Yet, even within a period dominated by one particular aspect of the Roman myth, there often exist many subtle nuances and exceptions to the general rule. Absolute monarchs in Baroque Europe, for example, may sponsor operas and commission paintings inspired by the most republican of Livian figures, works whose ideas were potentially revolutionary in their original context. On the other hand, the imperial aspect of Roman mythology may surface in an era of staunch republicanism when it is least expected. Any account of the evolution of the myth of Rome must, therefore, be sensitive to changes of taste and style, to the different and sometimes conflicting demands of different artistic media, and even to individual whim, if we are to present an accurate portrait of the myth's odyssey through our culture.

THE REBIRTH OF THE
MYTH OF ROME IN THE
EARLY RENAISSANCE

By the second and third centuries of the Christian era, the numerous heroes of the Livian model had already become secular saints, cultural heroes whose exploits were cited to inspire imitation. Citizens of the Roman empire soon began to feel that their own era could never match the achievements of the early republic, but they continued to look back nostalgically toward the distant past, guided by a similar nostalgia found in most of the Roman historians they read. An analysis of the twenty-seven major figures cited most frequently in classical Roman historical texts reveals that not a single figure postdates Julius Caesar (d. 44 B.C.).[1] Most Romans felt that the majority of the admirable characters in Roman history belonged to the heroic early days of the fledgling republic. Pagan antiquity thus viewed Lucretia, the first Brutus, and Manlius Torquatus in much the same manner as the early Christians venerated their saints and martyrs.

The myth of Rome which evolved from the Roman historians reflected a secular and essentially pagan vision of the world. With its political and ethical ideals embodied in a number of key historical events or heroic individuals, this complex value system soon found itself in conflict with the otherworldly, transcendent character of Christianity. Of course, Latin remained the language of the church and of scholars or intellectuals during the Middle Ages, and the late twelfth century even witnessed a renewal of interest in Roman law, rhetoric, and literature. But medieval Christian culture could not accept the worldly imperatives of the myth of Rome.

Nowhere is the Christian opposition to the mythology of Rome more eloquently and authoritatively argued than in The City of God by St. Augustine (A.D. 354–430). Augustine composed The City of God after the sack of Rome by Alaric's Goths in A.D. 410. Many non-Christian Romans blamed this disaster upon the neglect of the older pagan gods and the rise of Christianity. Augustine thus aimed his work directly at pagan culture and its secular saints, contrasting their achievements (many of which he admitted to be laudable) to the even more praiseworthy behavior of Christian martyrs, saints, and virgins. Point by point, he attacked the possibility of a political or ethical code based upon patriotism, love of country, and exemplary heroic figures.

Augustine devoted an entire chapter to the central tale of Lucretia and her suicide. He shifted Livy's emphasis from the political results of her act (the liberation of Rome by the first Brutus and the establishment of a republican form of government) to a discourse on suicide and virginity. Augustine agreed that Lucretia no more committed adultery than did the Christian virgins ravished during the sack of Rome, but he asked rather ingenuously why Lucretia received, in effect, the greater punishment of death. He suggested the possibility that Lucretia may have killed herself out of a consciousness of guilt, that she took involuntary pleasure in the violent sexual act of aggression. At any rate, her suicide was certainly a result of a false sense of Roman pride unacceptable to Christian morality: "As a Roman woman, excessively eager for honor, she was afraid that she should be thought, if she lived, to have willingly endured what, when she lived, she had violently suffered" (1.19).[2]

After undermining the fundamental myth of the Livian republican model with this critique of Lucretia's character, Augustine proceeded to criticize a number of other key episodes in Livy's history. Quite naturally, he censured the Romans for the rape of the Sabines (2.17). He condemned Horatius for the murder of his sister, bereaved over the death of the Curiatii: "In my view, this one woman had more human feeling than the whole population of Rome" (3.14). The heroism of Marcus Atilius Regulus is discounted, since he lost his life in the service of false gods and was rewarded for this fidelity to them with "torture of unexampled cruelty" (1.15). His critique of the republican myth of Rome included almost the entire catalogue of major figures—the first Brutus, Marcus Curtius, Mucius Scaevola, Manlius Torquatus, Camillus, and many others. Given the obviously immoral and scandalous behavior of many of the Roman emperors, Augustine felt no pressing need to attack figures taken from the imperial mythology indebted to Tacitus.

Augustine admitted that the Romans possessed secular virtues far superior to other pagan peoples. But it was precisely the secular nature of Roman culture he rejected. For Augustine, human history was not shaped primarily by the heroic deeds of particular individuals but was, rather, part of a grander design controlled by divine providence. Because of their outstanding secular virtues, the true Christian God chose the

Romans as the vehicle for His providential plan in human history (5.12). But their essential defect as a people was their worldliness: "In early times it was the love of liberty that led to great achievements, later it was the love of domination, the greed for praise and glory" (5.13). Augustine concluded this devastating attack upon the foundations of the myth of republican Rome by exhorting his fellow Christians to live in such a fashion that their conduct would eclipse even the illustrious secular exempla of the pagans: "If we do not display, in the service of the most glorious City of God, the qualities of which the Romans, after their fashion, gave us something of a model, in their pursuit of the glory of their earthly city, then we ought to feel the prick of shame" (5.18).

The influence of Augustinian thinking upon the Middle Ages cannot be overestimated. Augustine viewed man as a fallen being. Human virtue was the result of God's grace alone, certainly not a reflection of individual merit. Secular or political virtues, such as love of country, self-sacrifice for the commonweal, and the like—all embodied in the heroes of the Livian model—were vainglorious attempts to wrest control of human destiny from an all-knowing and all-providential God and were doomed to failure. Had God's plan for human history been slightly different, Augustine seems to imply, another people, such as the Carthaginians, would have served equally well as the vehicle for historical development rather than the Romans. And thus, all of the illustrious collection of Roman exempla would have been meaningless and eventually forgotten by posterity. Augustine's critique of classical Roman culture represented an imposing obstacle erected against revival of the republican myth of Rome. A true rebirth of Roman mythology would be impossible until the essential secular nature of this mythology was understood, accepted, and assimilated into Western culture once again. And there is no doubt that the central figure in shaping this momentous intellectual revolution in European thought was Francesco Petrarca (1304–74) or Petrarch (figure 1).

Petrarch's contribution to the revival of Roman mythology was enormous. Every aspect of Roman mythology was influenced by his life and works: historiography, classical scholarship, archaeology, literature and belles lettres, the arts, even practical politics. Moreover, his international fame as a poet and a scholar allowed him to become the confidant or friend of every major political leader, churchman, or intellectual in Italy as well as in Europe. The very idea of a "Renaissance" was a concept largely of Petrarch's creation. He was responsible for the conceptualization and popularization of a radical view of history which would be ac-

1. Altichiero, Petrarch at his study (fresco
in the Sala dei Giganti, Padua).
Soprintendenza per i beni artistici e storici del
Veneto.

cepted by poets, artists, and historians for centuries to come. While Christians such as St. Augustine had contrasted the "dark" era of pagan religion to the "light" of Christianity, Petrarch reversed this dichotomy. He defined the "dark" ages as the period stretching from the fall of the Roman empire to his own day. Thus, the revival of classical antiquity, which was at the base of his every intellectual effort, was equated with a rebirth or Renaissance of Roman values.

Petrarch's very definition of modern historiography placed Rome at the center. As he put it, "What else, then, is all history, if not the praise of Rome?"[3] But Petrarch intended more than mere veneration of the Roman past or bookish interest in classical history. He urged active emulation of the Roman example in a variety of fields. In short, he advocated for his contemporaries a revival of the true secular spirit embodied in the myth of Rome. Rome had not fallen forever. The spirit that built the imposing ruins Petrarch admired so much in the Eternal City could be revived in the present. And, as a patriotic Italian, Petrarch fervently believed that Italians of his own time could restore the grandeur associated with ancient Rome if only they realized their human potential: "For who can doubt that if Rome should commence to know itself it would rise again?"[4]

The European Renaissance, a period guided by Petrarch's renewed vision of the Roman past, represented more than mere admiration of classical antiquity. It was an active program, a consciously willed choice of a particular past—that of pagan Rome—as a model for action in the present.[5] A profoundly Christian spirit with a great respect for the works of St. Augustine, Petrarch nevertheless rejected Augustine's Christian critique of Livy's republican model. His program of viewing classical antiquity afresh became an integral part of the fundamental intellectual reform of medieval Christian culture we know today as Renaissance humanism. And the humanist movement which recognized Petrarch as its founder was directly responsible for spreading Petrarch's influential views on Rome throughout early modern Europe.

Petrarch's fascination with the massive remains of past Roman history, the marble ruins scattered everywhere around the Eternal City, led him to an original appreciation of their significance that was instrumental in the founding of the science of classical archaeology. As one historian aptly remarked, Petrarch was certainly the grandfather of Roman archaeology, if not its father.[6] The letters describing his first visits to the city between 1337 and 1341 reflected the inspiration the poet drew from these sites and began a tradition of writings on Roman ruins which later attracted Goethe and Stendhal, not to mention numerous lesser figures. Unlike his Romantic successors, however, ruins did not cause Petrarch to speculate on the futility of human endeavor. Instead, they evoked for him images of the greatest heroes of the classical tradition, who seemed to come to life again among the ruins as if the poet had traveled back through time:

> Here was the Battle of the Triplets, Horatius and his brothers . . . here the unhappy Lucretia, escaping from her violation to death, fell upon her sword; here Brutus prepared vengeance for his offended honor . . . and Mucius, who punished his own right hand for its misdeed . . . here Cincinnatus was plowing when he was summoned to be dictator . . . here was the lewd tribunal of Appius, from whose lusts Verginia was saved by her father's sword . . . here Curtius threw himself down in full armor . . . here Caesar triumphed, here he died. In the temple, Augustus saw the kings of earth prostrate and the world at his feet.[7]

Petrarch's knowledge of ancient topography was far less impressive than his profound understanding of ancient literary texts, but his passionate belief in the possibility of a revival of ancient virtue was always encouraged by his interest in Roman ruins.

If Petrarch's ability as a Roman archaeologist was precocious but limited, there is no question as to his important contributions to the revival of Roman tradition in European literature. No single individual in the history of classical scholarship did more to pull together the various threads which constituted the diverse manuscript traditions of extant classical works. The printed editions of Livy which eventually formed the backbone of a liberal education in Western Europe and provided the basis of Roman republican mythology in the modern world owed a great deal to Petrarch's efforts to reestablish a reliable text from surviving manuscripts.[8] But Petrarch was more than a mere antiquarian or manuscript collector; he also aspired to create imaginative literature in the spirit of his Roman predecessors. Imitation of such Roman models as Virgil, Livy, Cicero, and others became an integral part of his poetics, and this in turn became common practice in European art and literature until the nineteenth century. In both his Latin and Italian compositions, Rome played a central role. His Latin epic, *Africa*, for example, begun in 1338–39 just a year after his first visit to Rome, aimed to rival Virgil in its presentation of a perfect Roman hero, Scipio Africanus, the conqueror of Hannibal and Carthage. Petrarch based his hopes for future literary fame on this Latin poem, which even included a vision of Petrarch as the future epic poet of Scipio in the concluding Book 9. Despite its being little read today, it had a tremendous impact during Petrarch's lifetime and for a century after his death. The catalogue of Livian heroes scattered throughout the composition helped to popularize this newly revived Roman republican mythology. And a long digression in Book 5 treating the love of Masinissa for Sophonisba was the forerunner of the many Roman theatrical and operatic productions in later centuries which combined Roman political themes with Roman love affairs.[9]

His collection of Latin pastoral poetry, the *Bucolicum carmen*, was further evidence of his debt to Roman poetry. Eclogue 5, for example, was dedicated to Cola di Rienzo (ca. 1313–54), the Roman revolutionary and demagogue, and represented a political allegory of Rome.[10] In Italian, the very popular *Triumphs* (written sometime after the death of his beloved Laura in 1348) presented a series of symbolic processions, the imagery of which was so appealing that it was to prove an important influence upon Renaissance painting. One section of this poem in Dantesque terza rima, "The Triumph of Fame," portrayed the entire cast of the Livian mythological model. While Scipio Africanus and Julius Caesar stood at Fame's right hand, Petrarch's poem described a procession which included the two Brutuses, Marcus Atilius Regulus, Cincinnatus, Manlius Torquatus, Camillus, Marcus Curtius, as well as several of the most virtuous figures from the empire (Trajan, Marcus Aurelius, Hadrian, Vespasian).[11]

Perhaps the single most significant work Petrarch wrote to popularize his renewed vision of the myth of Rome was a compendium of classical scholarship, legend, and literature called *De viris illustribus* (*On Illustrious Men*), which he began around 1338 or 1339—again, shortly after his first visit to Rome. Initially, the book included some twenty-three "illustrious men," all taken from Livy's account of the early republic. Here, Petrarch examined the figures we have come to expect from Livy's repository of fable and legend: Romulus, the first Brutus, Horatius, Cincinnatus, Manlius Torquatus, Camillus, Fabius Maximus, and others. Eventually the work would include longer lives of Scipio Africanus and Julius Caesar. A few notable figures from the Old Testament (Moses, Adam, Isaac, and Joseph), plus two Greek heroes (Jason and Hercules) were also added. But Roman heroes dominated the book, and not a single individual after the demise of the republic or the establishment of the empire was ever mentioned. Nor were any representative medieval figures—knights, saints, martyrs—deemed worthy of such august company. Toward the end of Petrarch's life, he planned a definitive edition of the work, a selec-

tion of thirty-six lives to match the figures his patron, Francesco da Ca-
rarra, planned to have painted in a room of his Paduan palace. These
frescoes, now almost completely destroyed, were completed between
1367 and 1379. Some of them were painted under the very eyes of Petrarch. It was Petrarch's influence that caused the hall, the *Sala virorum
illustrium*, to have a predominantly Roman republican tone.[12] It was partially his reputation which established the vogue for such republican decorations in Italian public buildings. The fashion soon spread throughout
Italy to Verona, Rome, Florence, Siena, and Umbria, and it became particularly important in communes with republican traditions of their own.

Rome and its example represented a constant ideal for Petrarch and
dominated his thinking about almost every area of human activity. But
nothing reveals to us how deep such a sentiment was than the occasion
of his coronation as poet laureate in Rome on 8 April 1341. Amidst the
events described in his voluminous correspondence with friends and
patrons, Petrarch described the incredible "coincidence" of receiving not
one but two invitations to receive the poet's laurel crown on the same
day—the first from the senate of Rome, the second from the chancellor
of the University of Paris (*Letters on Familiar Matters* 4.2; dated 1 September
1340).[13] After much feigned hesitation, Petrarch opted to be crowned
upon the Capitoline Hill in Rome. He thus consciously chose to revive
and reshape Roman mythology by his example. His rejection of Paris
implied a conscious rejection of the medieval scholasticism and theo-
logical speculation which was so central a force at the university. The
example of republican Rome, and not that of St. Thomas Aquinas, the
philosopher of scholasticism, constituted the core of Petrarch's Renaissance humanism.

The oration he delivered on that occasion might well be taken as a
clear dividing point between the sensibility of the Middle Ages and that
of the early Renaissance. In his speech, Petrarch provided three motives
for his poetic aspirations: "first, the honor of the Republic; second, the
charm of personal glory; and third, the stimulation of other men to like
endeavor."[14] He first explained that he was obliged to select Rome over
Paris in order to continue the noble tradition of the poet laureate, which
had been abandoned after the selection of Statius under the Emperor
Domitian. Then, Petrarch declared that this desire to achieve personal
glory was not a result of overweening pride but that it was "innate not
merely in the generality of men but in greatest measure in those who are
of some wisdom and some excellence." And finally, Petrarch unabash-
edly offered his own example to his contemporaries, just as he had prof-

ited from the illustrious models of the Roman past (found in Virgil, Cicero, Livy, and others). Thus, the very quest for earthly fame that St. Augustine's *City of God* criticized in the republican heroes of Livy now constituted the only legitimate goal for virtuous men at the dawn of a new historical era. Even more interesting is the choice of the specific verse from Virgil's *Aeneid* (6.823) that Petrarch cited in his argument: "Love of his fatherland has conquered, and the immense desire for praise." Virgil referred here to the first Brutus, the liberator of republican Rome from the Tarquinian tyrants and the man who sacrificed his sons for the commonweal. It is not reading too much into this oration to assume that Petrarch hoped his listeners would identify his accomplishments with those of the first Brutus and would consider him the founder of a new humanistic culture imbued with the true spirit of Roman mythology, just as Brutus had earlier given Rome's first republic life with his selfless patriotism.

Perhaps the most unusual episode in Petrarch's life was his friendship with the Roman demagogue and revolutionary, Cola di Rienzo. No other relationship among the many important friendships Petrarch cultivated tells us as much about his veneration of the Roman past. Cola was not the first Italian to raise objections to papal authority in the Eternal City. Years earlier, Arnold of Brescia (ca. 1090–1154), another demagogue who hoped to curb the church's temporal powers, had attempted with initial success to engineer a coup d'état against the Roman city government. In so doing, Arnold had a vague notion of reestablishing republican rule in the city, but his secular goal was perhaps less compelling to him than his desire to return the church to its early apostolic piety and simplicity. At any rate, his plan failed when an Englishman, Nicholas Breakspear, ascended to the throne of St. Peter, taking the title Adrian IV (1154–59). Adrian destroyed the fledging republic by placing the city under a papal interdict. Arnold fled and was captured and eventually executed for heresy, his ashes scattered in the wind to prevent veneration of his corpse.[15]

Cola di Rienzo, however, was far more interested in reviving republican grandeur in the Eternal City. Although, according to the anonymous chronicle of his life composed around 1358 in Romanesco (the dialect of Rome), he was of humble birth, Cola was mesmerized by the vision of past Roman achievements that lay in ruins all around him, and he was a voracious reader of the classics:

From his youth he was nourished on the milk of eloquence: a good grammarian, an excellent speaker, and a good scholar. Lord, what a fast reader he was! He was well acquainted with Livy, Seneca, Cicero, and Valerius Maximus; he loved to describe the great deeds of Julius Caesar. Every day he would gaze at the marble engravings which lie about in Rome. He alone knew how to read the ancient inscriptions. He translated all the ancient writings; he interpreted those marble shapes perfectly. Lord! How often he would say, "Where are those good Romans? Where is their high justice? If only I could live in such times!"[16]

Cola and Petrarch first met in Avignon in 1343, when Cola was part of a group of envoys from the Roman city government sent to speak with the pope. At that historical moment, commonly known as the Babylonian Captivity of the Church, the pope and his court had been temporarily moved to that French city and were dominated in large measure by the French monarchy. Nevertheless, the pope continued to represent secular rule in the Eternal City, and his representatives in Rome still governed. The pope denied the requests Cola's group made for more popular participation in the city's affairs, but the visit resulted in a friendship between the ambitious young Roman notary and the Italian poet. Cola held steadfast to his dream of reviving past republican glories, and four years later (19–20 May 1347) a well-planned coup made him master of Rome. At first, Cola shrewdly cloaked his revolution against papal reprisals by naming the pope's vicar as his corector, but a few days after the initial upheaval, Cola had himself named tribune with dictatorial powers. Shortly after hearing the news of Cola's revolution, Petrarch addressed at least two letters to him, although more may well have been written. He also composed the fifth eclogue of the *Bucolicum carmen*, which praises the tribune's accomplishments in an allegory: wild animals represent the noble families who prey on the sheperd's flocks, the Roman people; the songs of a young shepherd symbolize Cola's new republican laws.

In the first letter, Petrarch praised Cola for having combined the best aspects of the first Brutus and Cicero, patriotism and eloquence. In the second, Petrarch was swept away by the power of his imagination and his enthusiasm for a revival of Roman republican virtue in his own lifetime. Cola's actions, in his view, had surpassed even those of the first Brutus as well as those of the second Brutus: "There are now three of the name of Brutus celebrated in history. The first is he who exiled the proud Tarquin; the second, he who slew Julius Caesar; the third, he who has visited with exile and with death the tryants of our own age. Our third Brutus, then, is the equal of both of theirs, in that in his own person he has united the causes of the double glory which the other two divided between them."[17] Cola is further compared to Romulus, Brutus, and Camillus: like these three heroes, he had refounded the city of Rome, freed it of tyrants by restoring its liberty, and rescued it in the midst of a perilous danger. The tone of this famous letter (*Epistolae Variae*, 48) was not merely that of a private message. It was clearly intended to be read to the Roman populace, a stirring call to action from their poet laureate. Petrarch then recited the entire litany of Livian republican figures—Marcus Curtius, Mucius Scaevola, Horatius Cocles, Marcus Atilius Regulus, and many others—in urging the Roman people to sacrifice everything for the love of their native city.

Petrarch's estimation of Cola di Rienzo's abilities proved to be far from accurate. Although Cola was a talented orator and a master at evoking the grandeur of Rome's past achievements—two characteristics which could not fail to impress Petrarch—he was also something of a charlatan, a megalomaniac avid for power, and more of a showman than a serious political leader. Perhaps an intimation of what was to follow could have been discerned in the pompous title he bestowed upon himself: "Nicholas the Severe and Clement, Tribune of Liberty, of Peace, and of Justice, Liberator of the Holy Roman Republic."[18] Then, Cola began dating all official documents and correspondence from the first year of his Roman revolution. After a number of spectacular cavalcades through the city, during which Cola appeared on a white horse (a color traditionally reserved for the pope) and dressed in white garments trimmed with gold, the Roman tribune rode to St. John Lateran in late July 1347 and bathed in the great fountain in which, according to legend, the Emperor Constantine had been cured of leprosy and converted centuries earlier. On the next morning he was knighted and issued a decree which bombastically asserted Rome to be the "head of the world" and that the right of election of a Roman emperor belonged only to the Roman people. Any kings, dukes, emperors, princes, and persons of whatever rank who disagreed with this decree were summoned to Rome to plead their argument during the Feast of Pentecost on the following year! It must have seemed to Petrarch that humanism's dream had finally been fulfilled. Here was a man who seemed capable of reestablishing the ancient grandeur of republican Rome and of reclaiming its sovereignty over the entire world.

Cola's downfall only a few months after his revolutionary rise to power in Rome was largely due to his own flawed personality. He had underestimated the power of the papacy, the tenacity of the Roman noblemen, and the fickle favors of the Roman crowds. Moreover, he seems to have suffered from a fit of nervous exhaustion and severe nightmares. After the issuance of so many antipapal decrees, he ultimately and quite unexpectedly submitted to papal authority, renounced his titles, and cancelled his imperious proclamations. After living in the Castel Sant'Angelo for a month, he left Rome to become an exile for the next several years.

Cola was not to vanish from the Roman scene entirely. After several years in the Abruzzi hills far from the Eternal City, he traveled to Prague, where the Emperor Charles IV imprisoned him and eventually transferred him to Avignon to await a trial by Pope Clement VI. With Clement's death in 1352 and the rise to the papal throne of Innocent VI, the new pontiff not only acquitted Cola of charges lodged against him by his predecessor but even returned Cola to Rome to champion papal authority and to put down the uprising of the boisterous feudal barons, who constantly contested the pope's temporal power in the city. Thus, on 1 August 1354—seven years after his original rise to power as a radical republican opponent of the papacy—Cola di Rienzo reentered Rome, now ruling as senator in the name of Pope Innocent VI.

The man who returned to Rome was not the same romantic firebrand who had engineered an earlier political upheaval guided by the myth of the ancient Roman republic. His exile had made him capricious, cruel, self-indulgent, and decadent, even though his oratory still possessed the power to move the Roman crowds. The mob, the source of Cola's strength, ultimately proved to be his undoing. Instigated by the feudal nobles, an angry mob assembled around the Capitoline Palace under the pretext of protesting high taxes. Once again, Cola lost his nerve at a crucial moment. As the anonymous chronicle puts it, he had two choices: "The first plan was to die honorably, dressed in his armor, with his sword in his hand, like a magnificent and imperial person. . . . The second plan was to save his life and not die. . . . These two desires fought with each other in his mind. The winner was the desire to save himself and live. He was a man like any other; he was afraid to die." Disguising himself as a commoner, he attempted to pass through the crowd, all the while shouting "death to the traitor." And, master showman that he was, he almost succeeded in escaping. But his disguise was given away by a single small detail: the splendor of the gold jewelry he wore under his shabby dress belied his apparent lowly station. Cornered and recognized, Cola relied on his charisma to hold his captors at bay for over an hour before one of them cravenly stabbed him in the stomach. This first blow led to many, and his mangled, headless body was dragged about, hanged by the feet from a balcony, and then burned.

Thus ended on 8 October 1354, only sixty-nine days after his reentry into the city of Rome, the extraordinary career of Cola di Rienzo. For Petrarch, Cola had seemed to provide proof that the dreams of a renascence of ancient Roman virtue could be effected in the contemporary world. Cola's vision was a noble and dignified one, shared with the greatest intellectual of his age. It was a vision which Petrarch would pass on to the humanist movement of the fifteenth century. But the person embodying this vision was a flawed vessel, a man who substituted rhetoric for substance, oratory and ostentatious displays of grandiloquent symbolism for carefully organized and executed programs of a concrete and durable nature. One of the most entertaining, if uncharitable, assessments of Cola—by the Italian journalist Luigi Barzini—identifies Cola's fatal flaw with a perennial defect in the Italian national character: "He never for a moment suspected that it was not enough to build a life-like persuasive facade. The facade and reality, for him . . . were one and the same thing."[19] Even the anonymous chronicler who serves as the source for Cola's biography was disappointed by Cola's cowardly demise: the last lines of his narrative juxtaposed Cola's embarrassing death with the nobility of the Roman senators who, in 390 B.C., dressed in their finest garments before facing the invading Gauls, too proud to disguise themselves even to save their lives (figure 2).

Cola di Rienzo had little practical impact upon the historical development of Italian politics in the late Middle Ages. His importance lies elsewhere—as a reflection of the power the emerging Roman mythology would hold over the Western imagination for centuries to come. Cola had attempted to plant a seedling in infertile ground, the communal government of Rome, which was very much different in composition from the other potentially republican city-states of northern and central Italy. His appeal remained one of the heart. The temptation to see practical politics as a means to realize the dream of a Roman revival would remain potent, although many of those who later followed his lead ended as badly as he did. His memory would be perpetuated primarily by poets and artists. Lord Byron dedicated part of *Childe Harold* (1812) to him. Wagner was inspired by his life to compose the opera *Rienzi* (1842). Bulwer-Lytton wrote a popular novel based upon his life, *Rienzi, the Last of the Roman Tribunes* (1835). And Gabriele D'Annunzio sketched a biography of Cola (1906) that reflected his own fascination with the myth of Rome.

2. Cola di Rienzo (statue on the steps of
the Capitoline Hill, Rome).
Soprintendenza per i beni artistici e storici per la
provincia di Roma.

Petrarch's dream would find more suitable soil in the humanist movement of the early fifteenth century in Italy, which was deeply indebted to his admiration for Rome and his studies of the classics. Moreover, the city-state republics these humanists often served provided economic and social buttresses for an emerging republican ideology that enabled these men to transfer their ideas from the scholar's study to the chancellories and public meeting halls of actual political institutions. Livian republican mythology provided these writers with ammunition to substantiate their claims that republican government was superior to all available alternatives in its promotion of selfless citizenship, patriotism, and the defense of the fatherland. The negative Livian models or those from the Tacitean imperial tradition supplied proof that an inordinate concentration of unbridled power in the hands of one man or an oligarchy led to political and moral corruption or tyranny.

The myth of Rome was particularly important in the city of Florence. The intellectual circle that grew up around Coluccio Salutati (1331–1406) began the transfer of Petrarch's Livian republicanism to a predominantly Florentine setting. The movement continued with important works by other Florentine chancellors, in particular Leonardo Bruni (1369–1444) and Poggio Bracciolini (1380–1459). While these scholar-diplomats wrote primarily in Latin, as was typical of almost all important intellectuals in Italy before the sixteenth century, their works were read and imitated all over Italy. They accepted Petrarch and his veneration of Livian republicanism as the basis for much of their work but applied his more general view of the Roman past to a particular political situation in Florence.

It was Salutati, more than any other writer, who helped to establish the basis for what modern scholars call "civic humanism." He held an unfaltering belief that Florence was heir to ancient republican Rome, that it was the bulwark of liberty in Italy and the implacable opponent of tyrants such as Giangaleazzo Visconti of Milan or papal politicians such as Pope Gregory XI.[20] Salutati was responsible for the development of an argument which rejected the medieval view (held by Dante and others) that Florence had been founded by Julius Caesar and was therefore a product of the Roman empire and its corrupted mores and decadent institutions. Instead, Salutati argued that the city had a more virtuous republican origin during the era of Sulla. In a major work, *On Tyranny*, composed around the turn of the fifteenth century, Salutati defined a tyrant as a man who usurps a government or who rules unjustly without regard for the law and declared that tyrannicide was indeed justified. However, he then discussed the vexing question of whether Dante was correct in placing the murderers of Caesar (the second Brutus and Cassius) in Hell for their role in the assassination. This issue was not merely an academic exercise in Florence. Dante was the city's greatest poet, and the claim that Florence had inherited the tradition of Roman republican liberty might be compromised by Dante's condemnation of Caesar's republican assassins. If Julius Caesar could be seen as an entirely admirable politician, would it not also be possible to praise the Visconti rulers of Milan, whose power the Florentine humanists opposed so violently? Salutati's solution to this dilemma was ingenious: he declared that Caesar had obtained power legally and that his murder was unjustified. In this way he preserved Dante's estimation of a man sometimes seen as a tyrant without coming into conflict with the emerging republican ideology of civic humanism.

Salutati's disciple, Leonardo Bruni, enlarged upon the interpretation of Rome and its republican political mythology that he inherited from his master. He accepted Salutati's proposition that Florence had been founded under the republic, not the empire. But Bruni was unafraid to classify Caesar as a tyrant and the Roman empire as a corrupt form of government, which destroyed liberty not only in Rome but in a number of earlier Etruscan city-states, the existence of which he argued for in his *History of Florence*. And in his *Panegyric to the City of Florence*, he stated that the republican origins of Florence had caused its inhabitants to harbor an unending hatred for tyranny of all forms: "The men of Florence especially enjoy perfect freedom and are the greatest enemies of tyrants. So I believe that from its very founding Florence conceived such a hatred for the destroyers of the Roman state and underminers of the Roman Republic that it has never forgotten to this very day. . . . fired by a desire for freedom, the Florentines adopted their penchant for fighting and their zeal for the republican side, and this attitude has persisted down to the present day."[21]

Bruni had access to a manuscript of Tacitus which had been brought from the library of Monte Cassino to Florence a generation earlier and which contained the first books of the *Histories* and the second part of the *Annals*. A key passage which he cites from this important manuscript moved Bruni to conclude that Roman virtue declined drastically after the Roman republic was reduced to the rule of a single individual: "Now, after the Republic had been subjected to the power of a single head, 'those outstanding minds vanished,' as Tacitus says." As modern commentators have noted, Bruni misread the line, perhaps willfully, for Tacitus referred here to the disappearance of great *historians*, not great Romans. Bruni generalized Tacitus's verdict into a general indictment of the moral effects of the empire, thus setting what he considered to be the more virtuous accomplishments of the republic into sharper relief.[22] But given the voluminous condemnation of imperial corruption in Tacitus's history, only a fraction of which Bruni had at hand, his distortion of a single line of his text nevertheless remained true to the spirit of Tacitus.

The republican writings of these "civic humanists" had a profound impact upon the political ideologies of fifteenth-century Italy. The city-states of northern Italy—Florence, Venice, Siena, Perugia, Lucca, and other lesser towns—saw the elevation of the Roman republic over the Roman empire as a prefiguration of their own very real political struggles with princely dynasties in such states as Milan. They turned to the new humanist learning to support the republican form of government precisely because they believed, as Livy had, that such a government produced more virtuous citizens. These Italian city-states were, of course, oligarchies, controlled by a relatively small group of prominent families, usually engaged in banking, trade, and manufacturing. But since the Roman republic was similar in its oligarchic makeup, that was only more reason to praise its accomplishments as a model to follow in contemporary practice.

We can measure the impact of such republican ideals in a number of places. In Perugia, for instance, in the Archives of the Collegio della Mercanzia (the Merchants' Guild), there is still preserved from the late fourteenth or early fifteenth century an interesting manuscript which testifies to the link between the economic or political power of the republican city-state and Roman republican mythology (figure 3). The picture of a griffin, the symbol of Perugia, is shown rampant upon a bale of wool, the source of the city's wealth and the basis of the economic power of the prominent families of central Italy. Underneath this illustration is an admonition in Latin to the members of the government: "From Brutus, the First Consul of the Romans, each Consulate should derive a prudent, just, strong, and temperate example."

In only a few generations, the dream of the humanist Petrarch had thus taken concrete form in central Italy. Contemporary Italians saw themselves and their political problems mirrored in the historical narratives of Livy and Tacitus. Ancient history seemed to repeat itself, as republican city-states struggled against the concentration of power in the hands of only a few powerful men. As a result, political discourse was animated by the conflict of republic and empire, liberty and tyranny, and virtue and vice. These terms constituted the vocabulary of social theory until the

3. Detail of a manuscript from the
Collegio della Mercanzia in Perugia, with
the inscription referring governmental
leaders to the example of the first Brutus.
Soprintendenza per i beni artistici e storici per le
provincie di Siena e Grosseto.

mid-sixteenth century. Only with the eventual demise of the city-state as a viable political form and the rise of national monarchies across the Alps and principalities within the Italian peninsula would the imperial myth of Rome arise to challenge the supremacy of the republican image.

An even more interesting early example of the influence of the new republican mythology can be found in the Republic of Siena, the city-state which for many years was Florence's rival for cultural and political hegemony in Tuscany. Siena and its republic also embraced the myth of Rome as a means of self-expression. In its famous Palazzo Pubblico, the center of Siena's republican government, the city commissioned Taddeo di Bartolo (ca. 1362–1422) in 1413 to complete a cycle of frescoes in the antechapel depicting Roman heroes, a work which was completed in the following year. As scholars have noted, Taddeo's work provided the model for at least two other such Roman fresco cycles (in Lucignano and in the Palazzo Vecchio of Florence) and is itself obviously indebted to the Petrarchan figures painted in Padua. His work is remarkable for a number of reasons. First and foremost, it is a painting in which only republican heroes are honored. No imperial figures are mixed with the virtuous figures of the early republic. Secondly, the individuals portrayed span the history of the early republic to its demise—from the first Brutus to Caesar and the second Brutus. Four secular virtues are personified—Justice, Prudence, Fortitude, Magnanimity—and are accompanied by the figure of Religion. All of these moral qualities are illustrated by famous republican heroes. The frescoes appear on two levels. On the upper level, the virtues appear in lunettes surrounded by a frieze with medallions of the famous men. On the lower level, full-length figures of famous men cover the wall facing the chapel and inside the arches leading to the chapel and to the adjoining Sala del Mappamondo (under this arch, they appear beneath figures of pagan gods and a map of Rome).

On the wall facing the entrance to the Sala del Mappamondo, a figure of St. Christopher, painted six years earlier, was allowed to remain but has nothing to do with the frescoes by Taddeo. Only three of the figures in the group are non-Roman: Judas Maccabeus; the Blessed Ambrogio Sansedoni, a Sienese patron saint; and Aristotle. Aristotle stands in a special position, for he introduces the famous men to the citizens entering the antechapel from the larger Sala del Mappamondo. And he is juxtaposed to the twin figures of Pompey and Julius Caesar on the opposite wall.

A number of inscriptions in Latin, and one large inscription in Italian, accompany the figures. Aristotle addresses the onlooker with two Latin inscriptions. A scroll reads: "As a civic example, I show you these men; if you follow in their sacred footsteps your fame will grow at home and abroad and liberty will always preserve your honor."[23] Below Aristotle is written: "I am the great Aristotle, and I tell you in hexameters about the men whose virtue made Rome so great that its power reached to the sky." A central inscription on the main wall, written in Italian rather than in Latin to ensure comprehension by the less learned, reads: "Take Rome as your example if you wish to rule a thousand years; follow the common good, and not selfish ends; and give just counsel like these men. If you only remain united, your power and fame will continue to grow as did that of the great people of Mars. Having subdued the world, they lost their liberty because they ceased to be united."

Caesar and Pompey are clearly excluded from the exempla of ancient virtue (figure 4). Instead, they are negative illustrations of the consequences of blind ambition, which plunged the republic into a civil war and eventually destroyed Roman liberty after the rise of an imperial form of rule. Because the frescoes in the antechapel criticized Julius Caesar and glorified not only the first Brutus but the second as well, they reflected in graphic terms the republican myth of Rome as modified by the Florentine civic humanists. In fact, the frescoes were commissioned by the Sienese republic at a moment when it was allied with the Florentine republic against hostile forces from the Kingdom of Naples. There is every reason to believe that the ideals of civic humanism already discussed in the works of Leonardo Bruni may very well have influenced the Sienese in commissioning such an embodiment of Roman republican mythology.

Many of the famous Romans arranged in the work are already familiar to us (figures 5 and 6). Titus Manlius Torquatus is associated with Fortitude, as is Marcus Junius Brutus (the second Brutus); Lucius Junius Brutus (the first Brutus) is linked to Prudence because of the madness he feigned before he drove the Tarquin tyrants from Rome. Elsewhere, Mucius Scaevola and Cicero are connected to Justice with other lesser figures, while associated with Magnanimity we find Marcus Atilius Regulus, Camillus, Scipio Africanus, and a lesser known consul, M. Curtius Dentatus. This last individual and Camillus were especially important to the Sienese, as the inscriptions make clear, because they provided a direct historical connection between ancient Rome and Siena. According to ancient tradition, the colony of Senae (the basis for the future city of Siena) was founded during the consulate of M. Curtius Dentatus, and the

4. Taddeo di Bartolo: *Julius Caesar and Pompey* (frescoes in the antechapel of the Palazzo Pubblico, Siena).

Soprintendenza per i beni artistici e storici per le provincie di Siena e Grosseto; photograph by Edna Southard.

5. Taddeo di Bartolo, Roman *exempla*:
Cicero, M. Porcius Cato, P. Scipio Nasica
(frescoes in the antechapel of the Palazzo
Pubblico, Siena).
Soprintendenza per i beni artistici e storici per le
provincie di Siena e Grosseto; photograph by Edna
Southard.

6. Taddeo di Bartolo, Roman exempla:
Curtius Dentatus, Furius Camillus, Scipio
Africanus (frescoes in the antechapel of
the Palazzo Pubblico, Siena).
Soprintendenza per i beni artistici e storici per le
provincie di Siena e Grosseto; photograph by Edna
Southard.

Sienese also believed that Camillus played a role in the foundation of their city.

Thus, Taddeo di Bartolo provided a visual manifestation of the nascent Roman republican mythology that was so integral a part of the Italian city-state republics of the early Renaissance. Upon entering the antechapel, the citizen of Siena was admonished by "the master of those who know," the legendary sage Aristotle, that Roman republican exempla, if understood and imitated carefully, would guarantee the internal stability and external freedom of their state. Only the blind ambition of men such as Caesar or Pompey could destroy a republic based upon love of country, patriotism, and self-sacrifice, ideals embodied in the memorable deeds of the numerous Roman heroes pictured there, who also personified the more general virtues. Furthermore, the ties between the origins of Siena and these illustrious Roman figures would also have been evident to the careful onlooker.

Siena, Florence, and to a lesser extent, other city-states in central and northern Italy, thus exploited the political potential inherent in the Livian myth of the early Roman republic. In this manner, the ideals of civic humanism and the images associated with works such as the ones by Taddeo di Bartolo became an integral part of the dominant ideology of these republican regimes. This intellectual development took place during an era when the greatest artists of the day—Filippo Brunelleschi, Donatello, Leon Battista Alberti, Masaccio, Lorenzo Ghiberti, and many others—were evolving a new style in sculpture, painting, and architecture, one heavily indebted to a revived interest in ancient Rome, its art, and its extant ruins. Thus, both humanism and the arts guaranteed an ever expanding role for Roman myth in almost every area of Renaissance culture. Livy and Livian republican mythology had not only been revived but had been incorporated into a political ideology that reflected not just the daydream of a fanciful worshipper of Roman ruins, such as Cola di Rienzo, or even the scholarly vision of a poet such as Petrarch. The myth of Rome had become part of a battle of ideas, a struggle for the allegiance of the best minds of the day in early modern Europe.

THE MYTH OF ROME IN

THE HIGH RENAISSANCE

AND THE REFORMATION

In Florence, interest in the myth of Rome had been reawakened by the humanist followers of Petrarch. Their Latin works, important and seminal contributions to the myth of republican Rome though they were, reached only a small, erudite public. However, with the establishment of the Florentine republic that followed the first expulsion of the Medici family from Florence in 1494, the Livian model influenced a larger audience and became not only a central feature of great works of art but also an element of the most original political theory of the time.

There had always existed a very intimate relationship in Florence between art and politics. Immediately after the expulsion of the Medici, for example, Donatello's famous statues, *David* and *Judith*, originally private commissions for the interior of the Medici palace, were removed. Both works were set in public view in front of the Palazzo della Signoria to signal the end of Medici tyranny. Republican opponents of this influential family viewed David and Judith as archetypal Old Testament tyrannicides, Hebrew counterparts to Livy's first Brutus. They seemed unconcerned that the Medici tyrants they had expelled from the city and who had commissioned the statues for their private collection had no such interpretation in mind. Nevertheless, an inscription added to the pedestal of *Judith* by the anti-Medici revolutionaries made evident to all who viewed the works on public display that the two biblical figures were now to be interpreted within a highly politicized republican context: "Exemplum salutis publicae cives posuere MCCCCXCV" ("Erected by the citizens as an exemplum of the public salvation, 1495").[1]

With a cultural milieu as highly politicized as Florence's, it is not surprising to find a flowering of art indebted to Livian republicanism. The Florentine republic was understandably obsessed with its survival, and no single tale seemed to strike the citizens' imagination more than the story of Lucretia, her rape, and the subsequent founding of the Roman republic. A rich iconographical tradition on this subject grew up in only a few years, apparently without any historical precedent elsewhere in Europe. A number of these Lucretia panels survive, all containing a narrative of the main elements of the Livian tale. The most important of them is The Tragedy of Lucretia, by Sandro Botticelli, which is preserved in Boston[2] (figure 7). In addition to this group of works devoted to Lucretia and the first Brutus, there exists a related series of works that expounds the very similar tale of Verginia. They were probably intended as a set of companion pieces to images of Lucretia and also include an example by Botticelli, now in Bergamo's Accademia Carrara.

No two of Livy's stories were more appropriate to the republic's ideological needs. One described the Roman republic's founding, while the other showed how a corrupted republic could be revitalized by a citizen's bold actions. Botticelli's two panels were most likely executed as pendants for the decoration of a palazzo chamber. There has been much scholarly debate over the date of the two paintings and the patron for whom they were intended. The best and most recent study of Botticelli places the works unequivocally after the removal of Donatello's statues in 1495 and before 1504—squarely, therefore, in the middle of the period of Florentine republicanism.

In both of these panels, Botticelli aimed at a tragic, dramatic excitement far removed from mere decorative function. Indeed, some scholars have found clear links between contemporary treatises on stage design and the architectural structures within which Botticelli places his republican protagonists. Most important is the fact that in the Lucretia narrative, Brutus, and not the unfortunate Lucretia, emerges as the central figure. On the left, Tarquin seizes Lucretia, while a dark accomplice (his servant) watches in the extreme left foreground. Above this scene over the lintel of the doorway is a relief in ochre narrating the biblical story of Judith and her slaying of Holofernes. The narrative then moves to the far right, where Lucretia receives her relatives. It is noteworthy here that there is no visual evidence of Lucretia's suicide in this portion of the painting. She merely faints into her relatives' arms. Above this scene is an ochre relief of Horatius Cocles defending the bridge across the Tiber against the invading troops of Lars Porsenna. In the center of the painting, Brutus incites the Romans to vengeance near the dead body of Lucretia. Behind him on a porphyry pedestal is a porphyry column supporting a marble statue of David wearing Roman armor and a helmet. Behind the statue rises a triumphal arch with a number of statues and reliefs. In the lower relief above the left arch, Mucius Scaevola attacks the camp of Lars Porsenna, killing the king's secretary by mistake. In the lower relief above the right arch, Porsenna confronts Mucius Scaevola, who is holding his right arm, still clasping a dagger, in the flames. In the upper relief above the left arch, Marcus Curtius, dressed in full armor, leaps into the chasm in the Roman Forum.

The figures of both Lucretia and Verginia might be construed as merely typical illustrations of pudicitia, female chastity, just the kind of theme that suited the decoration of the traditional wedding chests or cassoni so popular a gift in Renaissance Italian culture. But Botticelli's two panels are too large for cassone panels and are too obviously political for such a purpose. The painter underlines his republican intentions clearly when he includes both Judith and David (biblical symbols of tyrannicide) in the work, as well as a large number of the traditional Livian republican figures. There is little doubt, therefore, that Botticelli hoped to draw a parallel between the ancient establishment of Roman liberty by the first Brutus and the emergence of the Florentine republic during his own day. A careful examination of the scene behind the triumphal arch reveals not a classical style of architecture but, instead, a number of palaces in the Florentine style and a city gate reminiscent of Florence's Porta San Niccolò. Since the painting focuses upon Brutus, the righteous anger of the Romans over Lucretia's death, and the oath the Romans swear to drive out the Tarquin tyrants, Botticelli obviously intended to commemorate the expulsion of the Medici through his treatment of this Livian myth familiar to all.

Botticelli's republican message continues in his Verginia panel and includes a similarly complex narrative structure. The center foreground shows the Roman army incited to revolt against the injustices of the cruel Appius Claudius and the decemvirs. Verginia is accosted by Marcus Claudius, the henchman of Appius Claudius, on the extreme left. Left of center, Verginia is led before the tribunal by Marcus Claudius. Appius Claudius delivers the unjust verdict that Verginia is a slave, subject to his whim, in the center left. Right of center, Verginius kills his daughter with a butcher knife rather than allow her to be dishonored. And on the extreme right Verginius departs for the army to begin the revolt. In this painting as in that devoted to Lucretia, the central and concluding event of the narrative sequence appears in the center of the picture, as opposed to a natural left to right progression. And in each instance the political purpose of the work, its obvious appeal to a Livian republican ideology as a source of the Florentine republic's own government, de-

7. Sandro Botticelli, The Tragedy of Lucretia (tempera).
Isabella Stewart Gardner Museum, Boston.

emphasizes the personal, feminine tragedy of Lucretia or Verginia by stressing images of masculine republican heroism, that of Brutus or Verginius.

The republican fervor that inspired Botticelli can also be detected quite clearly in major works by Domenico Beccafumi (1486–1551) and Michelangelo Buonarroti (1475–1564). We have already discussed the interesting republican frescoes by Taddeo di Bartolo in the Palazzo Pubblico in Siena. Beccafumi covered the vault of the Hall of the Consistory in the same building with a series of Roman republican frescoes between 1529 and 1535. Taddeo di Bartolo's earlier work was notable for its acceptance of the basic Livian ideology associated with Leonardo Bruni and the "civic humanists." In Siena, the government the tyrant Pandolfo Petrucci established in 1487 had finally been replaced by a republic in 1524. The republicans then heroically defeated an invading Florentine army in 1526. The Republic of Siena had good reason, therefore, to celebrate its survival and to glorify its own institutions, and the government commissioned a work that was purely Livian in inspiration. Many of the exempla pictured on the ceiling of the Hall of the Consistory were collected together in the *Factorum et Dictorum Memorabilium libri ix* by Valerius Maximus. This text, written in the first century A.D., was designed as a handbook for rhetoricians and contained a listing of private or civic virtues and vices, all of which were illustrated by anecdotes from the lives of famous men. It became popular in the late Middle Ages (Cola di Rienzo was an avid reader), and the first printed edition appeared in 1471. It quite naturally contained the entire range of tales concerning Livian heroes and villains.[3]

Beccafumi's frescoes were by far the most elaborate republican work of art produced until that time. In a room used by the republican government functionaries, the three civic virtues of Justice, Love of Country, and Good Will are personified on the vault. The deep coves that slope from the ceiling are covered with a series of major scenes (rectangles, octagonals, *tondi* shapes), and these scenes run around the four walls. Above the two long walls of the room are three narrative scenes symmetrically arranged, and each of these major narratives concerns Justice. Other scenes over the shorter walls treat Love of Country and Justice. All of the ten frescoes devoted to Justice (six of which are narratives) deal with the terrible retribution received for crimes committed against the Roman republic. And, as we might expect, the scenes recall many episodes from Livy's history.

Over one long wall, the cove contains the depiction of three major episodes. The first shows the tribune Publius Mucius burning nine of his colleagues who opposed a free election. In the center (figure 8), Spurius Cassius, who encouraged the nine men and who harbored kingly ambitions, is decapitated under the symbol of Justice, which is depicted in the center of the ceiling. The third fresco pictures the execution of the sons of Postumius Tubertus by their father, who found them guilty of attacking the enemy against his command. This is, of course, similar to the more famous episodes from Livy concerning the first Brutus and Manlius Torquatus. It is no accident that the first Brutus is shown by himself in one corner angle, with the heads of his two sons at his feet.

Three episodes decorate the cove along the other long wall. We first encounter Spurius Melius, an ambitious aspirant to kingship in Rome, at the feet of an implacable executioner. Directly across from the narrative of Spurius Cassius is a magnificent image of the ignoble end of Marcus Manlius. He is being hurled to his death from the Tarpeian Rock, where earlier he had performed heroic exploits in defense of the Capitoline Hill (figure 9). The sixth narrative concludes the sequence with the tale of Saleucus, who fixed blindness as the penalty for adultery, then was forced to carry out his punishment on his own son. His only concession to parental love was to sacrifice one of his own eyes in place of one of his son's.

The paired pictures devoted to Spurius Cassius and Marcus Manlius that face each other from either side of the cove are quite remarkable. In the first place, their illusionistic style is quite probably indebted to a similar oculus of Mantegna's Camera degli Sposi in Mantua (which will be discussed later in this chapter). Here, however, the effect serves to underline a more serious theme—death sentences imposed on traitors to the republic. All of the cove narratives, and these two especially, were meant to serve as a warning to the members of the Sienese government who met underneath them in the Consistory Hall. Such would be their fate if they weakened in their devotion to free self-government in their city-state! To underscore his message, Beccafumi also created an amusing visual pun in his presentation of the story of Marcus Manlius. His title "Capitolinus," as well as the location of his execution (the highest point of the Capitoline Hill) are ultimately derived from the Latin word for head. Appropriately, Spurius Cassius across the room loses his head, while Marcus Manlius falls headlong to his death from the location that was, to the Romans, the head of their government.

Although there is a subtle bit of mischievous humor contained in the painting, the Sienese were deadly serious about their liberty and their

8. Domenico Beccafumi, Decapitation
of Spurius Cassius (fresco in the Hall
of the Consistory, Palazzo Pubblico,
Siena).
Soprintendenza per i beni artistici e storici per le
provincie di Siena e Grosseto.

9. Domenico Beccafumi, Execution of
Marcus Manlius "Capitolinus"
(fresco in the Hall of the Consistory,
Palazzo Pubblico, Siena).
Soprintendenza per i beni artistici e storici per le
provincie di Siena e Grosseto.

republican form of government. Besides defeating an army sent against them by Pope Clement VII (a Medici) in 1526, they drove out troops commanded by the Emperor Charles V on several occasions, the last in 1552 after three days of vicious street combat. Ultimately Siena and its possessions fell to the army of Cosimo I de' Medici of Florence in 1555 after the town had first been reduced to only 8,000 citizens. Six hundred families led by the Florentine republican exile and fierce opponent of Medici rule, Piero Strozzi, fled to the small town of Montalcino, and this bastion of Sienese republicanism survived for four more years. In 1559, the entire Sienese territory was ceded to the Grand Duchy of Tuscany by the Treaty of Cateau Cambrésis, and a republican form of government would not exist again in the region until the nineteenth-century Risorgimento and the unification of Italy.[4]

Republican ideals in Siena and the Sienese territory, however, were fiercely entrenched in its citizenry. Although Montalcino is remembered by most people today only as the source of one of Italy's noblest red wines, even now in Siena, during the traditional processions which open the famous Palio horserace in the city, the flag of Montalcino takes precedence over all others as testimony to its role as the republic's last bulwark against foreign tyranny.

In Florence, the Medici family extinguished similar republican ideals, but only after even more ferocious repression. When the Medici family returned to power in Florence in 1513 and sent Niccolò Machiavelli into enforced retirement for his service to the republic, Machiavelli could count himself among the lucky republican survivors. Paolo Boscoli was condemned for his part in an anti-Medici conspiracy which falsely implicated Machiavelli. Just before his death, Boscoli called out to his friend Luca della Robbia: "Ah! Luca, pluck Brutus from my mind, that I may pass from the world a perfect Christian."[5]

The anti-Medici republican opposition, exiled from the city and actively conspiring all over Italy against the rulers of their native Florence, embraced Roman republican mythology, especially the cult of the tyrannicide, the second Brutus. Thus, when Lorenzino de' Medici murdered his cousin, Duke Alessandro, on a January evening in 1537, he defended his actions as a modern revival of the classical act of tyrannicide. After fleeing to northern Italy, Lorenzino had a medal struck of himself as Brutus. On the reverse side, the coin pictured the Phrygian or liberty cap between two daggers. This coin was a replica of one minted in the classical period by the assassin of Julius Caesar. The Florentine exiles, led by

Filippo Strozzi, saw Lorenzino's act in the same light and hailed Lorenzino, proclaiming him the "Tuscan Brutus." Although nothing came of their futile gesture, the exiles continued to embrace republican ideals. When Strozzi killed himself in a Medici prison in 1538, after his defeat at the battle of Montemurlo, he left a bloodstained letter for the Emperor Charles V in which he compared himself to another great republican suicide from antiquity, Cato of Utica. On each side of this deadly political struggle, ideological opponents expressed their aspirations and values in a strictly Roman vocabulary—the embattled and outnumbered republicans hailing Brutus as their inspiration, the imperial forces in the ascendency in Italy and Europe citing Julius Caesar or Caesar Augustus as worthy models for a stable and peaceful government after a time of troubles.

It is in the context of this fierce struggle over the future of Florence that Michelangelo and his *Brutus*, a magnificent marble bust sculpted in 1539–40, must be placed (figure 10). In spite of his great debt to the Medici, his patrons for the Medici Chapel in the Church of San Lorenzo, where Michelangelo worked between 1519 and 1534, the artist was imbued with a predominantly republican vision. Michelangelo was even given the responsibility of preparing the Florentine Republic's outer defenses between 1527 and 1530, and when the city finally fell to imperial forces allied with Pope Clement VII, he was forced to hide in San Lorenzo for some time until he was assured that his former Medici patrons would not have him executed.[6] Soon afterwards, Michelangelo was persuaded by the staunch Medici opponent Donato Giannotti, the last republican secretary of the Ten under the republic and the aide of Cardinal Niccolò Ridolfi, one of the most important anti-Medici exiles from Florence, to sculpt his bust of Brutus.[7]

Michelangelo's *Brutus* is a heroic, resolute, and defiant figure, even in the incomplete form in which it has come down to us after Michelangelo abandoned the bust and entrusted it to his pupil Tiberio Calcagni, who apparently worked on the chin, neck, back, and drapery. Obviously indebted to classical Roman busts, Michelangelo's *Brutus* shares with his greatest works an uneasiness, a restlessness, and an indignant moral fervor that typifies the republican zealots of the period. The ambiguity created by Michelangelo's abandonment of this defiant figure with its rebellious energy has raised much speculation about the work's intentions.[8] In one of Giannotti's *Dialogues*, Michelangelo's friend pictured the artist in Rome discussing Dante's journey through the afterlife with a group of friends. Giannotti and Michelangelo argue about the propriety of placing

10. Michelangelo, Brutus (marble bust
in the Museo del Bargello, Florence).
Soprintendenza per i beni artistici e storici per le
provincie di Firenze e Pistoia.

Brutus in Hell. And while Giannotti declares that every true citizen is obliged to murder a tyrant, Michelangelo argues that killing a tyrant does no real good if it brings no improvement.

Michelangelo was thus probably ambivalent about his support for the radical Florentine republic which emerged between 1527 and 1530, just as he was unsure about the ultimate significance of Brutus's desperate act. Yet he sculpted one of the most stirring images of the republican hero in the history of Western art. And if he harbored doubts about the political implications of his subject matter, there is no question that subsequent owners of the bust did not hesitate to see in his *Brutus* an ardently republican image of defiance to Medici tyranny. There is today a Latin inscription in bronze attached to the base of the bust. It advances the specious thesis that Michelangelo left the bust incomplete when he came to the sudden realization that Brutus's actions were reprehensible. There is universal agreement, however, that this plaque was affixed to the bust by order of Francesco de' Medici, Grand Duke of Tuscany, who acquired it between 1574 and 1585. This was obviously done in order to discredit the work's republican message and to convert Michelangelo, by then the glory of the capital of the Grand Duchy of Tuscany, into a staunch Medici supporter. While it most certainly does not respect Michelangelo's opinion, the inscription does testify to the strength of republican sentiment in Florence and the lengths to which later Medici rulers would go in order to undermine the appeal of nostalgic republicanism among their subjects.

Renaissance Florence also produced the most original political theorist of the era in Niccolò Machiavelli. Machiavelli's exciting but brief political career, and most of his life after his exile from power, would be devoted to the most systematic analysis of Livian republicanism since the classical period. Relatively little is known of Machiavelli's life before his election to the post of secretary to the Florentine chancery in 1498, an office he was to hold until 1512. In that year, the republican government he served was overturned, his patron Piero Soderini (the standardbearer of the republic) was exiled, and the Medici family returned to Florence in triumph to reassert its control of the city. As a major republican functionary, Machiavelli was purged from office on 7 November 1512. On 12 February of the following year, he was arrested and tortured because his name was found on a list of potential anti-Medici conspirators drawn up by two republican plotters (the same conspiracy for which Paolo Boscoli was subsequently executed). No conclusive evidence was discovered which could link Machiavelli to an active role in this plot. Therefore, after surviving several turns on the rack, Machiavelli was exiled from Florence and spent most of the rest of his life in the nearby Tuscan countryside, writing the political, literary, and historical works which would make him famous.

Machiavelli's interest in Livy began as a young boy. His father, Bernardo, obtained a rare copy of one of the first Florentine editions of Livy's history in return for laboriously copying an index of place-names for the printer. When Machiavelli entered the Florentine chancery, he worked in an intellectual environment which had been rendered illustrious by the distinguished group of Latin humanists (Salutati, Bruni, Bracciolini, and others) who had earlier played a determining role in the revival of Livy and the growth of "civic humanism" in Florence and Tuscany. Apparently, comparing contemporary politics with lessons learned from his studies of Roman historians was a natural tendency for Machiavelli. Early in his diplomatic career, when in Imola at the court of Cesare Borgia, he asked that a copy of Plutarch's *Parallel Lives* be sent to him. He was most certainly measuring Borgia against the heroes of classical antiquity. And in one of his first brief essays, *On the Method of Dealing with the Rebellious Peoples of the Valdichiana* (1503), Machiavelli juxtaposed the proper and successful Roman republican method of dealing with rebellious subjects to the incompetent and disastrous means employed by his own government. Even though his briefer treatise, *The Prince* (composed in 1513, posthumously published in 1532), achieved immediate fame all over Europe, there is no doubt that Machiavelli himself was more concerned with republican theory than with the principality. After his exile from active political life in 1512, Machiavelli continued to study the Latin historians and to frequent a literary and intellectual circle known as the Orti Oricellari, which boasted not only a number of eventual anti-Medici conspirators but also a number of Livian republican theorists.[9] Between 1513 and 1519, Machiavelli labored over his masterpiece of republican theory, a commentary on Livy's history entitled *The Discourses on the Decades of Livy*, which appeared in print shortly after his death in 1531.

Like Petrarch, Machiavelli believed that a revival of classical Roman political values was both practical and possible in his own lifetime and that the benefits a republican form of government could bestow upon his native city would be great. But Machiavelli was far too astute a political analyst not to realize that the rule of a single man also had its merits. He anticipated Edward Gibbon in his glowing tribute to the good Roman emperors, calling that period a "golden age": "Let a prince examine the times from Nerva to Marcus [Aurelius], and let him compare them with those which came before and afterward, and then let him choose during which period he would wish to be born or in which period he would like to be made emperor" (Discourses, 1.10). Nor did he accept Livy's narrative without critical reservations. His practical realism moved him to doubt the intelligence of trusting Rome's destiny to the prowess of the three Horatii in their duel with the three brothers from Alba. Livy's narrative might well provide a romantic version of Rome's conquest of Alba, moving enough later to be used as the basis of a tragedy by Corneille or the subject of one of David's greatest paintings, but Machiavelli believed that the Romans risked years of careful military preparations by entrusting the fate of the city to only three brothers (Discourses, 1.23). Moreover, Machiavelli was unwilling to use Horatius's bravery against the Albans as an excuse for his murder of his sister, since he felt that in a well-ordered republic a man's merits should never be employed to balance his faults. Thus, he always approved of stern punishments administered to former heroes who betrayed their trust, such as Manlius Capitolinus or Spurius Cassius, precisely because civic virtue, following stern Roman practice, had to be measured in absolute, not relative, terms. Elsewhere (Discourses, 3.5), Machiavelli left no doubt that he considered Livy's edifying story of the rape of Lucretia and the founding of the republic by the first Brutus to be somewhat misleading. For him, Lucretia's violation was a mere pretext for the political revolution undertaken by a clever and calculating Brutus.[10] Brutus, in effect, was Roman history's first recorded "Machiavellian."

Machiavelli's view of the Livian mythology of republican Rome was thus one of critical approval, with some crucial modifications. Since he believed in a cyclical development in human history, where there was no sense of progress but, instead, only eternal recurrence, he was convinced that even in the past, virtuous Romans were obliged to bring their republic back to first principles on a regular basis in order to preserve it from corruption and decay. In Book 3 of the Discourses, he argued that this necessary "return to first principles" could be brought about either by legal institutions or by the actions of a single man. But it is obvious from his examples—almost a complete list of virtuous heroes from Livy's history—that he believed a single striking action, such as the execution of the sons of Brutus, the courage of Atilius Regulus, or the execution of Manlius Capitolinus, could accomplish more in a single instant than all of the well-intentioned institutional tinkering imaginable. The exempla of

Livy thus became, in Machiavelli's hands, an integral part of a political theory designed to restructure contemporary governments after the form of the ancient Roman republic.

Machiavelli was aware that he was almost alone among countless theorists who praised the rule of kings or princes. He therefore addressed the question of why the thirst for liberty, seemingly so strong in the classical world and in late medieval Italy with its many city-states and republics, now seemed to be extinguished. Machiavelli paradoxically placed the blame for the downfall of the Roman republic on its very successes. The astounding military and political victories of the republic established the empire, and "the Roman empire, with its forces and its greatness, wiped out all the republics and all the self-governing states" (Discourses, 2.2). Civic virtue, therefore, required not only competition for rank and honors within a government, but also much the same kind of healthy competition between governments as well. Republics, Machiavelli shrewdly concluded, were schools of civic virtue that allowed the expression of liberty and produced the heroic men and women who demanded such an environment.

The popular image of Machiavelli's political theory is based upon a vulgar simplification of his thought. It is true that all of his works, and especially The Prince, discussed the necessity of separating traditional ethical or religious values from the imperatives of political power and hard-boiled realism. Yet, the essence of his thinking cannot be reduced to the phrase "the end justifies the means"—a statement erroneously attributed to Machiavelli by his detractors and unskillful translators. The clearest discussion of ends and means in all of Machiavelli's works may be found, in fact, in a key passage of The Discourses and not in The Prince. Here, Machiavelli discussed the murder of Remus by his brother Romulus and the founding of Rome, and in this specific and very important instance, Machiavelli did accept violence as a sometimes necessary means of pursuing political goals: "It is, indeed, fitting that while the action accuses him, the result excuses him; and when this result is good, as it was with Romulus, it will always excuse him; for one should reproach a man who is violent in order to destroy, not one who is violent in order to mend things" (Discourses, 1.9). Machiavelli stopped far short of justifying all political ends here. On the contrary, he praised an admittedly violent but unavoidable action on the part of Romulus only because it was performed in the public interest and not for private advantage. Moreover, it resulted in a specific, laudable, and historically unique end—the establishment of the most durable and powerful republican government in human history.

In developing his argument as a commentary on Livy's Roman history, Machiavelli was actually speaking out not only against contemporary practice but also against the weight of imperial classical and medieval political theory. With the exception of the Republic of Venice and several city-states in Tuscany, the fifteenth and sixteenth centuries in Europe were a period during which power was gradually consolidated in the hands of dynastic monarchies, principalities, or duchies, the most powerful of which organized their rule along national lines. A republican state would not become either philosophically respectable or even practically possible, in many instances, until the late eighteenth century.

Besides this practical obstacle to his theories, Machiavelli also had to overcome a prejudice inherited from the classical and medieval political thinkers—the belief that republican government was inherently unstable and potentially anarchic. Only the contemporary example of the Republic of Venice countered the antirepublican prejudice found in much of the period's theoretical writings. Renaissance philosophers generally criticized the concept of self-government because of the chaos which exists in such a state, while praising the rule of kings or princes as a more stable system. Rather than avoiding this issue by offering his reader a utopian vision of governments such as More's *Utopia* or states "that have never been seen nor known to exist in reality" (*The Prince*, 15), in *The Discourses* Machiavelli attacked such traditional beliefs.

In his argument, he presented a view of the cycle of governments, including the three good forms of states—principality, aristocracy, and democracy—and their three corrupt counterparts—tyranny, oligarchy, anarchy—which he found in the works of a number of earlier classical thinkers. For him, however, "all three forms of government listed are defective: the three good ones because of the brevity of their lives, and the three bad ones because of their inherent harmfulness" (*Discourses*, 1.2). As a result, he aligned himself with earlier thinkers (Polybius in particular) who felt a mixed form of government was the most stable. But political stability was achieved not merely by the absence of conflict or by a static social structure where no change is permitted, as in Plato's *Republic*. On the contrary, Machiavelli's close analysis of Livy's Rome led him to his most original thesis, that a healthy body politic was characterized by social friction and conflict, not rigid stability. In Roman history, liberty and a republican form of government not only survived but flourished as long as the social conflict between the patricians and the plebeians continued. Thus, Machiavelli's ideal republic was a government characterized by a dynamic equilibrium between opposing forces rather than the suppression of one interest group by another in order to create a false tranquility: "It seems to me that those who criticize the conflicts between the nobles and the plebeians condemn those very things which were the primary cause of Roman liberty, and that they pay more attention to the noises and cries raised by such quarrels than to the good effects that they brought forth" (*Discourses*, 1.4).

To bolster this daring attack upon the mainstream, Machiavelli posited a link between a free, republican form of government such as the early Romans enjoyed and a citizens' militia. Not only would free citizens defend their country better and more enthusiastically than mere subjects or mercenary troops, but such a force would also act as a defense against the rise of internal tyranny and would be, in effect, a school for republican virtue. This essentially Roman conception of the citizen-soldier was passed down from Machiavelli's works—in particular, *The Art of War*—and became one of the major forces behind the preference for a citizens' militia in the revolutions of England, France, and America during the seventeenth and eighteenth centuries.

Once a republic established itself and could defend its external independence, the next most urgent concern for the government was maintaining civic health and guarding against internal corruption. In the cyclic view of history held by Machiavelli, all forms of government eventually decayed and collapsed. Yet, the Roman republic endured for an unparalleled length of time. Machiavelli investigated the sources of civic corruption, and he uncovered a number of them. First of all, there was the lack of a sense of religion. Rome's pagan rituals provided the state with a defense by guaranteeing the observance of oaths and instilling courage in the citizenry (*Discourses*, 1.11). On the other hand, the Christian faith had glorified humility rather than courage or valor, and the Roman Catholic church's quest for secular power had rendered it unfit to act as the moral arbiter of Italy.

Another source of civic corruption was excessive wealth or excessive power in the hands of ambitious individuals. The corrupting nature of excessive wealth or power becomes clear when we realize that Machiavelli distinguished between different types of social conflict. In the relatively uncorrupted Roman republic (the subject of *The Discourses*), as opposed to the thoroughly corrupted republic of his own native Florence (the focus of Machiavelli's *History of Florence*), violent social conflicts were omnipresent. But Rome's social conflicts proved beneficial, because Rome's conflicts were between plebeians and aristocrats and were carried on, according to Machiavelli's reading of Livy, without "factions" or "partisans." Machiavelli believed factions arose when a private citizen acquired inordinate power, wealth, or influence and used this for purely private, rather than public, ends. The supporters of such an individual Machiavelli considered partisans, rather than citizens, for they undermined the very bedrock of the republican polis, the sense of a shared community of values and goals accepted by all citizens. Thus, Machiavelli felt nothing but admiration for a man such as Cincinnatus, the Livian hero who saved the republic on numerous occasions when asked to serve as temporary dictator, yet who always returned to the relative poverty of his farm (*Discourses*, 3.25). And he quite naturally condemned the leaders of dangerous political factions, such as Julius Caesar: "Nor should anyone be deceived by Caesar's glory, so very celebrated by historians [of his time], for those who praised him were corrupted by his good fortune and amazed by the duration of the empire which, ruled in his name, did not allow writers to speak freely about him." Instead, let the reader note how these historians praise Brutus, "as though, unable to criticize Caesar because of his power, they praise his enemy instead" (*Discourses*, 1.10).

Around this theoretical framework praising the revival of Livian virtues in Tuscany, Machiavelli analyzed a number of the key episodes in Livian mythology—the murder of Remus by Romulus, the emergency rule of Cincinnatus, the tyranny of Julius Caesar, the battle of the three Horatii, the tale of the rape of Lucretia and the founding of the first republic by Brutus, as well as the execution of the sons of Brutus, the evil Appius Claudius and his lust for Verginia, the restoration of the Roman republic following Verginia's death, and so forth. And Machiavelli also employed a number of paired historical figures to contrast different personality traits he found important for the cultivation of a revived Roman virtue in contemporary Florence. Here, once again, we find a number of exemplary Livian episodes: Camillus and the evil schoolmaster of Falerii (*Discourses*, 3.20); the harsh discipline of Manlius Torquatus juxtaposed to the humanity of Valerius Corvinus (*Discourses*, 3.22); the deaths of Manlius Capitolinus and Spurius Cassius, both executed for their seditious conduct though both had heroically defended the republic from foreign enemies on other occasions (*Discourses*, 1.8 and 3.7); and the contrast between Fabius Maximus, who advocated temporizing, and Scipio Africanus, who favored attack (*Discourses*, 3.4).

With the political theory of Machiavelli and the enduring republican images of the greatest Tuscan artists, Renaissance republicanism reached its apogee in the early sixteenth century. Like the protean political myth it was, the Livian model would return ascendant in successive centuries when the rising tide of republican sentiment called it forth once again. Livy's reputation had been assured in the Renaissance because of the efforts of Petrarch and his humanist followers to locate and edit Livy's surviving manuscripts. These edited Latin texts were therefore available to shape the art and social theory of the High Renaissance. Petrarch had remained ignorant, however, of the major extant Tacitus manuscript, which his friend Giovanni Boccaccio (1313–75) discovered quite by accident, probably in 1362, in the library of Monte Cassino.[11] Known as Mediceus II, this document contained major portions of the *Annals* (Books 11–16), and *The Histories*. By the first quarter of the fifteenth century, it enjoyed wide circulation among humanist intellectuals in Florence and elsewhere. The minor works of Tacitus, *The Agricola* and *The Germania*, reached Rome around the middle of the fifteenth century. There, the manuscript containing these two works was acquired by Eneo Silvio Piccolomini, Cardinal of Siena, a humanist intellectual soon to be elected Pope Pius II in 1458. The third major discovery, a manuscript known as Mediceus I (*Annals*, Books 1–4), was made in the monastery of Corvey by Angelo Arcimbaldo, who had been sent north by Cardinal Giovanni de' Medici on a manuscript search. When Giovanni was elected to St. Peter's Chair as Leo X in 1515, he sponsored the first complete edition of the entire writings of Tacitus, which appeared in that year. Even before this edition was printed, however, Tacitus had been avidly copied and read by humanists, beginning with the friends and correspondents of Leonardo Bruni, whose loosely construed quotation from *The Histories*, as we have already seen, helped to construct the ideology of "civic humanism." And with the rapid diffusion of printing, by the beginning of the seventeenth century, at least sixty major publications of Tacitus circulated in Europe, including translations in all major languages.

At the time of the discovery of his works, Tacitus's impact was immediately felt in the polemical religious debates which eventually culminated in the German Reformation. Eneo Silvio Piccolomini was responsible for injecting Tacitean ideas into European culture when he employed references from *The Germania* to bolster his view that the Germans should be more dutiful sons of Mother Church and pay their papal taxes without complaint. In a letter to Chancellor Martin Mayer of Mainz, he wrote: "Cornelius Tacitus, who lived in Hadrian's times, writes even more ferocious things about Germany. Indeed, the life of your ancestors in that time was scarcely different from that of beasts .... in this manner of living there was no knowledge of letters, no discipline of laws, no study of the fine arts. Even the religion was stupid and barbarous, fosterer of idols and, in fact, tottering with illusions of demons. . . . Everything was foul; everything was abominable, harsh, barbarous, and, to use the proper word, savage and brutal." [12] Piccolomini's letter was written in 1458 but circulated widely only after its publication in 1496. Piccolomini's intimation that Germany had only recently emerged from barbarism understandably angered many nationalistic Germans who opposed the corruption of the Italian papacy. Furthermore, German humanists were angered because they read works such as The Germania in a manner much different from their Italian humanist counterparts. Following the lead of Conrad Celtis (1459–1508), they felt The Germania furnished proof that ancient Germany provided a new standard of greatness, valor in warfare, and superiority in moral values over not only the ancient Romans but their Italian offspring as well. Just as the revival of Livian republicanism led to patriotic attempts by Italians such as Petrarch or Machiavelli to reestablish a new Roman republic in the modern world, the sudden appearance of the works of Tacitus caused an upheaval in the intellectual life of northern Europe.

Celtis, the poet laureate of Emperor Frederick III, was the first German humanist to lecture on Tacitus in a German university. In his Public Oration Delivered in the University of Ingolstadt (1492), he neatly reversed Piccolomini's Italian view of his nation's barbaric past. German vices of his own day, he asserted, were merely a reflection of the evil influence of Italy, which had caused the German people to stray from its pristine purity and natural goodness (not barbarism) as Tacitus had described it: "To such an extent are we corrupted by Italian sensuality and by fierce cruelty in exacting filthy lucre, that it would have been far more holy and reverent for us to practice that rude and rustic life of old, living within the bounds of self-control, than to have imported the paraphernalia of sensuality and greed which are never sated, and to have adopted foreign customs."[13] In the distant classical past, Rome had corrupted Germany; now the heir to Roman history and civilization, the Italianate papacy, continued this evil influence. The Germans should thus regard Rome's civilizing mission with indignation rather than the gratitude Piccolomini's original letter had demanded.

The search by German humanists for a past which was suitable to their religious or political concerns was thus encouraged by the publication of the works of Tacitus in 1515. There, for the first time, Germans could read in detail of Arminius, a chieftain of the Cherusci tribe, who led an uprising against the Romans in A.D. 9, annihilating three legions led by Varus in one of the greatest military disasters the Romans ever suffered in their lengthy history. The parallel between ancient history and contemporary times was not lost on those writers who were eager to strip Germany of Italian and papal influence. Reformers and Protestant sympathizers were busily producing a massive outpouring of polemical pamphlets, usually illustrated with woodcuts. Indeed, this period may be said to be the first era in which political propaganda was circulated on a massive scale. We see this use of blatant propaganda in a title verso added to the second edition of the New Testament of Erasmus (1519) by the famous printer from Basel, John Froben (figure 11). Placed in a position that could hardly be missed by the many readers of this popular work, the woodcut depicts Arminius commanding Varus (reduced metaphorically to the status of a viper) to "finally desist from hissing" ("Tandem vipera sibilare desiste").

This illustration, in turn, most likely encouraged another nationalistic German writer, Ulrich von Hutten (1488–1523), one of the most effective propagandists in Germany's battles with Rome, to complete his influential *Arminius: A Dialogue Taking Place in the Underworld* (1519–20). In a conversation between Minos, King of the Underworld, and four of the great warriors in his kingdom—Scipio Africanus, Alexander the Great, Hannibal, and Arminius—von Hutten painted a portrait of Arminius as the ideal German—honest, pure of spirit, courageous, uncorrupted by Roman or Italianate sensuality, obsessed with the love of liberty—and expressed his resentment of Latin and Italian claims to cultural superiority over Germany, either in the distant past or in the present.

Tacitus himself is brought out by von Hutten as a witness to read from his history the passage which treats Arminius and his victories. As a result, Minos concludes reluctantly that he cannot correct the traditional historical verdict that Alexander, Hannibal, or Scipio were the greatest of ancient warriors, since "my decision was made some time ago . . . and I am afraid that the order of things must stand." But Minos nevertheless agrees that Arminius shall be assigned "a place beside Brutus" and that he should henceforth be considered "first in rank among the great defenders of their countries' freedom." [14] Thus, an ancient German hero, assimilated into the heated religious debates of the Reformation with the Roman papacy, was eventually transformed into a German Brutus, a modern version of the archetypal hero of Livian republican tradition. Such a breathtaking feat of adapting a classical source from Tacitus to an ideological purpose far removed from the original source's intention was only one of many such intellectual *tours de force* which Renaissance and Reformation artists, thinkers, and writers performed in accommodating the repository of Roman mythology from Livy and Tacitus to their changing needs.

The revival of Tacitus in Germany among the Reformers was part of a much larger movement against the "paganism" rampant at the papal court of Rome. As the center of the Catholic religion, art, and humanistic learning, Rome was attacked as the capital of the Anti-Christ, the source of a basically non-Christian culture, and a city which had betrayed its special place in God's scheme for secular pursuits. We see this most clearly in a series of important woodcuts by Lucas Cranach and Hans Holbein made to illustrate several key Reformation texts. In the *Passional Christi und Antichristi* (1521), one of the most influential of the Reformers' illustrated pamphlets, the simple life of Christ is juxtaposed to the decadent life of a pope (who bears a not accidental physical resemblance to Leo X, the Medici pope of the day). In numerous scenes, Cranach contrasted Christ's washing the feet of his disciples with the kissing of the pope's foot by obsequious courtiers. Ultimately, and not surprisingly, the printmaker consigned the pope to Hell at the end of the book.

In another major set of Cranach's illustrations, this time for Luther's German Bible of 1522, Cranach linked the papacy and the city of Rome itself with Biblical images of corruption. A number of the animals in the illustrations for the Book of the Apocalypse sport the papal tiara, especially the Great Whore of Babylon. Objections from the Duke of Saxony forced the print to be modified, and the papal tiara was removed from the picture in a subsequent December edition of the book. Cranach also equated Rome and Babylon in his portrait of the destruction of Babylon, where he employed an earlier print of Rome (by Hartmann Schedel, 1493) as the model for his image of Babylon. This equation of Rome, papacy, and the Great Whore of Babylon from the Apocalypse was continued by Hans Holbein in his illustrations of the Thomas Wolff Bible, printed in Basel in 1523, where once again, the monster displayed the papal tiara and ancient Babylon bore obvious similarities to contemporary prints of Rome.[15]

We have already seen how early Christian apologists attacked the exemplary secular heroes of the Livian tradition in favor of the even more laudable actions of martyrs, virgins, and saints. Moreover, early Christians viewed the often scandalous historical narratives of the Roman empire as proof that the city's fall to the barbarians in A.D. 410 was at least in part a

DILECTO FILIO ERA
CRAE THEOLOGI

LEO

11. Arminius destroys Varus and his
Roman legions in Germany. Title verso
from the Second Edition of the New
Testament by Erasmus, 1519 (woodcut).
Lilly Library, Indiana University, Bloomington.

VARVS·QVINTILIVS·H

SPQR

TANDEM
VIPERA·
SIBILARE
DESISTE

1517·

AH·

ROTERODAMO SA⁄
ROFESSORI.
A   S
P · X ·

CARITAS

consequence of Roman immorality. German reformers attacked the Italianate Roman papacy in much the same partisan fashion. On 22 May 1526, Pope Clement VII formed the League of Cognac with Francis I of France and the Republic of Venice to prevent the domination of Italy by the German Emperor Charles V. However, the League was ineffectual, and its military ineptitude culminated in the fall of the Eternal City on 6 May 1527 to an imperial army that included some 10,000 ferociously anti-Catholic Lutherans from Germany. The occupation and sack of the city lasted for months, only subsiding in February of 1528. It delivered a severe blow not only to Pope Clement's temporal authority in Italy but also to the crucial role Rome was playing in learning and the arts. Moreover, it seemed as if ancient history was repeating itself. Rome, the capital of the ancient world, had been devastated by barbarian hordes in the fifth century. Now Renaissance Catholic Rome suffered a second martyrdom from the descendants of these same barbarians.

The Sack of Rome might well have prevented a rebirth of Roman mythology in early modern Europe had this collection of legends, virtuous examples, and mythic narratives been exclusively identified with the religious aspect of Roman culture or the specific geographical location of the Eternal City itself. But the myth of Rome had been endowed with a basically secular, political, and universal character from the date of its revival in early Renaissance humanism and had already proved capable of adapting to a number of very different geographical locations. As a result, the Sack of the Eternal City hardly diminished the enthusiasm humanists or artists felt for the lessons they had rediscovered in the works of Livy, Tacitus, and other classical writers. In fact, for a brief period of three years (1527–30), the Sack of Rome even sparked a heroic rebirth of republican energy in the city of Florence. There, anti-Medici forces took advantage of Pope Clement's inability to control his native city while German troops kept him imprisoned in the Castel Sant'Angelo in Rome. They proclaimed a republic which lasted only a short while, one even more radical than the earlier republic for which Machiavelli had labored. This later republic was the one that employed Michelangelo to design its fortifications. With its fall and the reestablishment of Medici hegemony in Florence and the hegemony of Emperor Charles V throughout most of the Italian peninsula, only the Republic of Venice remained as a major republican government. This change of political climate led to an eclipse of Livian models in Italian art and political theory that would not be reversed until the late eighteenth century. At that time the republican message would be brought back into Italy by revolutionary thinkers from across the Alps.

Even before this tumultous period in Italian history, the art indebted to the republican mythology characteristic of central Italian city-states stood in sharp contrast to the imperial Roman motifs employed by artists from other political cultures in the peninsula. No better example of such a different vision of the Roman past may be found than that of the town of Mantua, the seat of the noble house of Gonzaga. This family dominated Mantuan politics from 1378 until 1630, and the culture it nourished and patronized produced Roman images which would have been quite out of place in republican Siena or Florence. In the late fifteenth century, the favorite Gonzaga court painter was Andrea Mantegna (1431–1506), a remarkable artist whose interest in the classical past reflected the humanistic culture of the times. Mantegna completed two major commissions for the Gonzaga family that employed Roman motifs.[16]

In the earliest work, the celebrated Camera degli Sposi, completed by 1474, Mantegna portrays in spectacular portrait-frescoes a meeting that took place between Cardinal Francesco Gonzaga and his family in Mantua in 1472. Such an important occasion gave Mantegna the opportunity to represent a wide variety of figures, all of whom reflected the elegance and magnificence of the Gonzaga household. The noble family and its courtly retainers are pictured around the walls of the frescoed room. On the ceilings's center Mantegna painted an illusionistic vision of an oculus ringed with a crowd of spectators staring down from above upon the family, various figures leaning over an imaginary balcony. All around this daring construction, only a few years later to be recalled by Beccafumi's quite different republican frescoes in Siena, Mantegna placed lacunaria containing portrait busts in plaster of Julius Caesar and his first seven imperial successors (Augustus, Tiberius, Caligula, Claudius, Nero, Galba, Otho). Art historians quite rightly emphasize the originality of the frescoed figures on the walls in the Camera degli Sposi. But the Roman theme on the ceiling was essential to the intention of the entire project, even if it is a secondary motif. With the portrait busts, Mantegna linked the Gonzaga family to the Roman emperors of the Claudian line. These imperial figures stood as a courtly compliment, a visual assertion that the glory and majesty of the Caesars had been equaled in Mantua by the Gonzaga family.

This association of a ruling family with the power and prestige of the Roman empire found even greater expression in a second project which

Mantegna began before 1486—a series of nine canvases entitled *The Triumphs of Caesar*. As originally conceived, they depict a pageant moving from right to left and emerging from behind a row of painted pilasters. Triumphant Caesar on his chariot in the final section is the culmination of an orgy of imperial imagery (figure 12). Mantegna had carefully studied classical art that was preserved or recently unearthed in Rome: the friezes on the Column of Trajan and the decorations of the Arches of Constantine and Titus. His *Triumphs* contain a wealth of detail in the Roman armor, vehicles, dress, and weapons unmatched by any other work of the period. And here, unlike the ceiling of the Camera degli Sposi, where the Roman motif served a secondary role, Mantegna intended these enormous canvases to link in bold and striking fashion the might and majesty of imperial Caesar with the might and majesty of the ruling Gonzaga clan.

The Gonzagas continued to use imperial imagery in the next century. During the rule of Duke Federico II (1500–1540), Raphael's protégé Giulio Romano (1499–1546) moved from Rome to Mantua in 1524 to decorate the many halls of the Gonzaga Palazzo del Te and the Ducal Palace. Federico II was a close ally of Emperor Charles V, who named him commander of his Imperial troops in Italy in 1529 and raised him from marquis to duke in the following year. Far from fearing the republican uprisings of a politicized citizenry such as threatened the Medici rulers of Florence throughout much of the sixteenth century, the Gonzaga dynasty was concerned primarily with threats from foreign invaders, usually as non-republican and absolutist in their rule as they were.

The Gonzaga court, now allied with an imperial dynasty, commissioned a type of art designed less to make a political statement than to dazzle important guests, such as Charles V, who visited Mantua in 1530. Mantuan art was devoted to decoration and the iconography of imperial power, and consequently the political propriety of the images, so crucial to works in republican Siena or Florence, was not insisted upon. In one room of the Palazzo del Te, for instance, the so-called Hall of Atilius Regulus, we find works depicting the horrible death of the Roman general in Carthage, as well as Horatio at the bridge, two notable episodes from Livian republican tradition. Yet, in the nearby Hall of Caesar, we find wall paintings devoted to ancient emperors and military commanders. That Federico's commissions were primarily decorative rather than intended to make political or ideological statements is confirmed by another room Giulio designed in the Ducal Palace between 1536 and 1540, the Councilroom of the Caesars. This room was built to house twelve

12. Andrea Mantegna, Final section of
Triumphs of Caesar showing Julius
Caesar in his chariot (tempera on canvas
in the Royal Palace of Hampton Court,
London).
Lord Chamberlain's Office (St. James' Palace) and
Rodney Todd White, Limited, Photographer.

portraits of the Roman emperors by Titian, the same twelve figures treated in the history of Suetonius. They were all eventually sold to Charles I of England, then sent to Spain, where they were destroyed by fire in the eighteenth century. Beneath each portrait, Giulio painted twelve narrative scenes from the lives of the men Titian portrayed. Pictures of Nero playing while Rome burned, for example, were no more intended as positive exempla than were the earlier busts of such evil figures in Mantegna's Camera degli Sposi. In a city where political participation was virtually nonexistent, art employing Roman mythology could narrate stories from the distant past only to provide entertainment or decoration.[17] At most, its purpose was simply to associate the present with an imperial age.

The striking difference between Mantuan and Florentine culture in their use of Roman mythology may be further demonstrated by a series of paintings in Florence completed after its republic was only a distant memory. In the beautiful Medici villa at Poggio a Caiano outside Florence, there is a magnificent hall which was worked on by a number of artists, including Andrea del Sarto (1486–1531) and Franciabigio (1482–1525). It was completed between 1579 and 1582 by Alessandro Allori (1535–1607). Even though the government of Florence had become by this time a hereditary grand duchy and the city's republican traditions were essentially moribund, the power of the once dominant political ideology was such that the paintings in the hall, chosen from Roman history to commemorate important events in Medici family history, were all taken from the Livian republican tradition rather than the imperial tradition employed by the Gonzaga family in Mantua. Thus, The Return of Cicero from Exile (figure 13) made reference to the return from Venetian exile of Cosimo il Vecchio in 1434, the date which may be said to mark the beginning of Medici domination in Florence and the end of its internal liberty. Another painting, The Consul Flaminius in Council with the Achaeans alluded to Lorenzo il Magnifico's successful diplomacy at the Diet of Cremona, where he upset Venetian schemes against his rule. Julius Caesar Receives Tribute from Egypt used a classical incident to symbolize the magnificent gifts (including a giraffe) which the Sultan of Egypt sent to Lorenzo in 1487. Finally, Syphax of Numidia Receives Scipio, Victor over Hasdrubal in Spain was an allegory of Lorenzo's courageous diplomatic voyage to Naples, which saved his regime from foreign and domestic enemies.

The questionable taste in choosing such themes to celebrate the rule of an absolutist grand duchy was no doubt obvious to everyone. But perhaps it was less bad taste or ideological confusion than the basic fact

13. Frangibiagio, The Return of
Cicero from Exile (fresco in the
Medici villa at Poggio a Caiano).
Soprintendenza per i beni artistici e storici per le
provincie di Firenze e Pistoia.

that by the end of the sixteenth century, republican sentiment had simply ceased to express a practical political program in most of Renaissance Europe. In an age characterized by absolute monarchies and princely rulers, the republican myth of Rome was expressed in less polemical, less political contexts until the upheavals of the eighteenth century revived its dormant revolutionary potential.

Livian republicanism in the arts and political theory thus had become something of an embarrassment. With the fall of republican governments, doubts naturally arose about the applicability of Livian political ideals. These reservations were usually expressed as praise for the practical historical lessons garnered from a reading of works by Tacitus. Machiavelli, the archrepublican thinker, anticipated this development in an interesting remark on conspiracies in The Discourses (3.6): "And truly golden is this maxim of Cornelius Tacitus, which states: men must honor past things and obey present ones; they should wish for good princes, but they should endure whatever sort they have."[18] Here, Machiavelli provided his reader with a rather free translation of a passage from The Histories (4.8) in which Tacitus discussed Marcellus Eprius, Nero's prosecutor in his reign of terror and treason trials. In his discussion, Machiavelli made the obvious point, one he felt was bolstered by Tacitus's description of the dangers of living under a cruel tyranny, that great caution must be exerted under such rulers.

In the mid-sixteenth century, an image of Tacitus came to the fore which fit the tenor of the times. Tacitus's historical works, which could just as easily have been exploited by republican thinkers to attack the despotism typical of nonrepublican governments, became a practical guide for adjusting to the tyranny of the age. In fact, from the middle of the sixteenth century until the end of the seventeenth century, it is possible to speak of "Tacitism" as one of the major genres of European political theory and to chart Tacitus's impact not only in political thought but also in literature, melodrama, and painting.

An important figure in the spread of Tacitean ideas to counter the republican values of Livy was Andrea Alciati (1492–1550), a Milanese legal scholar responsible for the most popular edition with commentary of Tacitus's complete works, Annotationes in Cornelium Tacitum (1517; reprinted in 1519, 1535, and 1554). In the course of citing Tacitus frequently as an authority for the study of Roman law, Alciati elevated Tacitus over Livy not only because of his superior style but, more importantly, because Tacitus seemed more appropriate in an age of despots, intellectual conformity, and few personal freedoms. "Livy becomes shabby before us, compared to Tacitus, when the latter lays down for us, in the example of famous men, many precepts for our instruction: how crimes are turned upon the heads of their perpetrators, how much fame we ought to seek from steadfastness and fortitude of soul, how we ought to behave cautiously with evil princes, how it is fitting to proceed modestly with everyone." [19] In an age where the well-ordered model of a free Roman republic was a utopian dream sustained only by embittered political exiles, late Renaissance readers might learn more of value from the story of a past era that in so many negative ways more closely resembled their own.

Another side of Alciati's antirepublican stance may be viewed in what became one of the period's most popular books, the *Emblemata* (1531; subsequent editions in 1534, 1546, 1551, and many reprintings thereafter). This book spread the fashion of the emblem as a literary genre and contained several hundred epigrams, each with a woodcut illustration, a caption, and a commentary. One particular epigram is of interest here and bears the caption "The Republic Liberated." Its illustration pictured a huge coin set against a landscape; on the coin are inscribed the words "Of the Name of Marcus Brutus." (figure 14) The accompanying Latin verse may be translated as follows:

> The destruction of Caesar; as if this were
>   the regaining of liberty!
> Rather, for the Brutish leaders,
>   it was but a matter of this coin.
> Short swords in the front ranks—though hovering
>   over: the slave's skullcap of liberty,
> Which, the slaves, when emancipated, put on.[20]

It would be difficult to overestimate the distance we have traveled from Machiavelli's fervent praise of Livian heroes, especially for the assassin of Julius Caesar, and the stirring images indebted to republican mythology by Beccafumi or Michelangelo to Alciati's sneering, contemptuous epigram with its broadside attack on the value of republican revolution and the character of the greatest of republican tyrannicides. While the writings and influence of Livy still found a welcome audience among those republicans dedicated to changing the political situation in Italy by violent means if necessary, Tacitus, especially in the Alciati commentary, seemed to offer wiser and more widely accepted counsel: patience, acceptance, caution, and resignation to a fate which could not be changed by the actions of mere mortals.

This Tacitean pessimism in the face of the impossibility of political

Respublica liberata.

EMBLEMA CL.

14. *Andrea Alciati*, Emblemata (1531) (*woodcut*).
Lilly Library, Indiana University, Bloomington.

reform found its greatest expression in the writings of Francesco Guicciardini (1483–1540), a Florentine diplomat, historian, and essayist who was not only one of Machiavelli's most intimate friends after his retirement from politics in 1512 but also one of the architects of the reestablished Medici rule after the fall of the second Florentine republic in 1530. Although perhaps better known for his monumental *History of Italy* (1561–64), the most widely read history written during the Renaissance, Guicciardini produced the first informed reaction to Machiavelli's Livian theories—*Considerations on the "Discourses" of Machiavelli* (1529–30)—as well as a series of maxims and practical political observations, the *Ricordi* (1513–30), which call into question the very foundations of Machiavelli's republican ideals.[21]

Guicciardini, always the practical diplomat suspicious of abstract, intellectual schemes imposed upon political phenomena, questioned Machiavelli's reliance upon Roman exempla or even the model of the Roman republic. "How mistaken," he remarked, "are those who quote the Romans at every step. One would have to have a city with exactly the same conditions as theirs and then act according to their example. That model is as unsuitable for those lacking the right qualities as it would be useless to expect an ass to run like a horse" (*Ricordi*, 110). Machiavelli's most innovative idea—that social conflict, such as the kind which occurred in Livy's Rome, might be beneficial rather than destructive—was brushed aside with another pithy aphorism: "to praise disunity is like praising a sick man's disease because of the virtues of the remedy applied to it" (*Considerations*, 1.4). The traditional exempla of the entire classical tradition, both those from Livy and those from Tacitus, were entirely meaningless: "If they are not exactly alike in every detail they are useless, since every slightest variation in the case may make a very great difference in the result, and to distinguish these minute differences requires a keen and perspicacious eye" (*Ricordi*, 117).

Guicciardini cited Tacitus a number of times in the three different versions of his *Ricordi*, and in every instance Guicciardini linked the Latin historian with advice for survival under the rule of tyrants, as in the following statement obviously indebted to a reading of Alciati's *Annotationes*: "Cornelius Tacitus explains very well how those living under a tyranny may live and conduct their affairs with prudence, just as he teaches tyrants the means by which they may found their tyrannies" (*Ricordi*, 17). Unlike Machiavelli, who believed in the power of books, classical precedents, and abstract ideals, Guicciardini relied solely upon practical experience—his celebrated *discrezione*, or discretion. Taken as an accurate portrait of life in an era much like Guicciardini's, rather than a guidebook for the reconstruction of a revived Roman republic (as Machiavelli construed Livy), Tacitus's histories could teach the wise but prudent man how to survive in a dangerous world.

The view of Tacitus as a useful handbook in a time of troubles spread quickly in the late sixteenth and early seventeenth centuries, largely as the result of the efforts of two non-Italian intellectuals: a Dutchman named Joest Lips, better known as Justus Lipsius (1547–1606); and a Frenchman, Marc-Antoine Muret (1527–85). Both men traveled to Rome and were active at the court of Pope Paul III, where Tacitus was widely read. Muret gave three celebrated public lectures on Tacitus in 1580–81, while Lipsius published an edition of Tacitus in 1575 and a major political treatise, Six Books on Politics, in 1589 that relied heavily upon Tacitus. By the end of the sixteenth century, these two men had created a groundswell of interest in Tacitus. Over one hundred commentaries on Tacitus appeared between 1580 and 1680. Forty-five editions of the Annals and The Histories were published in the sixteenth century, followed by 103 editions in the seventeenth century.[22]

Lipsius and Muret continued the line of development already outlined in Guicciardini and Alciati. For Lipsius, Tacitus perfectly suited an age of book burnings, inquisitors, and religious terror: "How prudent Tacitus was about those things, and how apt for our time with its heretics going around burning books! Indeed, he wrote that when a certain man wrote something too freely about Cassius and Brutus, he was condemned by Tiberius, and his writings were confiscated by the aediles and burned."[23] This statement was read by Lipsius in 1572 during his inaugural lecture (Oratio) but published only in 1607. Muret described both Pope Paul III and Cosimo I, Grand Duke of Tuscany, as avid readers of Tacitus and also advocated the reading of Tacitus not only for his stylistic qualities but also for his moral value: "Although, thanks be to God, our age has no Tiberiuses, Caligulas, or Neros, it is good to know that, even under them, good and prudent men were able to live, and to know in what way and to what extent they were able to bear up under their vices and were able to dissemble."[24]

Political debate in an era dominated by absolute rulers and severely restricted freedom of expression thus accepted Tacitus as a writer whose practical advice was well worth heeding. Livian republicanism became, to say the least, dangerous in such a climate. Even in Florence, the birthplace of so much republican sentiment and so many contributors to the republican myth of Rome, the appeal of Livy and of Machiavelli's commentary upon Livy was weakened by practical considerations. This is evident in the works of Scipione Ammirato (1531–1601), a writer whose dependence upon Medici court patronage underlined the change in Florentine intellectual life after the establishment of the Grand Duchy of Tuscany. Ammirato became interested in Tacitus largely for his usefulness in combatting what he considered to be the evil influence of Machiavelli, whose republican ghost still gave the Medici rulers of Tuscany nightmares. In his *Discourses on Cornelius Tacitus* (1594), Ammirato used Tacitus not only to demonstrate, at least to his own satisfaction, that the rule of princes or kings was inherently more beneficial than that under an unstable Livian republic but also to contradict point by point the historical observations Machiavelli offered in his commentary on Livy. Instead of praising the kind of informed and active citizenry suggested by Livy or Machiavelli, Ammirato decided that political activity was primarily the responsibility of a prince, not his subjects. The image of Tacitus as a sage offering the advice of prudence was employed by Ammirato to defend the status quo in late sixteenty-century Italy, justifying the domination of the Spanish, the oppressive force of the Church, and enforced obedience to despotic rulers: "Exemplary punishment always contains an element of injustice. But individual wrongs are outweighed by the advantage of the community" (14.44).[25] Ammirato cited this line from Tacitus and agreed with it completely.

Ammirato's commentary on Tacitus was more popular, if not ultimately more important, than even Machiavelli's republican commentary on Livy. It went through six editions in twenty years; two Latin translations were published for German audiences in 1609 and 1618; four French editions were in print by 1642. Ammirato's message was very simple and suited the atmosphere of the times. Forget politics, since political participation is only the province of princes and beyond the realm of human control. Do not peruse classical histories for exempla to guide practical affairs, since the past is useful only for its moral or philosophical value as a source of amusement or intellectual delight.

Only one voice during this period saw in Tacitus something more than a classical precedent for contemporary apologists of despotic rulers. Traiano Boccalini (1556–1613), in his celebrated *Advertisements from Parnassus* (1612–13) and in a *Commentaries on Cornelius Tacitus* which appeared posthumously in 1677, reflected the fascination for Tacitus that characterized the entire century. Boccalini, however, was a fanatic supporter of the

Venetian Republic and a rabid opponent of Spanish domination in Italy and clerical oppression—all parts of the status quo a Tacitean writer such as Ammirato sought to defend. For Boccalini, Tacitus taught more than mere patience and caution. He revealed as well the hidden secrets of tyrannical princes and the true art of politics. The imperial historian thus provided his reader with "political spectacles" (occhiali politici) through which one could discern the secret motives and the concealed machinations behind the murky facade of current events. Tacitus and Machiavelli both led their readers to the same truths about the nature of power through their realistic assessments of politics as it was actually practiced. That Boccalini's message was considered a dangerous and subversive opinion may be demonstrated by the fact that most contemporary accounts claim he was poisoned by Spanish assassins in 1613 in order to silence his polemical pen.

The plays devoted to Roman themes by the period's greatest writer, William Shakespeare (1564–1616), provide a noteworthy exception to the general tendency during the Renaissance and the Reformation to embrace only a single aspect of Roman mythology, either republican or imperial. Very few manifestations of the myth of Rome in any period or any artistic medium have been as sensitive to the many serious political or philosophical problems the entire range of Roman history poses as these dramatic masterpieces. The first serious indication of the playwright's fascination with the drama of republican and imperial Rome may be found in an early poem, The Rape of Lucrece (1594). This work represents a formal defense of Lucretia's chastity in some 1,850 lines, elegantly composed in rhyme royal. In spite of the genius of Shakespeare's language, the poem often becomes sententious and overly moralistic—a common failing of long narrative poetry of the epoch.

Shakespeare presented the story in such a manner that a "fatal element of moral uncertainty," in the words of a recent critic, was introduced into the poem.[26] St. Augustine was supremely aware of the philosophical argument underpinning his Christian critique of Lucretia's suicide as he attacked pagan admiration for the woman's bloody deed. Many of the republican representations of Lucretia to follow Augustine in the Renaissance departed from his Christian perspective to embrace the decidedly Roman republican view that Lucretia's suicide was a highly noble, moral act. When Brutus comments on Lucrece's suicide in Shakespeare's poem, however, he ignores the woman's vexing moral dilemma and criticizes her actions. Apparently for him, the only sensible response to Tarquin's lust would have been to murder the rapist, not to die a suicide:

Such childish humour from weak minds proceeds:
Thy wretched wife mistook the matter so,
To slay herself, that should have slain her foe.

(1825–28)

Shakespeare's refusal to take an unequivocal position on the meaning of Lucrece's suicide, neither accepting nor completely rejecting the Augustinian or the pagan vision of his protagonist, leaves the modern reader with a sense of incompleteness and moral confusion. Yet, Shakespeare's sensitivity and even uncertainty in the face of such starkly juxtaposed value systems would bear better fruit in the three major "Roman" tragedies which were to follow *The Rape of Lucrece*, as he analyzed in brilliant fashion the transition of Rome from a small republic composed of citizens of extraordinary personal virtue to an enormous empire covering the entire known world. One play spanned the early republican period celebrated in Livy's exemplary historical narratives (*Coriolanus*, 1608–10); a second examined the gradual erosion of republican values during the period of power struggles among great military leaders that Plutarch had immortalized (*Julius Caesar*, 1599); and a third dealt with the final establishment of an imperial dynasty under Augustus (*Antony and Cleopatra*, 1606–07).

With *Coriolanus*, Shakespeare offered a meditation on the meaning of Roman citizenship and republican virtue. Caius Marcus (Coriolanus), a Roman patrician and a fierce opponent of extending citizenship to the plebeians, is summoned to battle against a neighboring people, the Volsci, in 493 B.C. During this period the plebeians have been demanding that their rights be defended by the newly created tribunate. The tribunes of the plebeians, Sicinius and Brutus, hate Coriolanus and manage to turn the people against him by exploiting his intemperance and his innate hatred of the commoners. After an outburst against the lower classes, Coriolanus is banished. He goes to fight on the side of the Volsci and only the intervention of his mother Volumnia saved Rome from his wrath. He is betrayed by Aufidius, a leader of the Volsci whom he trusted, and he is eventually assassinated.

Shakespeare's Coriolanus embodied the uncorrupted patrician virtues of the early republic. He sought to pursue a Roman ideal of honor, and in his absolutism and refusal to compromise lay his tragic flaw. As his friend Menenius remarks: "His nature is too noble for the world: / He would not flatter Neptune for his trident, / Or Jove for's power to thunder. His heart's his mouth: / What his breast forges, that his tongue must vent" (3.1.256–58). Unwilling even to feign familiarity with the common herd, Coriolanus desired honor but refused to realize that Roman honor was a public quality, dependent upon the approval of an audience of fellow citizens. Thus, the very approval Coriolanus required was unacceptable to him because of its tainted source in the vulgar mass of ordinary men, who could be persuaded by rhetoric and emotion to confuse the appearance of virtue for its substance. When he heard that he had been banished, Coriolanus turned the tables on his accusers and banished them from his presence: "You common cry of curs! whose breath I hate / As reek o' the rotten fens, whose loves I prize / As the dead carcasses of unburied men / That do corrupt my air, I banish you; . . . Despising, / For you, the city, thus I turn my back: / There is a world elsewhere" (3.3.120–23, 133–35). Shakespeare's protagonist attempted to live a life of Roman virtue outside the boundaries of the city-state, the source of public and civic recognition such virtue required in order to be meaningful to a republican hero. In the process, he destroyed himself. *Coriolanus* certainly demonstrates many serious defects in democratic government (in particular, the tendency to demagoguery), but the play also reveals the flawed character of a popular leader who is temperamentally incapable of ruling successfully.

In *Coriolanus*, Shakespeare was fascinated with an individual who manifested a basic flaw in the proud and potentially destructive nature of the Livian hero. In *Julius Caesar*, he examined a group of ambitious men, all of whom were vying for control of the Roman state in the twilight of the republican era, confronting an issue which carried increasingly greater world-wide significance—the conflict between a leader's private morality and his public responsibilities. *Julius Caesar* is as much a play centered upon the second Brutus, the classical world's most famous tyrannicide, as it is upon the man he murdered. But Shakespeare's Brutus was far removed from the defiant and resolute image of Michelangelo's sculpture, which symbolized republican aspirations for the Florentine Renaissance. He embodied a far more complex and questionable set of motivations and personality traits. Cassius and the other conspirators lured him into their plot precisely because he was a man with the purest of motives but one who failed to realize that other mortals might not act on such disinterested intentions. While Brutus worked for a noble end—the defense of the Roman republic—his heroic character was undermined when he selected an ignoble means, that of assassination, to achieve this goal. And it is clear in the play that Caesar's assassination occurred long before any real acts of tyranny had been committed. All the conspirators, save Brutus, had selfish personal motives for killing Caesar. Only Brutus acted in order to forestall any future tyranny: "It must be by his death: and for my part, I know no personal cause to spurn at him, but for the general. He would be crowned. How that might change his nature, there's the question" (2.1.10–13).

A man whose motives are as pure as those of Brutus may nevertheless commit serious tactical errors, as Brutus did when he allowed Mark Antony to pronounce the famous funeral oration that turned the masses against the conspirators. Ironically, it was the honorable nature of this purest of conspirators which provided Mark Antony with the rhetorical ammunition for his oration, which swayed the crowd with its constant repetition of the phrase, "And Brutus is an honourable man." Tragically, Brutus attempted to combine his own private morality, that of an austere republican citizen, with a public act of tyrannicide, but in the process, the purity of his personal motives was compromised by the self-interested actions of his coconspirators. His motivation may be best expressed in his own remarks introducing Mark Antony to the crowd:

> If then that friend demand why Brutus rose against Caesar, this is my answer:—Not that I loved Caesar less, but that I loved Rome more. . . . As Caesar loved me, I weep for him; as he was fortunate, I rejoice at it; as he was valiant, I honour him; but, as he was ambitious, I slew him. There is tears for his love; joy for his fortune; honour for his valour; and death for his ambition (3.1.20–22, 25–29).

It was because of Brutus's tragic purity that Mark Antony could declare of him, after his suicide on the battlefield of Philippi, that he was, indeed, the "noblest Roman of them all" because only he acted for the general welfare. And yet, the tragedy of Brutus makes it clear that Shakespeare felt such purity of motives was insufficient for the ideal ruler and republican citizen if the means he chose to express his political ideals were flawed and incapable of preventing the rise of a single imperial ruler and the transformation of the republic into a dynastic empire.

With *Antony and Cleopatra*, the third and final stage of the historical drama of Rome unfolded. If *Coriolanus* revealed the dangers inherent in a republican system dependent upon the prideful virtues of Livy's warrior heroes, and *Julius Caesar* dramatized the inevitable conflict of private morality and public deeds when such individuals clashed, then this third great drama moved to a broader dimension, employing its two main characters to embody diametrically opposed ways of life. Over and over again, Antony is identified with Rome when his reason dominates his lust and his passion, while Cleopatra is constantly addressed as "Egypt" and as the very personification of Oriental, non-Roman sensuality and irresponsibility. Here, duty and love clash in a manner only superficially similar to the way in which this theme provides a narrative structure for so many melodramas of the period following Shakespeare, for the love experienced by Antony and Cleopatra takes on a metaphysical dimension that rivals politics and state business in its intensity, if not in its importance.

There is no doubt that Shakespeare believed the Roman republic moved toward the creation of a dynastic, imperial rule precisely because Roman republican virtue was slowly becoming corrupted. This is sharply revealed in a remark by Ventidius, a soldier in Antony's service who has defeated a Parthian general but who is strangely concerned over his very success:

> O Silius, Silius,
> I have done enough; a lower place, note well,
> May take too great an act; for learn this,
>   Silius;
> Better to leave undone, than by our deed
> Acquire too high a fame when him we serve's
>   away.
>
> (3.1.12–16)

Ambition in the old republic usually found a means of expressing itself within the framework of the city-state's republican institutions, and rewards for faithful service to the state were, at least in principle, assured. However, in an era when the sole source of civic approval rested not with a group of like-minded citizens but, rather, upon the whimsical favor of a single and probably capricious ruler, particular expressions of personal valor, no matter how beneficial they might prove to the commonweal, could also prove fatal.

We have traveled a long distance from the Rome of the early republic. Now bold and heroic deeds endanger the life of their executor because the moral and political fiber of Roman republican institutions have been corrupted. Ambition, which once expressed itself through legitimate channels, must now turn to palace intrigue and conspiracy. A political career is thus inevitably less attractive under an empire than under a republic, and when political service loses its attractions, the world of erotic love, in *Antony and Cleopatra* a general metaphor for all those forces standing in contrast to the old republican virtues and responsibilities, now seems more appealing. Love, a private affair, has been transformed into a public spectacle by this regal pair of lovers, thus shifting the arena of public valor to a realm completely out of keeping with republican custom. Before her suicide, Cleopatra declares that political ambition is nothing, that Fortune and chance continue to control man's destiny: "'Tis paltry to be Caesar" (5.2.2).

Beginning with the historical materials he found in Livy, Plutarch, Tacitus, and Suetonius, Shakespeare's dramatic genius raised the level of discourse about the myth of Rome to an unparalleled level of complexity. His three Roman tragedies are remembered today, long after the dozens of lesser dramatic works based upon Roman themes from the Renaissance and the baroque era have been forgotten. Ultimately, Shakespeare demonstrated that either Rome, republican or imperial, might be the source of human tragedy.

ROMAN MYTH AND MELODRAMA

IN THE BAROQUE AND

NEOCLASSICAL AGES

D uring the baroque and neoclassical periods, including most of the seventeenth century and the first half of the eighteenth, Europe was characterized by the rule of absolute monarchs. Italy's republican city-states, which fostered a revival of Livian virtues, had all but disappeared. As a result, the Roman image of imperial power and majesty derived from the Tacitean model gained strength and prestige in European culture. While Livian values encouraged active and heroic citizenship, imperial values favored the acquiescence of obedient subjects or the adulation of an all-powerful sovereign by his admiring courtiers. Although this period is not an era which favored republican art or political theory, it is remarkable how the republican ideal managed to survive, nevertheless, in a number of interesting forms.

In the period under discussion, Roman themes became of central importance to the theatre, particularly in a new artistic form invented by the Florentines, the operatic melodrama. Most tragedies or operas employing a Roman setting—with the notable exception of Shakespeare's Roman tragedies—simplified the complex political and moral issues embodied in either the Livian or the Tacitean tradition. In many plays and melodramas, problems such as the nature of citizenship, the conflicting demands of family and state, and the philosophical questions concerning historical change, decay, and rebirth—all traditionally at the heart of the myth of Rome—were subordinated to the theme of tragic love and were deprived of any practical political intent. Nevertheless, one original subject popularized during this period in both drama and opera constituted a distinctly new contribution to the evolution of the Roman myth—the theme of the clemency, generosity, and magnanimity of an all-powerful ruler. Such a variation on imperial Roman mythology was obviously intended to appeal to the nonrepublican, aristocratic audiences at the courts and palaces where such works were commonly performed.

Increased attention to the imperial aspect of Roman myth also changed how the traditional republican myths were interpreted. Much of the specifically political or ideological intent of republican mythology was modified, rendering it more personal and therefore less objectionable. Instead of viewing one of Livy's heroic figures as a potential political model, for example, it became more convenient to view such a character as an ethical model, a paradigm for *private* moral conduct and the pursuit of *personal* virtues. In a sense, such an apolitical interpretation rendered these narratives socially neutral and, therefore, ideologically harmless. This approach to Livian mythology explains why so many major artists and writers continued to decorate the walls and ceilings of their kingly patrons with pictures of such individuals and to produce dramatic and operatic performances in which such characters play major roles even when the values such heroic individuals represent were in direct contrast to those of their audience or patrons.

The treatment of the theme of Lucretia and Brutus, from the late sixteenth century until the eve of the French Revolution, underlines quite dramatically how a once politically significant republican myth was modified to suit different sensibilities.[1] The Florentine republicans had emphasized the masculine figure of Lucius Junius Brutus, the man who used Lucretia's rape and suicide to establish the first Roman republic. After the middle of the sixteenth century, however, the best known representations of this legend omitted Brutus entirely, concentrating upon the tragedy of Lucretia and her inner suffering. Excellent illustrations of this development may be found in four paintings by European masters: *Tarquin and Lucretia* (1570) by Titian (1480–1576); *Lucretia* (1580–85) by Paolo Veronese (1528–88); *Lucretia* (1666) by Rembrandt (1606–69); and *Tarquin and Lucretia* (1745–50) by Giovanni Battista Tiepolo (1696–1770).

Titian took the first step away from the Florentine republican tradition by eliminating political meaning. Titian's painting (figure 15) does not focus on the momentous results of Lucretia's suicide, as in Botticelli's work, where the violated woman symbolizes Rome and Brutus's vengeance leads to the founding of the republic. His emphasis is rather upon Tarquin's threat to kill Lucretia if she did not give in to his libidinous demands. By including the slave in the left of the picture, Titian also invites us to share the experience of watching the rape, and this voyeuristic, essentially male perspective undercuts almost completely the moral and political impulse behind the story as recounted by Livy or painted by Botticelli. Furthermore, the contrast between the clothed ravisher and

15. Titian, Tarquin and Lucretia (oil on canvas).
Fitzwilliam Museum, Cambridge.

the half-naked, vulnerable woman and the juxtaposition of Tarquin's forceful right knee and upraised knife with the helpless woman's arms, underlines Titian's appeal to prurient interests.

It would be natural to assume that a version of the story by a woman artist named Artemisia Gentileschi (1597–1651) might change the masculine perspective of Titian or reveal Lucretia in a more active and positive role. This is especially true since we know that this young artist suffered an experience similar to Lucretia's. In 1611, she was raped by her teacher Agostino Tassi. The courts acquitted the man after torturing the woman to test the veracity of her testimony! Yet, her version of the legend, *Tarquin and Lucretia* (1645–50), only repeats the iconography of Titian's version.

Only a few years later, Veronese moved even further away from the original Livian story (figure 16). Lucretia is now pictured standing alone, isolated, and apparently caught up completely in her private tragedy. The entire social context of her plight—both the presence of the rapist and the historical events that followed her death—has been obliterated by the artist. The rich jewelry, ornate clothing, and curtains surrounding the woman suggest a Venetian patrician of the sixteenth century rather than the virtuous and heroic symbol of ravished republican liberty. And the moment of Lucretia's death has been softened by the reticent manner in which her clothing envelopes the fatal dagger, as if she hesitates to stain or soil her exquisite body with the metal and the blood.

By far the most enigmatic version of Lucretia's demise was provided by Rembrandt, whose Lucretia continues the solitude established in Veronese's portrait but is even more ambiguous and suggestive (figure 17). The younger woman has already stabbed herself (the bloodstain is evident through her clothing, although the dagger itself seems to be unsullied), but her reaction is quite puzzling. Her left hand clutches a rope—suggestive either of a bellcord used to call a servant or perhaps a curtain being raised or lowered. Has she changed her mind in the midst of her suicide and called her servants or relatives to her aid? Or, is she raising a curtain on her gesture as if to dramatize its theatrical nature? Both Veronese and Rembrandt, of course, completely altered the original story by showing Lucretia in solitude rather than in the midst of her friends and relatives, once again emphasizing the private, personal dimensions of what was no longer construed as a politically significant act.

Even more openly sensuous an interpretation of Lucretia was offered by Tiepolo (figure 18), whose rapist leers and whose suit of armor contrasts even more dramatically than in Titian's painting to the nakedness and vulnerability of the woman. Moreover, Tiepolo cleverly conflated

16. Paolo Veronese, Lucretia (oil on canvas).
Kunsthistorisches Museum, Vienna.

17. Rembrandt, Lucretia (oil on canvas).
Minneapolis Institute of Art.

18. *Giovanni Battista Tiepolo*, Tarquin
and Lucretia (*oil on canvas*).
Magdalene Haberstock Collection, Augsburg
Museum.

two moments of the rather complex Livian narrative—that of the threat with the dagger and the later suicide with the same weapon—by the ambiguous manner in which the arms of the two figures are intertwined. At an initial glance, the viewer can imagine both that Tarquin is threatening Lucretia with a knife *and* that the woman is about to thrust the knife into her abdomen. In either case, the dagger which generations of republican revolutionaries viewed as the symbol of the founding of the first Roman republic by Brutus has now been transformed into a cleverly drawn phallic symbol.

Thus, Livy's dramatic political fable was radically transformed by a number of major European artists. Lucretia's individual suffering may actually have achieved greater stature in these works. We empathize with her helplessness in Titian (although we are also asked to enjoy the spectacle); we wonder at the concealed and mysterious motives which move her to end her life in the private, existential dramas of Veronese and Rembrandt; and we are even amused at the ambiguous visual punning in Tiepolo. But we have moved an immeasurable distance both from the political and ethical intention of the original source as well as from the earlier works and discussions of the legend that were informed by republican values.

The transformation of the Lucretia story underscores the modification of a tale with historical and political significance into one with a predominantly erotic flavor. Other equally radical transformations of Roman republican and imperial narratives from the classical histories of Livy, Tacitus, and others took place in the same period, although these transformations did not consist of a shift away from moral and ethical grounds. The best examples of such works of art are found among the many neoclassical scenes painted by Nicolas Poussin (1594–1665), considered the greatest figure in the so-called "Grand Manner" style. With the establishment of the French Royal Academy in 1648 and its influential Rome branch in 1666, historical genre painting, referred to as *exemplum virtutis*, was elevated to the pinnacle of artistic forms, and Poussin's early Italianate work contributed to its popularity, which was to remain high until the French Revolution.

Painting in this style concentrated upon those historical scenes and iconographical choices that stressed moral lessons. The selection of a topic from republican or imperial history was less motivated by its political message than by its salutary moral tone. This is apparent in two great canvases by Poussin—*The Death of Germanicus* (1627) and *Camillus and the Schoolmaster of Falerii* (circa 1635). The earlier work had a noble, ecclesiastical patron (Cardinal Francesco Barberini), while the later canvas was done for one of France's wealthiest financiers, Louis Phélypaux de La Vrillière.[2] In *The Death of Germanicus* (figure 19), Poussin produced his first masterpiece. The story is taken from the *Annals* of Tacitus and depicts a deathbed scene made popular by the widespread circulation of translations of Tacitus and tragedies based upon his works. Germanicus, a nephew of the Emperor Tiberius and a man reputed to have a preference for the old republic, was sent by Tiberius to govern the eastern provinces. With him Tiberius sent Calpurnius Piso, who was also apparently assigned the task of checking the activities of the popular Germanicus if he should become a threat to Tiberius. While in Antioch, Germanicus fell ill. He suspected that he had been poisoned by Piso on the orders of Tiberius, and Tacitus reports that Germanicus asked his generals to swear that they would avenge his death.

Poussin has carefully staged this potentially dramatic scene within a rigid, austere setting. The stark, neoclassical architecture is softened only by the vivid colors of the cloaks, the generals' bright armor, and the garments worn by the mourning family. Yet rather than emphasize the revolutionary content of the scene by underlining the cruelty of an all-powerful emperor and the martyrdom of a republican hero, Poussin chose instead to accentuate the gravity and the moral dignity of the dying man. As a result, the painting praises the art of dying well and the moral advantages of accepting the inevitable demise of all earthly things, rather than asking the spectator to make an ideological response to the historical facts represented on the canvas. The grandeur of the setting and the dignity of the figures within the composition seem designed to counsel temperance rather than rebellion. Much the same message can be gleaned from Poussin's *Camillus and the Schoolmaster of Falerii* (figure 20). This incident from Livy's account of the life of the republican hero originally had an exclusively political meaning. Camillus was the prototype of the virtuous military leader who punished treachery and double-dealing. In Poussin's painting, such issues take second place to compositional form. Unethical behavior, embodied in the twisted and distorted nude figure of the evil schoolmaster in the center, surrounded by his young charges, is juxtaposed to the literally upright and well proportioned Camillus. Rather than prompt us to an imitation of Camillus's actions, we are asked merely to contemplate the difference between shapeless ugliness and harmonious form. Political issues have been replaced by aesthetic ideals.

A similar movement away from political themes can be seen in the theatre of the period. Shakespeare's portrait of the Roman experience

19. Nicolas Poussin, The Death of
Germanicus (oil on canvas).
Minneapolis Institute of Art.

20. *Nicolas Poussin*, Camillus and the
Schoolmaster of Falerii (*oil on canvas*).
The Norton Simon Foundation, Los Angeles.

represented a unique attempt to understand the multifaceted evolution of the Eternal City from its republican origins. This comprehensive and highly nuanced historical panorama found few imitators among the many baroque and neoclassical playwrights, librettists, and composers who subsequently treated Roman myth in tragedy, melodrama, and opera. Like the artists of the period, they, too, stripped Roman myth of its political significance and employed it as a noble backdrop for labyrinthine love affairs or emotional and moral crises of a strictly private nature. This attitude toward the Roman past, either republican or imperial, was first articulated in the French classical theatre and is evident in masterpieces by Pierre Corneille (1606–84) and Jean Racine (1638–99). This treatment of Rome would also color the countless dramas and musical productions devoted to Roman themes, from those of Claudio Monteverdi (1567–1643) to those produced on the eve of the French Revolution, after which the political import of Roman mythology would be revived on the stage.

The sort of drama we label "classical" has been well defined by an English scholar as "a play which relies for its effect on regularity of form, on unity of impression, and on absence of physical action. In it we expect to enjoy words and not to watch fisticuffs. Conflicts, there are, as in all drama, but mental rather than physical, symbolic rather than realist. We watch a clash of opinions, of attitudes rather than individuals; we hear a language which is rare rather than racy; we are not reminded of real life but allowed to escape from it."[3] Rather than explore the historical or philosophical aspects of a dramatic situation, which Elizabethan tragedy does so brilliantly and with a dramatic language that spans the entire range of tones and stylistic registers, French classical theatre concentrates upon the mental and poetic dimensions of an action, employing all of the persuasive powers of rhetoric that could be drawn from the Alexandrine couplet, which was its elegant and refined medium of expression. The focus on the implications of mental actions produced at its best a drama of intense emotional power and poetic beauty.

Within this drama of ideas and emotions, the history of republican and imperial Rome served primarily as a noble backdrop. Corneille's best work, Horatius (1640), more than any other work of this period, helped to set the tone for the treatment of Rome on the post-Renaissance stage. While the play recalls Shakespeare's Coriolanus in its definition of Roman identity in the early Republic, Corneille divested the Livian story of the heroic battle between three brothers from Rome and Alba of much of its historical particulars, transforming the classical source into an abstract confrontation between the widely divergent points of view embodied by the major characters. In order to add additional dramatic conflicts and complications to the original story, Corneille added new characters or developed minor figures as foils for or confidants to the main protagonists. In his version of the tale, a sister on each side is engaged or married to a member of the opposite family: Sabina, the sister of the Curiatii, is married to Horatius, while Camilla, the sister of the Horatii, is betrothed to Curiatius. *Horatius* is thus only superficially about Roman history, as one recent critic has noted. Its true subject is the play of different temperaments, personal attitudes, and abstract ideals of conduct, set in motion and directed toward violent conflict by the skillful dramatic construction and the moving rhetoric of the poetry.[4]

Sabina, torn between two rival families and countries, expresses an un-Roman distaste for the warlike, masculine values of her husband Horatius. When Curiatius confronts Horatius, and both learn that they have been chosen to defend their native cities, their different reactions juxtapose almost too neatly conflicting views of the world—that of republican Rome (at least as seen by Corneille) and that of the non-Roman world. Horatius, the perfect Roman soldier, believes that to die for one's country is the noblest death imaginable, and he is quite willing to forget his friendship and the possibility of closer kinship with Curiatius for a higher duty. Curiatius, on the other hand, follows Sabina in his loathing for this internecine warfare, since Rome and Alba have the same origins. He argues with Horatius: "And yet your hardness is a little savage: / Few, even of the greatest, would make boast / Of reaching immortality this way. / However high these fumes will waft your name, / Obscurity is better than such fame. / . . . / This sad, proud honor moves but does not shake me: / I greet its gifts but pity what it takes; / And if your Rome demands a loftier valor, / I render thanks to Heaven that I am not Roman, / To cherish still some trace of being a man" (1.3.456–60, 478–82).[5]

It would never have occurred to earlier republican writers to juxtapose, as Corneille does in *Horatius*, Roman values to those of humanity at large. On the contrary, for earlier manifestations of republican mythology, Roman values represented the very *essence* of humanity. When Camilla learns of the death of her fiancé Curiatius by her brother's hand, she determines to reject his deed in the name of humanity, calling down upon Rome and her champion a treasonous curse. This causes Horatius to fly into an irrational rage. He murders his sister (offstage, carefully avoiding the offense a visible action might have caused his audience), and the final act of the drama turns upon the question of his guilt or innocence. Valerius, a Roman also in love with Camilla, argues that Horatius must be punished for his crime, just as he was properly honored by his glorious deeds. This, in fact, was the usual practice in Livian mythology, as in the example of Marcus Manlius Capitolinus. Livy's account excuses the exception made for Horatius, but Corneille goes somewhat further in exonerating Horatius, perhaps in deference to the absolute monarchy then governing his native France. He brings forth King Tullus, who declares that in this special instance, the law must be silent, since in the founding of Rome, even Romulus was forced to kill his own brother: "Then live, Horatius, our noble warrior: / Your valor puts your fame above your crime" (5.3.1759–60).

A number of the characteristics of Corneille's play inform most of the baroque or neoclassical representations of Rome in drama and music. The complex, intricate political situations that fascinated Machiavelli or Shakespeare now have been reduced to abstract intellectual problems between conflicting ideals. We have already seen the same phenomenon in the canvases of Poussin, although composition and color rather than the rhetoric of poetic langauge rendered such tensions there. And with this narrowing of focus and heightening of emotional power, there was also an accompanying move away from any practical application of the Roman exempla exployed. Corneille's republican hero, unlike Michelangelo's Brutus, would find himself just as comfortable at the court of Louis XIV as in a revolutionary republic. Since his Roman identity was presented as an abstract ethical principle, Horatius could exist in the grandiose world of Corneille's poetry without ever arousing troublesome ideological issues among the audience.

Just how similar the treatment of republican and imperial Rome could be may be seen from a comparison of Corneille's play with two works devoted to the Emperor Nero: Monteverdi's opera L'incoronazione di Poppea (1642) and Racine's tragedy Britannicus (1669). Monteverdi's opera, blessed with a great libretto by Francesco Busenello (1598–1659), was unusual in accepting energetic sensuality rather than condemning passion as a source of moral corruption. It was, moreover, the first opera to treat a historical theme (Nero's love for Poppea and the influence of passion upon his imperial rûle) rather than a mythological subject. From the opening prologue, where the goddesses of Virtue, Fortune, and Love argue over which of them possesses the greatest power over mankind, we realize that Monteverdi has shifted the focus of his portrait of imperial Rome from the realm of moral choices to that of the senses (figure 21). As in the tragedy by Corneille, the plot is complicated by a byzantine

21. Claudio Monteverdi, Prologue to
L'incoronazione di Poppea: "Love
asserts her hegemony over Virtue and
Fortune" (New York City Opera
production, November 9, 1977).
New York City Opera and Fred Fehl,
photographer.

network of interconnected personalities: Ottone returns from a war and discovers that his mistress, Poppea, has taken Nero as her lover; the Empress Ottavia, jealous of Poppea and fearful of her position, persuades Ottone to murder Nero. The plot, however, is uncovered and foiled. Ultimately, Nero banishes the Empress, orders his tutor Seneca to kill himself when he opposes his amorous schemes, and finally marries Poppea.

Unlike Corneille, Monteverdi displayed a marked cynicism in his treatment of human experience as well as an acceptance of destructive human passion, which is allowed to dominate all other aspects of life. The victors in the lyrical drama are those who are ruled by an elemental thirst for power and sexual passion—Nero and Poppea—while the figures who would traditionally be praised for their virtuous Roman qualities—the moral teacher, Seneca; Ottone, the faithful lover; and Ottavia, the spurned wife—are all defeated and serve, in many respects, only to set in relief the two passionate lovers. Nothing in Tacitus, the original source, can match in emotional power the triumph of Eros at the close of the opera. This triumph is embodied in a magnificent duet sung by Nero and Poppea: "I gaze on you, I rejoice in you, / I embrace you, I chain you to me, / I suffer no more, I die no more, / oh my life, oh my treasure. / I am yours, you are mine. My hope, say it, say, / you are alone my idol, / yes my darling, yes my heart, / my life, yes" (3.6).[6]

Racine's *Britannicus* approaches the character of Nero from a much different perspective. Inspired by the same source in Tacitus that Monteverdi used as a starting point for his opera, Racine restricted his narrative even further to a single moment in the emperor's youth: his decision to murder his stepbrother Britannicus and tear himself away from the oppressive influence of his mother, the Empress Agrippina. Nero's mother announces this sudden transformation in the opening scene of the tragedy: "Nero has moved against Britannicus. / The impatient Nero is done with self-restraint; / he is weary of inspiring love; he would now / be feared. Britannicus tortures him, I in turn, / feel my own presence daily more troublesome."[7] As Racine put it in the first preface to the play, Nero represented not the mature and totally depraved tyrant he would later become but, instead, a "budding monster."

By limiting the historical action in the drama, Racine achieves a tremendous concentration upon a single incident, which itself represents the central, recurring conflict in Nero's life: whether or not to commit a crime. He is pressured by his confidants: Burrhus advises him to be a strong, moral ruler, while Narcissus uses seductive words to corrupt him.

He is jealous of his rival, Britannicus, who had been disinherited by his mother and removed from the royal succession to make way for Nero. But Britannicus is more fortunate in love, because Junia loves him rather than Nero. And Nero is both afraid and resentful of the domineering and treacherous Agrippina, who has controlled his freedom during the first three virtuous years of his reign. Racine's genius in this psychological portrait of the birth of a moral monster consists in convincing us that Nero's understandable desire for personal freedom and independence can be purchased only at the price of crime. His tragedy—and Nero is portrayed here tragically rather than being attacked for his future failings —is that he can find no means of asserting his personal identity save those which would initiate a career of brutality and murder.

In both *L'incoronazione di Poppea* and *Brittanicus*, Nero emerges as a far more sympathetic figure than in subsequent treatments of his life in literature or film. In the opera, his passion and sexuality triumph over reason and restraint; in the tragedy, his will to power overcomes family ties and the demands of just government. And yet, the figure of this imperial ruler, who allows either his passion or his cruelty to overcome his better instincts, never moves very far from the demonic heroism of Corneille's republican warrior, Horatius. The Roman world these characters inhabit—whether republican or imperial—consists of abstract moral choices or highly charged emotional imperatives and sharply juxtaposed personal ideals or ambitions rather than specific historical problems or particular political institutions. And whether it is the rhetoric of the French poetry or the magnificent music of Monteverdi, the narrow focus of the story line—narrow, that is, when compared to the Roman tragedies of Shakespeare—permits a stronger emotional concentration upon a single, well-defined moral choice. The tremendous influence of Racine and Corneille upon European theatre and Monteverdi upon operatic melodrama guaranteed that Roman subjects would be among the favorite topics chosen by baroque or neoclassical composers and playwrights throughout much of the late seventeenth and mid-eighteenth centuries.

It was also in the tragic theatre of Corneille and Racine that a highly original theme was added to the evolution of Roman mythology: the clemency, generosity, or magnanimity of an all-powerful Roman ruler. The genesis of this theme may be found in Corneille's *Cinna* (1641) and in Racine's *Berenice* (1670). In the first play (inspired by Seneca's *De Clementia* 1.9), the Emperor Augustus's life is threatened by a plot hatched by his trusted protegée Emilia, who desires revenge against Augustus for the execution of her father. She is assisted by Cinna, a relative of Pompey, who has been repeatedly pardoned and honored by Augustus in the past. The death of Augustus becomes the price Cinna must pay for Emilia's hand in marriage.

When the guilt of the pair of lovers is discovered, Augustus, rather than executing them, pardons them both on the advice of his wife Livia. He thus asserts his superiority over the other characters by exercising not only control over the entire world but also over himself and his righteous indignation: "I'm master of myself as of the world; / I am, I will be. O posterity, / Preserve forever my last victory! / Today, the holiest anger I subdue / Whose memory might reach right down to you! / Let us be friends, Cinna, I wish it so: / I gave you life once, when you were my foe" (5.3.1693–99).

The same sort of imperial self-control is celebrated in *Berenice*, which treats the Emperor Titus's ultimately successful struggle to place his duties as ruler of the world above his passionate desire for Berenice, a foreign princess. Unlike Mark Antony or Julius Caesar, whose oriental escapades cost them prestige and power, Titus proves worthy of the challenge to his self-control, conquers his emotions, and triumphs, as Augustus does in *Cinna*, more over himself than over his opponents.

This emphasis upon the clemency displayed by all-powerful rulers was obviously designed to edify the aristocratic audiences at the courts of various European monarchs. This and other Roman themes were typically employed in the performances of *opera seria*, so popular as courtly entertainment. Following the example of the noble melodrama of Monteverdi, eighteenth-century lyric theatre in the years before the French Revolution attempted to recreate the tragic effects of the French neoclassical works by Corneille or Racine in the opera. The popularity of Roman themes in the melodrama of the period was considerable. Without taking into account the many hundreds of unpublished operas produced during the period from Monteverdi's *L'incoronazione* to 1796 (the year of Napoleon's first Italian campaign at the height of the French Revolution), no less than twenty-one major operas treating republican and imperial Roman topics were produced by some of the greatest composers and librettists of Europe: Henry Purcell (1659–95); Alessandro Scarlatti (1660–1725); George Frederick Handel (1685–1759); Johann Adolph Hasse (1699–1783); Giovanni Battista Pergolesi (1710–36); Antonio Vivaldi (1678–1741); Christoph Willibald Gluck (1714–87); Domenico Cimarosa (1740–1801); and Wolfgang Amadeus Mozart (1756–91).[8]

The subjects of such operatic compositions were varied, including Arminius, the German Brutus (Handel, Hasse); Julius Caesar (Handel); Cleopatra (Cimarosa); Sulla (Mozart); Cato of Utica (Hasse, Vivaldi); Titus Manlius (Vivaldi); Horatius and the Curiatii (Cimarosa); the Emperor Titus (Mozart); and many others. With the demise of *opera seria*, the popularity of Roman subject matter in European lyrical drama declined rapidly. In spite of the many efforts by composers and librettists of obvious genius, *opera seria* never matched the tragedies of sixteenth-century England or seventeenth-century France. One explanation may be found in the genre's nontheatrical conventions. Employing only recitative, arias, and solo ensembles, interior dramatic development was difficult, and thus *opera seria* became primarily a "display piece for singers." [9] So long as the music was organized in such a manner that all sentiment or emotion remained limited to the formally organized musical sections (duets, arias), while all action was left to be conveyed in recitative, *opera seria* remained an essentially static and actionless, though beautiful, lyrical genre. Exhibiting wonderful virtuoso flights by individual performers, it never achieved true tragic proportions and usually remained a somewhat fixed collection of set pieces rather than a convincing, unified dramatic action.

Nevertheless, a number of the best "serious" operas have been revived quite successfully in the past decade, and three of these works contain visions of Roman clemency: Vivaldi's *Tito Manlio* (composed for the 1719 carnival season in Venice); *Lucio Silla*, written by Mozart in 1772 with a libretto by Giovanni de Gamerra (1743–1803); and the most popular of all the "serious" operas, Mozart's *La clemenza di Tito*, composed just before Mozart's death in 1791 to celebrate the coronation of Emperor Leopold II as King of Bohemia.

Vivaldi's *Tito Manlio* represents a fine example of how the *opera seria* genre treated Roman myth. The simple story from Livy—the stern decision of the consul to execute his son (also named Tito Manlio) for disobeying orders—becomes a labyrinth of convoluted amours and conflicting demands, often at variance with Roman history. The death of Geminio, the Latin commander, at the hands of the consul's son sets in motion the elaborate plot, which, like so many other operatic story lines from the period, relies upon juxtaposition and opposition. The sisters of Manlio and Geminio, never mentioned in Livy, complicate matters with their amorous attachments to members of the other's family. Manlio's sister Vitellia loves Geminio and therefore supports her father in his harsh decision to execute her brother. Geminio's sister Servilia is in love with Manlio and thus opposes the execution. Vivaldi's fantastic plot reminds the viewer more of Corneille's *Horatius*, which had indeed influenced the composer, than of the original Livian legend.

Perhaps the most interesting modification of the classical source occurs at the conclusion of the opera. Manlio is saved at the last minute by the intervention of the Roman army, which refuses to allow the consul to execute his sentence, just as in Corneille the king saves Horatius. As the consul admits at the end of the last act, "the will of the army is law to the law" (3).[10] Such a conclusion obeyed the period's insistence upon a happy ending (*lieto fine*), but it also falsified Livian history. The elevation of the army over republican institutions reflected, no doubt, the lack of any real historical empathy for Roman republican values on the part of Vivaldi's aristocratic audience, as well as their interest in elevating political decisions above the whim of individual rulers.

In Vivaldi's opera, the act of clemency usually performed by an all-powerful, benevolent imperial ruler was carried out by the army. In Mozart's *Lucio Silla* and *La clemenza di Tito*, similar and even more surprising acts of generosity are performed under both republican and imperial rule. It is a measure of how far the neoclassical period has moved from the Renaissance understanding of Roman myth that the difference between the world of the republican dictator Lucio Silla (or Sulla, as he is usually known) and the Emperor Titus hardly interested the composer or the librettist. In *Lucio Silla*, Mozart employed historical events from Rome's civil wars. Lucio Silla, dictator of Rome, has proscribed Cecilio, a Roman senator. Cecilio learns from his friend Cinna that Silla is courting his wife Giunia, who believes Cecilio to be dead. After Cecilio's attempt to assassinate Silla fails, the dictator magnanimously pardons Cecilio, reunites him with his wife, Giunia, and restores Rome to its former liberty. In this coup de théâtre, very poorly prepared by a rather weak libretto, Silla declares: "Cinna, I no longer wish you / to be the witnesses, before all Rome, / of my crimes and cruelty, / and here I shall reveal the heart / of Silla." And to Giunia, he announces: "The godless Silla, the haughty tyrant, / hateful to all men, decrees / that Cecilio shall live to be your husband. / What I have seen has taught me / that the soul prefers innocence and a virtuous heart / to deceitful splendor" (3).[11]

One of the few *opere serie* that managed to rise above the rather stilted and nondramatic character of the genre was *La clemenza di Tito*, not only because it is filled with magnificent music but also because its libretto, based upon an older tragedy by the librettist and court poet of Saxony, Caterino Mazzola, provided a far more convincing dramatic structure than did other libretti of the period. Furthermore, in this case the theme matched the occasion of composition perfectly, as it was intended to be performed at a king's coronation. As one recent Mozart biography described the work, it was a "symbolic" act, wherein the personified wisdom and kindness of the Emperor Titus was intended to demonstrate the magnanimity of his modern counterpart.[12] Nevertheless, in spite of its great music—notably the march and chorus, "Servate, oh Dei custodi" ("Oh gods, guardians," 1), and a number of magnificent arias sung by Titus—even the Empress Maria Louisa of Spain denounced the premier performance as "una porcheria tedesca" ("German hogwash"), an opinion that has been echoed by not a few critics since Mozart's time.[13]

As we might expect, the opera's plot is a maze of intricate interrelationships, mixing political and erotic issues. Vitellia, daughter of the deposed Emperor Vitellius, believes she has a right to the throne and plans to kill the Emperor Titus, since he has not chosen her as his consort. She employs Sextus, who loves her, to achieve this end. Meanwhile, Titus gives up his plan to marry Servilia and declares he is ready to choose Vitellia as his empress. But Sextus has already gone to the Capitol to assassinate Titus. In Act 2, we are surprised to discover that the plot has failed and that Titus has given Sextus over to the courts for trial, even though he cannot bring himself to believe that his best friend would plan his death. Vitellia finally reveals herself to be the leader of the plot. Rather than sentencing the pair to the death their actions have merited, Titus magnanimously forgives them all, bringing the performance to a resounding finale with the expected lieto fine (figure 22).

Perhaps one reason that Mozart almost succeeded in revitalizing the opera seria in this work is that he had dramatized the theme of imperial clemency with a character whose emotional intensity rivaled that embodied by the Roman heroes of Racine and Corneille. Mozart's Titus controlled the entire known world, yet he was supremely aware that it was much more desirable to control his own emotions and to govern his own desires. His actions are heroic in the same sense that the tragic choices made by the characters of French classical tragedy are heroic. They are decisions that resolve conflicts of absolute, abstract moral values. His desire to be generous and forgiving drives Titus to become almost as demonic a character as Corneille's Horatius. Both men are single-minded, unidimensional figures who stop at nothing in pursuit of their ideals. In particular, the exit arias sung by Titus reveal the intensity

22. *Wolfgang Amadeus Mozart, Finale to
La clemenza di Tito: "The Emperor's
clemency triumphs over his desire for
revenge" (New York City Opera
production, November 15, 1981).*
New York City Opera and Fred Fehl,
photographer.

of his personality. Notable examples of such arias include one in Act 2 ("Del più sublime soglio"), which suggests that generosity is the only satisfaction to be found in high office: "This is the only satisfaction / of the highest office: / all the rest is but misery; and subjugation."[14] Equally memorable are "Ah, se fosse intorno al trono" ("Ah, if everyone near to my throne"), wherein Titus expresses his gratitude to his friends' assistance; "Se all'impero, / amici Dei" ("If a severe heart / is necessary to the empire, / oh gods, take the empire / away from me / or give me another heart"); and the concluding "Il vero pentimento" ("The true repentance / of which you are capable, / is worth more / than constant fidelity").

Even at the time Mozart wrote La clemenza di Tito, the opera seria and its particular means of employing Roman mythology had already fallen from favor. The new middle-class audiences that had begun to frequent the public theatres and opera houses in the late eighteenth century cared little for the opera illustrating the generosity or benevolence of an absolute monarch or dictator. Mozart may well have viewed clemency in either a republican dictatorship or an emperor as a virtue which transcended the particular kind of political institution or civic culture each individual represented. But in an age of revolution, such opinions would find increasingly fewer partisans. Far from being considered a virtue, a monarch's clemency only reminded his rebellious populace that they were subjects rather than citizens with inalienable rights of their own. And, during the evolution of the myth of Rome in an era of violent political upheaval, patriotic resolution in the face of adversity rather than a despot's clemency would be seen as the highest human virtue.

During this period, however, the republican myth of Rome was not entirely quiescent. Perhaps the greatest expression of the republican side of the myth of Rome in the eighteenth-century theatre may be found in Pietro Metastasio (1698–1782). Practically unknown and unread today, Metastasio was nevertheless Europe's most influential and popular dramatist during the first half of the century. In 1730, he moved from Italy to Vienna, where he became the resident court poet (poeta cesareo) under Emperor Charles VI. He remained there until his death, serving both Charles and Empress Maria Theresa. His lyrical dramas—classical in their observation of the dramatic unities and the strict theatrical decorum established by the French neoclassical theatre—were perfect vehicles for composers in search of opera subjects. And the memorable "little arias" (ariette) that characters declaimed just before their exit from the stage in his works would become the characteristic "exit arias" in the opera libretti based upon his plays. He is best remembered for Attilio Regolo (Atilius

Regulus, 1732) and for *La clemenza di Tito* (1732). The first play, generally considered to be Metastasio's masterpiece, was set to music by Johann Adolph Hasse in 1750. The second play has a remarkable history, serving as the source for some twenty operas, including one by Gluck as well as the version by Mozart already discussed.

Metastasio took the plot of *Attilio Regolo* from Cicero's account of the republican general taken prisoner in Africa in the war against Carthage. Regulus embodied for both Cicero and Metastasio the quintessence of republican morality and discipline. Not only did Regulus refuse any compromise with the oath he had sworn, but he even prohibited his Carthaginian captors from assisting him in obtaining his freedom, because in his eyes, any compromise would be made at the expense of his Roman honor. Regulus's instructions to his son reflected the stern severity of the republican tradition: "Our country is a whole of which we form the part. 'Tis criminal in he that bears the name of citizen, to weigh his private weal distinct from hers."[15] In the third and final act, the Roman populace blocked the path of the departing hero, crying "Regulus, stay" ("Resti, Regolo!"). But the tragedy concluded with the last words of the captive leader to his native city, which exhorted his fellow citizens to remember their Roman heritage. Yet Regulus's final utterance showed him overwhelmed by true emotion ("but why these tears—farewell!"), transformed from an almost unbelievable paragon of republican severity into a more sympathetic figure.

Despite the republican sentiment of this play, Metastasio's position as court poet at the Austrian court—the same government that consistently repressed Italian attempts to reunify the northern peninsula under a single national republic—naturally made him suspect among the young Italian firebrands and patriots of the eighteenth century, who would see the French Revolution as a means of transforming the political geography of Italy, driving out the Austrians as well as the native Italian principalities, duchies, and kingdoms, and establishing republican governments where none had existed for centuries. It is not surprising that Metastasio and his works, most written expressly for an absolute monarch's entertainment and certainly not composed to advocate practical political action, might be viewed with disfavor by republican zealots. Vittorio Alfieri (1749–1803), the preromantic tragedian and poet whose own dramatic works embraced a revived Roman republicanism and were perhaps the most important Italian expression of this newly emerging direction in the myth of Rome, indignantly commented upon Metastasio when, as a young man, he visited the Austrian court in Vienna:

I might during that stay in Vienna easily have got the acquaintance and frequented the society of the celebrated poet Metastasio. . . . I had been in the imperial gardens at Schoenbrun a witness of Metastasio making the customary slight obeisance to Maria Theresa, with a servile expression of completely adulatory satisfaction. I was a youthful Plutarch addict and so much given to exaggerating the abstract truth that I never would have consented to contract friendship or acquaintance with a Muse hired out or sold to the despotic authority that I so warmly abhorred.[16]

The passionate nationalism and insistence upon love of country in Metastasio's *Attilio Regolo*—a work originally composed to commemorate the birthday of an absolute monarch—would nevertheless continue to appeal to audiences of a far more revolutionary epoch. Alfieri must have been amazed to discover that in 1792, republican audiences in Rome applauded a revived presentation of this play that viewed the Roman general as the embodiment of the egalitarian ethics the French revolutionaries carried with them as they crossed the Alps into Italy. And even more radical and surprising transformations would occur in a number of art forms that employed the myth of Rome, republican or imperial, during the revolutions in America and France.

THE MYTH OF ROME

IN AN AGE OF REASON

AND REVOLUTION

Before Rome and its secular mythology could play a crucial role in shaping events which culminated in both the American and French revolutions, a major change in perspective would have to occur. During the baroque and neoclassical periods, Roman mythology had been stripped of its political import and in many cases reduced to a series of neutral, abstract ideals with little relationship to the practical world of everyday affairs. Both republican and imperial figures from Roman mythology in art, theatre, and melodrama existed in a rarefied universe set apart from the arena of human history. The Roman myth served more often as a source of courtly entertainment than as inspiration for political life. The practical value of republican ideas was, of course, lessened in an age of absolute monarchs, but even the imperial myths served only decoratively to link the rule of modern kings with their ancient counterparts. Within these very restricted parameters—restricted when compared to the much wider scope it enjoyed from the fourteenth through the mid-sixteenth centuries—Roman mythology nevertheless managed not only to survive but even to flourish.

The changes in the mythology of Rome occurred almost contemporaneously with the onset of the neoclassical period in the early eighteenth century. While many artists continued to produce work that employed the apolitical Roman mythology treated in the preceding chapter, a new historical perspective upon Roman history was forming in the works of a few key intellectuals whose writings would stimulate an entirely different interpretation of ancient Roman history in social thought, art, and literature. Signs of such a new historical consciousness of Rome can be found in a number of major philosophical or historical works from this period: *The New Science* of Giambattista Vico (1668–1744), first published in 1725 and definitively revised in a third edition of 1744; the *Considerations on the Causes of the Greatness of the Romans and Their Decline* (1734; revised edition in 1748) by Montesquieu (1689–1755); *The Social Contract* (1762) by Jean-

Jacques Rousseau (1717–78); and the monumental *Decline and Fall of the Roman Empire* (appearing in six volumes between 1776 and 1788) by Edward Gibbon (1737–94). Other books might be cited as having contributed something important to the newly emerging historical perspective on Rome and its mythology, but these four works were fundamental in establishing a very different climate of opinion from that which nourished the image of Rome in the French neoclassical theatre or in the melodramas and *opere serie* which took the theatre of Corneille and Racine as their models. With these four figures, Roman myth was transformed from a storehouse of moral exempla to be developed for imperial entertainments into a revolutionary force capable of stimulating political change and social transformation, as it had been during the Italian Renaissance.

The first step was establishing a new sense of historicism, that is, the belief that each successive age possesses its own peculiar artistic standards, philosophical assumptions, and political or social institutions that have evolved over time. This step was taken in Vico's somewhat eccentric work of genius. His *New Science* launched a broadside attack upon the aesthetic underpinnings of European neoclassicism and its belief in an absolute human nature unsullied by historical development or change. The most original contribution to European thought made by this treatise was a radically novel theory of cognition that distinguished between knowledge about the world of nature and what Vico termed "the world of nations." For Vico, metaphysical and scientific questions belonged to the world of nature. Although philosophy, mathematics, or physics might permit man an imperfect understanding of natural phenomena, these disciplines always produced incomplete knowledge because God, and not man, had created nature. Man might know only what he had made or produced with his own hands. Because man created the world of history (the "world of nations"), human knowledge must take the social sciences as its proper domain.[1]

After proposing this revolutionary theory of cognition, which stood so far outside the prevailing mainstream that Vico's originality was overshadowed for years by far less original thinkers, Vico then proceeded to analyze human history in terms of process and development. In his view, three completely distinct epochs of human history exist: a primitive "age of Gods," during which mankind possesses an essentially poetic sensibility and is governed by superstition, religion, and magic; a second "age of heroes," dominated by classical republics where plebeians and ruling oligarchies struggle for power; and a third "age of men," a democratic and rationalistic period in which equality is the governing principle of political and economic relationships. Moreover, human history reflects what he termed a *corso* (course) or *ricorso* (recourse): it is not unilinear but cyclical, moving by progressive stages to higher and higher levels of development, all the while guided by divine providence.

Vico held the post of professor of rhetoric at the University of Naples from 1699 until his retirement in 1741, and his thought was profoundly conditioned by his training in classical languages and literatures. The study of rhetoric was required preparation for a legal career, and *The New Science* literally overflows with minutiae (often quite tedious) about Roman law, customs, and institutions. However, because of the city's longevity, Rome provided Vico with the historical data he required for his cyclical theory of history. Vico believed human affairs evolved in a cyclical pattern from anarchy to oligarchy to democracy to monarchy before returning, after following an inevitable period of decadence, to anarchy. Roman history richly demonstrated this pattern. Its fall and the so-called Dark Ages announced the beginning of a new cycle slowly moving forward in Vico's own day toward the "age of men."

Vico's *New Science* provided European intellectuals with an epistemology that elevated social sciences and the topic of social change and evolution above even the weighty questions of metaphysics and the natural sciences. Roman history no longer represented merely a series of moral exempla from which one could choose whatever one desired. Vico's Rome now embodied the process of universal human history, a history which gave a privileged place to evolution and revolution rather than stasis. Vico's *New Science* emphasized changing tastes and institutions rather than permanence, and it celebrated a historicism that recognized the necessity of each successive age creating its own peculiar moral values and political ideologies. And although this new perspective on human history in general and Rome in particular was far removed from any practical goal, Vico's original interpretation of historical evolution laid the foundations for a new and more pragmatic vision of the Roman past, which would eventually produce concrete reforms and specific institutional changes.

Montesquieu was another thinker who furthered the reemergence of the republican myth of Rome. Few political theorists possessed the popular reputation Montesquieu enjoyed by the time of the outbreak of the American Revolution. He was not only widely cited by political writers influential in planning the tumultuous upheavals in America and on the continent, but he was a primary influence upon Edward Gibbon.

Considerations on the Causes of the Greatness of the Romans and Their Decline also marked an important revival of the republican ideals of Machiavelli, whose *Discourses* was one of the major sources for Montesquieu's treatise. Montesquieu, and Rousseau after him, would do much to change the image of Machiavelli as a "Machiavellian" counselor of tyrannical princes and to reestablish him as the modern era's most original republican thinker.

Montesquieu concentrated not just upon Rome's decline but also on its phenomenal success under the republic. Following Machiavelli (who echoed Livy), Montesquieu asserted that Roman power derived from Roman virtue, but unlike other major thinkers in the evolution of Roman myth, Montesquieu emphasized the strength of Roman institutions rather than the contributions of isolated, heroic individuals, such as the early republican warriors so prominent in Livy's history. In discussing the famous episode of Lucretia and Tarquin, for instance, Montesquieu remarked that "the death of Lucretia was only the occasion of the revolution which occurred," and that all the historical evidence showed Tarquin not to be a "contemptible man."[2] General trends and movements marking Rome's evolution from grandeur to destruction occupied his attention, not edifying vignettes shaped to appeal to the reader's emotions. Montesquieu agreed with Vico, furthermore, that the vast fresco that constituted Roman history did indeed reflect some rational meaning, if not a grand design or the touch of Divine Providence. As he remarked:

Here, in a word, is the history of the Romans. By means of their maxims they conquered all peoples, but when they had succeeded in doing so, their republic could not endure. It was necessary to change the government, and contrary maxims employed by the new government made their greatness collapse. It is not chance that rules the world. . . . There are general causes, moral and physical, which act in every monarchy, elevating it, maintaining it, or hurling it to the ground. . . . In a word, the main trend draws with it all particular accidents.[3]

Montesquieu thus believed historical change and process to be a completely natural phenomenon. Roman history—as in Vico's *New Science*—is valuable precisely because it has endured for a sufficient length of time to reveal long-term patterns and meaning. All of Montesquieu's explanations for Rome's greatness reflect sociological or economic causes. Rome's virtues—a love of liberty, hard work, and military discipline; internal strife limited by self-restraint; the refusal to admit defeat; the willingness to sacrifice private goals for the commonweal's benefit—thus are seen as the necessary products of a particular type of society, not merely as the result of special valor manifested in the characters of historically unique Livian heroes. Organized in the proper (Roman) manner, any society can produce such heroic figures. Montesquieu thus shifted attention away from the Roman exempla made famous by centuries of artistic and historical tradition toward the fundamental structure of society's institutions—both in ancient Rome and in contemporary Europe or America.

Thinkers of Montesquieu's era were engaged in heated debates over the question of social status and political equality. The *philosophes*, the French philosphers of reason, usually defended the natural equality of all citizens. Thus, it is not surprising to discover that Montesquieu believed equality of property and subsequently of political power to be the single most important factor behind the strength of the Roman republic. Moreover, when that equality in social, political, and economic relations disappeared in Rome, the republic's corruption and devolution into an empire followed as a necessary consequence. Thus, the Machiavellian view of republican Rome reemerges in several key sections of the *Considerations*. In addition, Montesquieu accepts Machiavelli's original interpretation of the internal social conflicts in Rome: civil strife in a republic is a sign of civic health, not corruption, whereas the "good order" of Augustus was, in reality, only a "durable servitude":

To ask for men in a free state who are bold in war and timid in peace is to wish the impossible. And, as a general rule, whenever we see everyone tranquil in a state that calls itself a republic, we can be sure that liberty does not exist there. What is called union in a body politic is a very equivocal thing. The true kind is a union of harmony, whereby all the parts, however opposed they may appear, cooperate for the general good of society—as dissonances in music cooperate in producing overall concord. In a state where we seem to see nothing but commotion there can be union—that is, a harmony resulting in happiness, which alone is true peace.[4]

Once republican institutions had been corrupted and the social relationships that guided Rome to her vast territorial conquests had been altered, the city's slow but certain decline under the Caesars was an inevitable and natural process having little to do with the heroics of figures from Livy or the evil deeds of Tacitean villains. These changes included a growing lack of public spiritedness, increasing inequality of wealth and political power, the rise of factions, the advent of enervating luxury, and the eventual loss of a shared sense of community as citizenship spread beyond the boundaries of the once tiny city-state. Ultimately, Montesquieu declared, Rome's decline came about as a result of its very success. After all its enemies fell before its victorious armies of citizen-soldiers, Rome destroyed itself by changing the social institutions and customs that had produced its phenomenal growth.

Montesquieu's treatment of Rome's rise and decline taught his readers to link the nature of a political society's institutions to the kinds of laws and individuals that society's government produced. Rome was a positive model for eighteenth-century republicans because it alone demonstrated how a proper mixture of institutions could create a durable commonwealth and how an improper combination of institutions could bring such an admirable political edifice to ruin. With Rousseau's *Social Contract*—perhaps the most important political tract published in the century—this attention to a society's institutions and the legacy of Rome was given further study.[5] Part of Rousseau's contention was his belief, shared by many of his generation, that Rome's downfall was precipitated by its very size: had the republic maintained its original, tiny, city-state character, its republican institutions would have remained pure. Rousseau remarked that the only country in Europe still capable of proper political organization, on the basis of its size, might well be Corsica: "The valor and perseverance with which this courageous people was able to recover and defend its freedom would well deserve that some wise man should teach them how to preserve it. I have a feeling that some day this little island will astound Europe."[6]

Naturally, Rousseau had no idea just how prophetic a remark he had written. Corsica would, indeed, astound Europe, but because of the exploits of its most famous son, Napoleon Bonaparte, and not for the superiority of its republican government. In fact, Napoleon would eventually provide a modern parallel to Julius Caesar, making the same transition from a republican government in France (which he served as consul) to an empire he later created for himself in imitation of Caesar Augustus.

The argument that republican government could not survive in a large territory was no mere academic debate. If size alone determined the virtue of a republic, then only small city-states, such as those of Switzerland or Corsica, ancient Greece or Renaissance Italy, could ever attain this status. It would thus be impossible to establish a republican government in a larger state such as France or Italy. One contribution the successful American Revolution made to political discussions of the eighteenth century was to provide practical proof that a republic, indebted to Roman models, could indeed be established over an enormous land mass.

Earlier, in his influential *Discourse on the Origin and Foundations of Inequality Among Men* (1755), Rousseau had stated that the Romans were the "model for all free peoples."[7] Almost the entire fourth and last book of *The Social Contract* is devoted to a practical consideration of Roman institutions. Basing his views upon those of Livy, Machiavelli, and Montesquieu, Rousseau praised the Roman censors, who helped forestall civic corruption, analyzed the positive contribution the tribunate made to the republic, considered the protection a temporary dictatorship might offer to the state, and supported Rome's tolerant view of religion while attacking the intolerance fostered during the Christian era. There is little doubt that a wisely organized republic following the general principles Rousseau laid down in *The Social Contract* would closely resemble the classical republican city-state of Rome or that revived Roman republican government envisioned in Machiavelli's *Discourses*.

Vico's philosophy of history helped to change the very notion of historical change during the Enlightenment. Both Montesquieu and Rousseau, in very different ways, taught men in the Age of Reason that the political institutions of a society could be modified and fitted to the culture desired by its members. Republican Rome, as always, seemed to be the model of a rationally organized political society that managed to evolve and change over time. It remained for Edward Gibbon to chronicle the mighty spectacle of the decline and fall of the Roman empire, the successor to the ancient republic. Gibbon first visited Rome in 1764, and his ambition to write a history of Rome arose, in part, from his reaction to the ruins he saw there. Unlike Machiavelli or Montesquieu, Gibbon was a conservative thinker, intrigued by the demise of the empire proper, not by its republican predecessor. In fact, his history of the Roman empire does not end at the fall of Rome to the Goths in the fifth century after Christ but continues until the demise of the eastern empire with the capture of Constantinople by the Ottoman Turks in 1453. Not surprisingly, Gibbon defined history in general as "little more than the register of the crimes, follies, and misfortunes of mankind."[8]

Nevertheless, Gibbon's diagnosis of the cause of imperial Rome's decline seems derived from both Machiavelli and Montesquieu: the Roman empire collapsed (or, rather, declined and fell over several centuries) not because of its failures but because of its dramatic successes. The creation of the golden age of tranquility and prosperity lasting from the death of Domitian until the accession of Commodus (A.D. 99–180)—"the period in the history of the world during which the condition of the human race was most happy and prosperous"[9]—caused Rome to grow soft. "This long peace, and the uniform government of the Romans, introduced a slow and secret poison into the vitals of the empire. The minds of men were gradually reduced to the same level, the fire of genius was extinguished, and even the military spirit evaporated."[10] The decline in public valor and virtue was soon followed by the corruption of the intellect: "a cloud of critics, of compilers, of commentators, darkened the face of learning, and the decline of genius was soon followed by the corruption of taste."[11]

When the barbarian invasions destroyed the empire, "the Roman world was indeed peopled by a race of pygmies"; the "fierce giants of the north broke in and mended the puny breed."[12] Besides the decline of Roman intellect and Rome's traditional sense of civic pride, Gibbon detected another and perhaps more mysterious cause of Rome's demise in the decline of religious tolerance enjoyed in pagan Rome. He regarded such intolerance as a specifically Jewish trait that, passed on to Christians, unsettled the mixture of peoples and cultures living within the widespread empire. Moreover, with the advent of Christianity, the pagan sense of duty to the res publica, the commonweal, was replaced by a growing concern with the afterlife. The active citizen, concerned with public affairs and expressing his humanity through political participation, was replaced by the mystic, the priest, and the monk.

Gibbon thus explained the fall of Rome as the dual triumph of barbarism and Christianity. Like Vico, Montesquieu, and Rousseau, Gibbon in his monumental history urged the reader of the eighteenth century to view the story of Rome as a whole, as a vast panorama which upon closer observation might well yield meaningful lessons for the present. Yet, unlike their Renaissance predecessors, and especially unlike Machiavelli (from whom they learned so much about Roman institutions), these four thinkers believed in the possibility of progress and historical evolution. While the Renaissance viewed Rome's classical past as a superior model that could only be partially matched in the present, the political philosophers of the Age of Reason were convinced that the Heavenly City of St. Augustine could be rebuilt on earth in the Roman stamp but with "more up-to-date materials," as Carl Becker put it.[13]

Two different but related developments in Roman mythology followed from the works of Vico, Montesquieu, Rousseau, and Gibbon. One, particularly evident in painting and etchings devoted to Roman subjects in the eighteenth century, treated Roman history and the decline of Rome in a philosophical manner. Another, less philosophical and more political, employed the reawakened interest in republican and imperial Rome to bolster the momentous revolutions in America and France and attempted to reestablish Roman institutions in the modern world.

Foremost among the artists of the century who employed the historical demise of ancient Rome as their theme was Giambattista Piranesi (1720–78), a Venetian printmaker. In Piranesi's hands, the myth of Rome takes on a mysterious quality. Piranesi's avid interest in topographical views of ancient and modern Rome was derived in part from his participation as a young artist-apprentice in the restoration of classical ruins at Rimini. With the spectacular discoveries of ruins at Pompei and Herculaneum from 1738 onward, Piranesi encountered the archaeological works of Johann Winckelmann (1717–68). Piranesi raised his sons on the edifying tales of republican heroes from the Livian tradition. There is a story that on his deathbed, Piranesi shunned the Bible and clasped to his breast, instead, a copy of Livy, declaring: "I only have faith in this!"[14]

Topographical views or *vedute* became quite popular in the period, and a typical participant on the European Grand Tour would purchase pictorial souvenirs of his visit to the Eternal City from Piranesi, usually adding them to views of Venice by Canaletto. The disparity between ancient republican Rome or that of the imperial Caesars, on the one hand, and the decadent eighteenth-century capital of an even more decrepit papal state, on the other, was not lost on Piranesi. Piranesi began the etching of the plates for his *Vedute di Roma* (*Views of Rome*) in 1748, and he was to continue working on this incredibly popular series of prints during the remaining three decades of his life, producing some 135 different views of ancient, Renaissance, baroque, and contemporary Rome.

Piranesi's etchings of ancient Rome are far superior to those views of contemporary Rome he included in his collection. In most cases, the prints of modern buildings retain a picture postcard style that lacks the original genius Piranesi displayed in his vision of the ruins from the distant past. In his portrayal of the Temple of Minerva Medica, the dominating metaphor is that of the struggle between organic growth (vegetation clinging to the architecture) and the massive masonry of the ancient Roman structure (figure 23). The print served to dramatize the survival of the past through the vicissitudes of many centuries of historical change. Piranesi's classical Rome, in the words of one recent critic, "is a mighty corpse overgrown with modern maggotry. For Piranesi, Rome is a vast dead mother, over whom (around whom, under whom) he clambers."[15]

The relationship between the classical ruins Piranesi drew and the hu-

23. Giambattista Piranesi, "Temple of
Minerva Medica" from Vedute di
Roma (etching).
Indiana University Art Museum, Bloomington.

man figures he placed within this imaginary landscape is always the same: the human figures (grotesque types indebted to the drawings of Giambattista Tiepolo) are constantly dwarfed by their surroundings, seem to have no real relationship to the ruins, and are always slightly ridiculous, comic figures, standing in sharp contrast to the decadent nobility and grandeur of the ancient monuments. Piranesi furthermore rejected any true pictorial realism in his prints. The tourists who purchased his etchings must have been struck by the contrast between the proportions of the monuments in Piranesi's prints and the actual structures they encountered on the archaeological sites of the Eternal City. An excellent example of how Piranesi confounded expectations may be found in the view of the Temple of Saturn in the Forum, with a corner of the Arch of Septimus Severus in the foreground (figure 24). Modern buildings are combined with those from the ancient world, and the result is more an image of the ancient contending for survival with the contemporary than an archaeologically accurate rendering of the republican Forum.

The view of the interior of the frigidarium at the Baths of Diocletian (an imperial rather than republican monument) reflects another of Piranesi's illusionistic tricks (figure 25). Everywhere in this edifice, which embodies, like the Temple of Minerva Medica, the never-ending struggle between organic vegetation and stone masonry, mysterious shadowy orifices—their original function in the bath complex long forgotten— invite the viewer into a labyrinth of mysterious adventures, not unlike the fabulous staircases of Piranesi's *Carceri* (*Prisons*), which appealed so strongly to the imaginations of De Quincey, Coleridge, Hugo, Baudelaire, and other Romantic poets.[16] To further dramatize this sense of mystery, the structure stretches off to infinity toward the right side of the print in a manner that is far out of proportion with the actual size of the structure as it was preserved in Piranesi's day. The artist's brilliant visualization of the course of classical Roman history, its lessons of human mutability, and the philosophical view of the ancient Roman ruins still preserved made Piranesi's work an important pictorial counterpart to the much less accessible writings of Vico or the tomes of Gibbon. They reflected the same uneasiness with the neoclassical perspective upon ancient Roman history that stressed changelessness and stasis. In Piranesi's case, his unique and highly personal style also pointed toward a romantic interpretation of classical ruins and landscapes.

In contrast to its effect on Piranesi, the myth of Rome evoked in the men who made the American Revolution and those who precipitated an even more bloody revolt in France a more pragmatic response. Their

24. Giambattista Piranesi, "The Temple of
Saturn with a Corner of the Arch of
Septimus Severus" from Vedute di
Roma (etching).
Indiana University Art Museum, Bloomington.

25. Giambattista Piranesi, "Baths of
Diocletian, Interior of the Frigidarium"
from Vedute di Roma (etching).
Indiana University Art Museum, Bloomington.

reinterpretation represented the most important flowering of Roman mythology since the Italian Renaissance. And like that earlier period, which combined great political ideals with important works of literature and art, the revolutionary upheavals in both countries produced artists and works of genius in the Roman stamp. In recent years, a wealth of historical evidence has established a pattern of influence that leads from Machiavelli's writings through republican theorists of the Commonwealth period in England directly to the American colonies.[17] Indeed, one major synthesis of this entire tradition, demonstrating the coherence of republican theory from Florence in the fifteenth and sixteenth centuries through the late eighteenth century in England and America, has called the American Revolution and the birth of the United States Constitution "the last act of the civic Renaissance."[18] The creation of the American Republic owed a great deal to Machiavelli's vision of a Roman polity, and his influence was spread not so much through the writings of the better-known contract theorists, such as John Locke, but instead through the avowedly republican works of a number of lesser-known thinkers who may be called "Machiavellian" republicans. These included James Harrington (Oceana, 1656); Henry Nevill (Plato Redivivus, 1681); Walter Moyle (Essay Upon the Constitution of the Roman Government, 1699); Algernon Sidney (Discourses on Government, published posthumously after the author's execution in 1683 for his republican views); and John Trenchard and Thomas Gordon (The Independent Whig and Cato's Letters, circa 1730).

Although none of these writers is popular today, in colonial America they were all widely read and discussed. Their republican theory, steeped in English constitutional history and indebted to Machiavelli and his vision of Roman republicanism, was crucial in forming the American Revolution. In 1776, John Adams was amazed at the average Englishman's ignorance of such thinkers, who were, after all, a crucial part of recent English political history: "A man must be indifferent to the sneers of modern Englishmen, to mention in their company the names of Sidney, Harrington, Locke, Milton, Nedham, Neville, Burnet, and Hoadly. No small fortitude is necessary to confess one has read them." Yet he went on to add that it was precisely these Englishmen—men in the Machiavellian republican tradition—who "will convince any candid mind, that there is no good government but what is republican." [19]

With few exceptions, the Founding Fathers were college or university graduates, and the level of their learning was remarkable. The curriculum that schools and colleges offered during the period was relatively standardized and consisted primarily of a solid grounding in the Latin classics. Washington's stepson, for instance, was expected to know thoroughly the following authors or works by the age of fourteen: Livy, Cicero, Terence, Horace, Martial, Grotius, the Greek Testament, Hooke's *Roman History*, Kennet's *Roman Antiquities*, and Blackwell's *Sacred Classics*.[20]

Much of the rhetoric of prerevolutionary American politics was thus colored by Roman values and concepts. Revolutionary figures often assumed classical republican names to underline their views or their beliefs. Those who owned slaves, ironically, quite often gave them Roman names (Brutus, Marcus, Cato) with Livian overtones. Another less ironic example of Roman influence was the code devised in the correspondence between Alexander Hamilton and Gouveneur Morris: Washington was coded "Scaevola," John Adams "Brutus," Jefferson "Scipio," and Madison "Tarquin," because he had gone over to the Jeffersonian camp. When George Washington demanded the surrender of General Burgoyne in August 1777, his words reflected the same language and many of the same values already examined in the republican sentiment of sixteenth-century Florence: "The associated armies in America act from the noblest motives, liberty. The same principles actuated the arms of Rome in the days of her glory; and the same object was the reward of Roman valour."[21] The name of a major American city, Cincinnati, expresses the colonial enthusiasm for this stalwart republican hero, who also inspired a Society of the Cincinnati, a revolutionary group dedicated to Roman republican principles. And it is no surprise that George Washington, military victor over the British, would be remembered by his contemporaries not only as another first Brutus, who had established the republic and expelled the tyrant king, but also as the "Cincinnatus of the New World," who had rejected supreme power for the attractions of hearth and home.

An examination of the debates which took place during the American Constitutional Convention in Philadelphia between 25 May and 17 September 1787, a meeting resulting in the document eventually ratified by all thirteen states in 1790, reveals the degree to which delegates fell under the spell of the republican image of ancient Rome. They invoked Roman heroes, cited Roman history and institutions, and discussed Rome's eventual transformation from a republic into an empire governed by a single ruler. Once again, as had been fashionable in sixteenth-century Europe, Rome was recalled in theoretical discussions about alternative forms of government: a republic was always preferred over a monarchy, and Rome's republic was clearly the authoritative model. Roman republican heroes were part of the litany of secular political saints that republican advocates recalled at Philadelphia. Furthermore, the discussions about particular governmental institutions to be created or famous figures from the classical past were joined to more philosophical or moralistic considerations concerning the fatal flaws and corruptive influences that eventually caused the demise of the Roman model. Although John Adams was unable to attend the meeting, he made sure that the delegates could read the first part of his lengthy *Defense of the Constitutions of America*, a work which contained encapsulated descriptions of republican constitutions and institutions from Florence, Venice, Athens, Sparta, Pistoia, Cremona, San Marino, Carthage, Argos, Crete, Switzerland, and the Netherlands, as well as abbreviated digests and critiques of the major theories of republican writers from Roman times through the Italian Renaissance and the Glorious Revolution in England. Such was the scope of learning and knowledge typical of our Founding Fathers!

A similar cult of republican antiquity grew up among the leaders of the French Revolution. Most of these revolutionaries had received a classical education at the colleges of France. In their speeches and polemical tracts, men such as Danton, Robespierre, Desmoulins, Marie-Joseph Chénier—to mention only some of the best known figures—often cited the Roman works they had studied in school. The cult of antiquity that influenced the leaders of the revolutions in America and France had, in France, popular expression as well. The Phrygian cap, the classical symbol for liberty in republican Rome, was revived and became a Parisian fad. Towns, streets, and neighborhoods were renamed, and even individuals changed their names to demonstrate support for the revolution. In many cases the new names bore testimony to the influence of republican Rome. Thus, there were towns called Montfort-le-Brutus (rather than Montfort-l'Amaury), or Brutus-le-Magnanime (rather than Saint-Pierre-le Moutier), as well as streets named Rue de Brutus, de Scaevola, de Manlius, de Cato, and the like. And while this popular outpouring of republican fervor was primarily an urban phenomenon—the majority of country folk continued to baptise their infants with the usual Christian names—in Paris there were literally hundreds of Brutuses registered in a brief space of time. Babeuf substituted the names Camillus Gaius Gracchus for his Christian names, François-Noel Toussaint Nicaisse and declared that in so doing, "I had the moral purpose, in taking as my patron saints, the most honorable men, in my opinion, of the Roman republic. . . . To erase the traces of royalism, of aristocracy, and of fanaticism we have given republican names to our districts, cities, streets, and to everything that bore the imprint of these types of tyranny."[22] It should be no surprise to discover that the favorite authors of the French revolutionaries were primarily Roman, rather than Greek, and that Livy, Tacitus, Sallust, Plutarch, and Cicero were their constant fare. Today, the republic of ancient Rome seems far too undemocratic to suit our notion of a properly or equitably constituted government. But the French revolutionaries turned to the Roman republic precisely because it was a more democratic republic than anything that existed in France or Europe at the time.

The cult of the first Brutus represented the most widespread use of Roman myth during the revolution. Busts of the defender of Lucretia's virtue and the founder of liberty were distributed in public places, and one rested near the orator's tribune in the National Assembly. In 1793, when the assembly moved to the Tuileries, the hall was decorated with statues of the first Brutus, Camillus, and Cincinnatus. The Roman fasces, the bundle of sticks bound around an axhead, the weapon carried by the lictors who escorted the republican consuls through the streets, was painted around the walls. The fasces also began to appear on the government's coins. Even the calendar was altered drastically. The new year was marked by the abolition of the monarchy on 22 September 1792: that date became Year One of the Republic, the dawn of a new era. All subsequent years would be divided into twelve months of thirty days each. The names of the months were changed, since two of them—July and August—referred to Roman imperial tyrants.

In the popular assemblies constituted during the revolution, talk of ancient Rome was as frequent as it was during the formation of the American Constitution in Philadelphia. As the revolution moved more and more violently to the left and the Reign of Terror began, however, many of the most fervent devotees of republican Rome were eventually devoured by the revolution. Camille Desmoulins, for example, opposed the Committee of Public Safety and its policy of terror, which Saint-Just and Robespierre supported. In his newspaper, he attacked the revolutionaries who advocated continuing the Reign of Terror by ironically pretending to provide a literal translation of Tacitus for his readers.[23] While offering descriptions of the cruel tyrannies of Tiberius, Nero, or Caligula, Desmoulins was able to attack the regime and to identify his own faction with that of moderation. Unfortunately for Desmoulins, the Committee of Public Safety—especially Saint-Just and Robespierre—lacked a sense of humor, and Desmoulins was condemned to die along with Danton and his followers on 5 April 1794. Ironically, even the dreaded Committee of Public Safety draped itself in a Roman toga: ten of the twelve members of this group who remained in Paris (two were posted to the provinces) were known as the decemvirs, recalling the group of lawgivers who reformed republican laws in Rome between 451 and 450 B.C. The republican trappings of the French revolutionaries reached the point that it became quite common to swear "on the head of Brutus" or to speak "*en Brutus.*"

As we have seen from our examination of art, literature, and opera in the seventeenth and eighteenth centuries, an apolitical Roman mythology was popular even before the actual outbreak of the American and French Revolutions. Artists of this period worked not to further ideological goals but to fulfill their patron's commissions. But very often, and particularly in the case of French art during the revolution, the social context of a work devoted to Roman myth could drastically alter its public reception and even change its ultimate significance. This is especially evident in the remarkable career of the painter Jacques-Louis David (1748–1825).[24] The painting David submitted to the Salon of 1789—the last salon exhibition held in Paris under the old monarchy—was a major work with a lengthy descriptive title: "J. Brutus, first consul, has returned to his home after having condemned his two sons, who had joined the Tarquins and conspired against Roman liberty; lictors bring back the bodies so that they may be given burial."[25] David's moving tribute to the founder of republican liberty in ancient Rome was commissioned not by a rabid revolutionary but, instead, by the very King of France against whom the revolution would soon be directed. But before the Salon opened in August of 1789, the Tennis Court Oath of the Third Estate took place, and on 14 July, the Bastille was stormed. Not until some years later, when the David painting was reexhibited in the Salon of 1791 amid an entirely different political climate, was the political message potentially present in this great work clearly perceived by the public. Begun as a royal commission, and completed only two months after the fall of the Bastille, it would become one of the most memorable symbols of republicanism in French art. David changed as well during the same period: he later voted for the execution of his royal patron when he served in the National Convention.

The interplay of art and politics during the revolutionary eras in Europe and America helped to reinforce the highly political potential of Roman mythology. At the Salon of 1785—some years before the old regime collapsed—a number of works displayed there by several artists of note announced a renewed attention to themes from the *exemplum virtutis* genre, themes which would easily be exploited only a few years later for their ideological potential. One of these paintings, Nicolas Guy Brenet's *Piety and Generosity of Roman Women*, pictured Roman matrons giving their jewels and wedding rings to the republic for its defense in a dire military emergency. Later during the beginning months of the revolution, David's wife joined some twenty-one wives or daughters of artists in offering their jewels to help pay the national debt. This was not to be the only instance of a revolutionary action committed in conscious imitation of a relatively unimportant event in Livian history.

Two other works exhibited at the Salon of 1785 were prophetic of changes to come. The first of these is by Jean-Simon Berthélemy (1743–1811) and was entitled *Manlius Torquatus Condemning His Son to Death* (figure 26). In the painting, the conflict between the republican duty of the consul and his paternal love for his disobedient son may be seen in the contrast between the consul's hands: while the right hand points toward the harsh punishment his son must receive for fighting against his orders, the left clutches his toga over his heart in anguish. As the shocked group of soldiers pleads with Manlius to have mercy, the presence of the fasces leaning upon the steps clearly signals his son's fate. This illustration of draconian severity in defense of the republic prefigured the moral absolutism which only a few years later would produce the Terror and hundreds of executions in the name of Liberty, Fraternity, and Equality. It was reexhibited in the revolutionary Salon of 1791 along with David's painting of the first Brutus and was at that time called an excellent example of "military discipline," obviously aimed at offering to the French public a political, rather than a moral, exemplum of the high personal costs that must be paid in supporting the new regime.[26] Born out of the apolitical *exemplum virtutis* tradition, such works were reshown and reinterpreted to serve an ideology quite different from that of their nonrevolutionary patrons. In this respect, republican salons repeated a practice first carried out with other works of art by Florentine republican revolutionaries in the late fifteenth century.

Another painting at the Salon of 1785, David's *The Oath of the Horatii*, is also worth mentioning here (figure 27). Like his famous painting of Brutus, it, too, was originally commissioned by King Louis XVI. The political oath fascinated David, for it symbolized, not only in ancient Rome but also in revolutionary France, a dramatic moment when the future was shaped by the conscious choice of political leaders rather than by the dead weight of tradition. In David's version of the Horatii's oath, there is a clear contrast between the manly Roman virtues of patriotism and valor on the left and the weaker, less desirable feminine characteristics of com-

26. Jean-Simon Berthélemy, Manlius
Torquatus Condemning His Son to
Death (oil on canvas in the Tours
Museum).
Cliché des Musées Nationaux, Paris.

27. Jacques-Louis David, The Oath of the Horatii
(oil on canvas in the Louvre Museum).
Cliché des Musées Nationaux, Paris.

passion and pity displayed by the women on the right of the canvas. All of our attention, and all of the emotional potential of this great republican work, focuses upon the center of the picture, where the gazes of the father and his three sons seem to intersect as do the outstretched hands and the three fatal swords. Later, when David exhibited his *Oath in the Tennis Court* at the more radical Salon of 1791—the exhibit at which both *The Oath of the Horatii* and *Brutus* were reexhibited—his reputation as a Jacobin artist was firmly established, and his canvases were reinterpreted as expressions of the ideological fervor that created the French Revolution. The influence of the earlier *Oath of the Horatii* upon the *Oath in the Tennis Court* is apparent in the preparatory drawing for the later work (figure 28). The various gestures of the figures comprise a series of variations upon the noble and selfless postures of the three Horatii. In this fashion, David clearly suggested to the perceptive spectator at the 1791 Salon, who could compare the two works on the spot, that an identity of values which transcended the centuries existed between republican Rome and revolutionary, republican France.

The same basic identity of values informs two masterpieces created in 1788 and 1789—the marble statue, *George Washington* by Jean-Antoine Houdon (1741–1828), and David's painting, *Brutus*. Each is remarkable for the perceptive manner in which it captured the character of the very different revolutions in America and France. It was Thomas Jefferson who, as Minister to France from 1785 to 1789, was the principal impetus behind the State of Virginia's decision to give the commission for the statue to Houdon (figure 29).[27] Both Houdon and Jefferson had originally preferred a figure in classical Roman garb, but it was Washington's express desire to avoid such an affected pose that eventually influenced Houdon's decision to dress him in his regimental uniform. However, everything else about the work recalled not only classical antecedents but a specific Livian hero, Cincinnatus. Washington's career, for his contemporaries, resembled no other republican figure so much as Cincinnatus. In 1783, Washington had retired as commander in chief of the American army after reportedly having refused repeated offers of a kingship. Later, after serving two terms as president of the newly formed republic, he stepped down from office, even though he could probably have retained supreme power for the rest of his life. Celebrations of his retirement, in the prints of the period, associated Washington with Cincinnatus for both of these rare actions, and there is no doubt that Houdon's statue meant to underline Washington's status as a modern

Cincinnatus who, like his Roman counterpart, triumphed in war but left power voluntarily and returned to the calmer pursuits of his farm.

Houdon's work captured the noble features of Washington, which many of his contemporaries saw as an incarnation of the physical and moral characteristics of Roman bust sculpture. Despite his non-Roman dress, Washington leans upon the most important symbol of the Roman republic, the fasces, to which his military sword has been attached. Behind the general is clearly visible the blade of a plow, symbol of Washington's return to the land and his identity as a modern Cincinnatus. As we view the statue from the front, it becomes extremely difficult to distinguish the plow from the fasces. Or, more properly, it seems as if the ax of the fasces, designed for the punishment of the republic's enemies, has been transformed into the blade of a plow. No more eloquent image of a noble warrior who has become a man of peace has ever been produced.

The genesis of David's Brutus was even more complex. David's work revealed a general indebtedness to the cult of Brutus, which flourished before and during the revolution among republicans of all nationalities and which had retained a certain popularity even under cultures dominated by absolute monarchs as a classical emblem of selfless patriotism. In addition, David was most probably influenced by the publication of Vittorio Alfieri's dramatic works, which included not only a treatment of the founder of the Roman republic in Bruto primo (The First Brutus) but also a consideration of Caesar's assassin in Bruto secondo (The Second Brutus). Alfieri's tragedy of the first Roman consul was published in Paris in 1788, precisely at the time David was completing his painting. The Italian patriot had written his play in large measure as a rebuttal to Voltaire's tragedy Brutus, originally composed in 1730. When Alfieri's mistress remarked that she had enjoyed a revival of Voltaire's work, Alfieri's angry reply to her innocent comment expressed all the hatred for tyranny, and especially for panderers to kings, that characterized his entire life: "What Brutus plays are these, Brutus plays by Voltaire? I will write plays on that Brutus theme and I will write on both of the Bruti. Time will show whether such subjects of tragedy are more suitable to me or to a Frenchman, who was born a plebeian and in all his signatures, over a space of seventy and more years, subscribed himself: 'Voltaire, gentleman in ordinary of the king'!"[28]

Alfieri viewed his play as more than a literary work. It was also intended to arouse in the hearts of his oppressed Italian countrymen the same love for liberty and republican government that characterized the

28. Jacques-Louis David, Tennis Court Oath (preparatory sketch)
(Versailles Museum).
Cliché des Musées Nationaux, Paris.

29. Jean-Antoine Houdon,
George Washington (marble statue
in the Virginia state capitol).
Virginia State Library, Richmond.

play's hero. In fact, the dedication of the play linked the first Brutus to a contemporary republican hero, George Washington: "Dedication to the most illustrious and free citizen, George Washington. The name of the deliverer of America alone can stand on the title page of the tragedy of the deliverer of Rome."[29] The tragedy of the second Brutus was dedicated to the "future people of Italy," and there is no doubt that Alfieri hoped for a revival of republican feeling in his native Italy, then occupied by Austrians or governed by a varied assortment of petty despots. Alfieri anticipated David's painting by his concentration upon the conflict between the consul's love for liberty and his affection for his family. While the first act opens with a report of Lucretia's death and the fall of the Tarquin tyrant, Lucretia's tragedy is almost completely ignored—only her dead body appears at the rear of the stage in Act 1. Alfieri is more concerned with the masculine virtues of the founder of the new republic, who sacrifices his sons for the commonweal. His Brutus emerges at the close of the work as a preromantic figure, a solitary patriot whose devotion to duty leaves him childless and isolated, as the last line of the tragedy emphasizes: "I am / The most unhappy man that ever lived."[30]

David's *Brutus* (figure 30) portrayed this same tragic moment in the life of the Roman hero. The head of Brutus is based on the Capitoline Brutus from Rome (of which David owned a copy), a classical bust which later inspired the marble bust of Brutus (1792) by Joseph Boiston that adorned the French National Assembly. If *The Oath of the Horatii* had emphasized one aspect of the republican oath, that of duty, David's interpretation of Brutus in this great work uncovered the terrible human cost of maintaining such oaths—the destruction of a man's family and its sacrifice on the altar of republican virtue. Alfieri's unhappiest man alive is rendered skillfully by the forceful personality of Brutus set within the dark, foreboding shadows that underscore his anguish. The heroic consul refuses to take even a cursory glance behind him at the bodies of his sons, which are being returned to their home by the lictors; a statue personifying the city of Rome stands between them. In his hand, Brutus holds the damning list of conspirators who plotted with the Tarquin tyrant. To the right and bathed in light in sharp contrast to the somber Brutus, are the women of the family. Unlike the stern patriarch and defender of his country, these women give vent to their emotions and lament the fate of the two young men. In David's view, a republican government clearly had need of sterner stuff in its citizens.

Art historians seem to be in agreement that *Brutus* was originally intended primarily to convey a moral or philosophical message—that of

30. Jacques-Louis David, Lictors
Returning Dead Sons to Brutus (oil
on canvas in the Louvre Museum).
Cliché des Musées Nationaux, Paris.

stoic resignation—and it would be surprising if the King of France had commissioned such a work with the understanding that its message was designed to advocate the downfall of his monarchy. However, after its exhibition in the Salon of 1791, the predominantly philosophical interpretation of the painting was radically transformed by the course of events, and the canvas, with its celebration of republican sacrifice, became something quite different for its public—a masterful portrait of the subject *par excellence* of revolutionary virtue: "avenger of woman's wrong, founder of liberty, restorer of law, inflexible magistrate capable of executing his own sons for the good of the state."[31]

Theatre during the French Revolution was radicalized in a more substantial fashion than even the plastic arts. We have already seen how David's *Brutus* was probably influenced by Alfieri's patriotic tragedy. The revolutionaries were steeped in classical history, encouraged the cult of Brutus, and one of the most important cultural events to increase interest in this Roman figure was a revival of Voltaire's tragedy *Brutus* in 1790. At its first performance, the large audience hailed Mirabeau, one of the early moderate leaders, as the "Brutus of France." Linking contemporary events or figures to similar events or characters from Rome's republican past in order to provide commentary on current events became fashionable. Soon, parallels between ancient and modern times provided popular artistic themes after the revival of Voltaire's play and the reexhibition of David's prerevolutionary Roman paintings. When King Louis XVI attempted unsuccessfully to flee Paris and was captured at Varennes in 1791, he was immediately branded as the French "Tarquin," because Tarquin had likewise fled Rome after the rape of Lucretia and Brutus's revolt.[32] Many of the plays of the day also reflected the dynamic interplay between Roman myth and the course of events. For example, Marie-Joseph Chénier's play *Caius Gracchus* (1792), a dramatization of the Roman tribune's heroic attempts to return to the Roman people rights usurped by the aristocratic senate, aimed at obvious parallels in contemporary France. Other plays, such as Joseph Aude's *Return of Camillus to Rome* (1789) and Doigny du Ponceau's *Verginia or the Destruction of the Decemvirs* (1791), attempted similar political statements. In Gabriel Legouve's *Epicharis and Nero* (1793), the playwright (with the apparent approval of Danton and his followers) implicitly attacked the Jacobin faction and its leader, Robespierre, by drawing a parallel between Robespierre's advocacy of the Terror and the evil career of the Roman emperor Nero.[33]

In retrospect, however, it seems that the plastic arts of the period best captured the essence of both the American and French revolutions. In both instances, the artistic vocabulary and the political language played on Roman republican imagery in order to visualize a new social order. Houdon's Washington embodied the conservative, reliable, moderate military leader, whose ambitions were limited to saving the republic through his military prowess. David's Brutus, even given its original philosophical intent, conveyed an implicit moral absolutism in the consul's willingness to sacrifice even his sons for the commonweal. Such patriotism, when carried to excess, would result in the Terror. As we look back upon the American Revolution, discovering what we now believe to be its essentially conservative character, it is perhaps altogether too comforting to assume that its stability was a foregone conclusion when it began. In fact, had the character of George Washington been more like that of Napoleon, and had the Founding Fathers been as greedy for personal power as some of the contemporaries of Robespierre in France, the iconography of the American Revolution might well have been profoundly different. We can see a glimpse of what might have been Washington's image in these circumstances in Giorgio Ceracchi's marble bust of Washington (figure 31). Washington is depicted not as the American Cincinnatus who returned power to his people and retired to relative obscurity on his farm but, rather, as the single ruler in whose hands was vested the sovereignty of the government. Unlike the majority of images of the Virginian soldier, Ceracchi's study of the general is not a republican hero but an imperial figure. Its style is clearly indebted to the many marble busts of Roman emperors that the Italian artist employed as models.[34]

Happily for the United States of America, Washington proved impervious to such temptations, and the republican image popularized by Houdon became the standard interpretation. Of the many such works, perhaps none expresses this perspective quite so well as the statue by Antonio Canova, which the State of North Carolina resolved to commission in 1815. Once again, Thomas Jefferson played a major role in obtaining the artist for the job, and in this instance, his preference for Roman garb was followed to the letter. As he wrote to Thomas Appleton (1763–1840), at that time American consul in Livorno, on 22 January 1816: "Who should make it? There can be but one answer to this. Old Canova of Rome. . . . As to the style or costume, I am sure the artist, and every person of taste in Europe, would be for the Roman, the effect of which is undoubtedly of a different order. Our boots and regimentals have a very puny effect" [an obvious reference to Houdon's *Washington*].[35]

The statue (figure 32) reached Raleigh in 1821, and by all accounts it

31. Giorgio Ceracchi, George Washington
in the imperial style (marble bust).
Gibbes Art Gallery, Charleston, S.C.

32. Antonio Canova, George Washington:
original destroyed by fire; present copy made from a plaster mold in 1971
(marble statue in the North Carolina state capitol).
North Carolina Division of Archives and History, Raleigh.

was considered the finest artistic treasure of the state or even of the nation until its tragic destruction by fire in 1831. What remains today is a copy made from a plaster cast retained by Canova in his Italian study at Possagno. It now stands in the capitol rotunda in Raleigh where the original once stood, and it pictures Washington, in classical Roman dress as either a consul or a tribune, writing on a tablet. The words on the tablet, faithfully reproduced in Italian when Canova's plaster cast was redone, reads: "Giorgio Washington al Popolo degli Stati Uniti 1796 Amici e concittadini" ("George Washington to the People of the United States 1796 Friends and fellow countrymen"). Visitors are often puzzled by Canova's Romanized republican figure of our first president composing in Italian, but the mystery is quite simply resolved. This inscription, part of the working model, was inadvertently reproduced when the plaster copy was made. However, the Italian inscription reminds the viewer that Canova considered Washington to be most clearly following Roman republican tradition when he left office after delivering his farewell address. Perhaps Washington's selfless act was not fully appreciated when it occurred, but by 1821, after Americans had witnessed the extraordinary events in France that led from the formation of a republic to the institution of a dictatorship under Napoleon and then to the restoration of a monarchy, Washington's deed seemed to embody the essence of republican heroism. An anecdote recounted by the American neoclassical artist John Trumbull (1756–1843)—the artist who provided a series of paintings for the rotunda of the Capitol building in Washington—reveals how strongly Washington's two resignations from power, first from the army and then from the presidency, had impressed republicans. In speaking with President James Madison about his choice for a painting, that of Washington's resignation, Trumbull declared that it was "one of the highest moral lessons ever given to the world." Trumbull reported in his autobiography that after a moment's reflection, Madison replied: "I believe you are right; it was a glorious action."[36]

Americans were justified in praising Washington's reluctance to pursue political power as the most unusual of all his republican virtues. Quite the opposite, of course, occurred in revolutionary France, where the course of events led swiftly from the founding of a republic modeled in part after that of ancient Rome to the rise of a dictator who seemed to embody both the military genius of Julius Caesar and the administrative skills of Caesar Augustus. Napoleon's rise to power began when he was appointed commander of the army in Italy on 2 March 1796. His brilliant victories on the peninsula reorganized the map of southern Europe and resulted in the establishment of a democratic republic in Venice (12 May 1797), followed by the Ligurian Republic in Genoa and Pisa (15 June 1797), the Cisalpine Republic in Milan and Lombardy (9 July 1797), a Roman republic in the Eternal City (15 February 1798), and the Parthenopean Republic of Naples (26 January 1799). Napoleon was far less interested in the ideology of the French Revolution or in spreading the new republican gospel throughout Italy than he was in consolidating the political influence he accrued back in France with his astonishing military victories. The Treaty of Campo Formio (18 October 1797) reflected both his cynicism and his political realism, for while his Austrian opponents were forced to recognize the Cisalpine Republic in Lombardy, a French ally, Napoleon gave Venice and most of the territory of the Venetian Republic to Austria in return. His willingness to abolish a fledgling democratic republic with the stroke of a pen shocked patriots in Italy and was the first of Napoleon's many ruthless acts on the road to supreme power in France. Napoleon's opponents might well have paid more attention to the lessons found in Roman history. The Cisalpine Republic that General Bonaparte formed in Italy took its name from the province the Roman senate had once given Julius Caesar to govern in 58 B.C.

When Napoleon did eventually seize power in the event known as the Eighteenth of Brumaire, Year 8 of the Republic (10 November 1799), he retained for some time the republican trappings that had become fashionable during the initial phases of the revolution and was named one of three consuls. Eventually, he was "promoted" to the rank of first consul, with the power to consult the people directly by plebiscite. This institution copied from the ancient Roman republic was later used in 1804 to affirm the final transfer of absolute power from the first consul to the office of emperor. By an overwhelming vote (some 99 percent), French citizens agreed that Napoleon should become emperor of the French and that his family should possess hereditary rights to the throne after his death. As almost an afterthought, the various Italian or Dutch republics with Roman republican names (Cisalpine, Ligurian, Parthenopean, Batavian) were transformed back into the Kingdoms of Italy, Naples, and Holland, and they were ruled by Napoleon's relatives or by Napoleon himself.[37]

Because Napoleon dominated European history from the turn of the nineteenth century until his eventual defeat and exile in 1815, he naturally had a major impact upon the role of Roman myth in the figurative arts. Some of the images preserved of him from this period by Houdon —notably a terracotta bust, The Emperor Napoleon (1806), and a marble bust of the same title (1808)—pictured a man who still retained a strong residue of republican character. The figure portrayed was, in the terracotta work, a thin, austere Roman in the republican rather than the imperial style. Houdon followed his interpretation of Washington by dressing Napoleon in a regimental tunic and portraying him as a serious, dignified figure. Indeed, many of the most famous early portraits of Napoleon show him in his office at work, dressed in his simple regimental uniform, seeming to retain some vestiges of his humble, republican origins. However, the temptation to move from a republican Napoleon, the protector and preserver of the French Revolution and the new republic, to an imperial Napoleon, the emperor of the French and founder of a new imperial dynasty, was irresistible.

The new imperial symbolism substituted the "lavishness of the Roman Empire for the sobriety of the Roman Republic that dominated Revolutionary imagery." [38] However, Napoleonic art bestowed upon the Corsican general not only all the virtues of the magnanimous Roman emperors but also those associated in the traditional iconography with Christ and Christian saints. If Brutus, Scaevola, or Cincinnatus had served as the patron saints for republicans, art in the service of the empire combined two traditions that stressed the clemency, benevolence, and magnanimity of all-powerful, absolute sovereigns. In two paintings, *Napoleon in the Pesthouse of Jaffa* (Salon of 1804) and *Napoleon at Eylau* (Salon of 1808), Baron Antoine-Jean Gros (1771–1835) depicted the appearance of the emperor at a pesthouse in Cairo and his later appearance upon a battlefield in a manner that clearly suggests the arrival of a Christ-like savior capable of healing the sick. Other artists followed similar themes or adopted a distinctly imperial iconography indebted both to the themes and motifs of imperial Rome as well as to the seventeenth-century tradition of the *exemplum virtutis*.

Although David had gained fame as the interpreter of Jacobin values during the French Revolution, he was almost as opportunistic as Napoleon in his ability to cultivate political alliances, and the painter soon began to produce a number of works in the emperor's service. One of these in particular, *The Distribution of Eagles* (Salon of 1810), returned to what was for him a familiar subject—the political oath. Earlier, even before the revolution, David had immortalized the fateful oath taken by the Horatii in defense of the republic; later, he depicted its modern counterpart at the Tennis Court. Now he treated a subject more befitting the imperial majesty of his new patron, the Grande Armée's oath of allegiance to Napoleon on 4 December 1804 after his coronation. The influence of Roman images throughout the course of David's career underlines just how intense and multifaceted was the impact of Roman mythology upon artists of the period.

With the coronation of Napoleon as emperor of the French, the stern, austere, sober images of the first Brutus, Cincinnatus, and the other Livian figures from the early Roman republic disappeared from European art. In their place arose entirely different imperial figures, such as the bust by François Pascal Simon de Gerrard on a Sèvres porcelain vase produced during the early years of the empire (figure 33). Unlike a court portrait, ceramic products were produced in quantity and were thus accessible to larger numbers of consumers. It is very likely that the image of Napoleon on the vase represented something of an official view, much like the photograph of the current American president that graces every public office or post office in the United States. Here, de Gerard portrays Napoleon as Augustus. Gone is the somber, somewhat emaciated republican hero, the typical image from Napoleon's early military career. Gone, too, is his simple regimental uniform, now inappropriate in the ruler of most of Europe. In their place, we have a more prosperous and well-fed personality, crowned by the imperial olive wreath and clad in ermine robes of state. The republican first consul, a French first Brutus, has been almost magically transformed into the French Caesar Augustus, emperor of the world.

33. François Pascal Simon de Gerard,
Portrait bust of Napoleon I in imperial
costume (enamel on porcelain vase,
Museo degli Argenti, Palazzo Pitti,
Florence).
Soprintendenza per i beni artistici e storici per le
provincie di Firenze e Pistoia.

ROMANTICISM AND

RISORGIMENTO

With the demise of the Napoleonic empire and the restoration of the ancien régime in most of continental Europe, the iconography associated with the imperial image of Napoleon did not entirely pass away. In fact, in France during the Restoration, it continued to be exploited by a number of artists who worked for royal patrons. Thus, at the Salon of 1840, Eugène Delacroix could exhibit a painting whose subject matter recalled the canvases devoted to the virtues of kings or emperors by artists whose patrons were absolute monarchs. The Justice of Trajan (figure 34) not only continued the imperial imagery associated with the now discredited Napoleonic empire, but it once again returned to the theme of an all-powerful ruler's magnanimity and generosity that was so important an aspect of baroque and neoclassical culture. Within the space of only a few decades, kings in France (and the Roman emperors used to symbolize their grandeur and munificence) had been attacked, executed, superceded, and restored. And at each stage in this historical dialectic between republicanism and monarchy, Roman myth had played a crucial role in providing visual images to explain, justify, or legitimize a particular point of view.

In the evolution of the myth of Rome, American contributions were relatively insignificant until the eighteenth century. The most memorable of the works of art treating such themes in the New World had been done by visiting European artists, who had inherited a long tradition of republican or imperial imagery from their national cultures. But in the romantic period, American artists considered a stay in Italy or Europe an essential part of their training, and these studies determined the continuing popularity of classical themes and genres in American art. The Livian tradition in American sculpture established by Houdon and Canova remained popular; courthouses and state capitol buildings all over America required decoration. But the most important embodiment of the myth of Rome in nineteenth-century America was the five-part, romantic evocation of the entire sweep of Roman history, both republican and imperial, entitled The Course of Empire (1833–36), by Thomas Cole (1801–48).

34. Eugène Delacroix, The Justice of
Trajan (oil on canvas in the Rouen Museum).
Cliché des Musées Nationaux, Paris.

Cole's fascinating interpretation of an entire historical cycle in the life of an ancient civilization would be impossible to imagine without some knowledge of the works of Montesquieu, Piranesi, or Gibbon on Rome, and given the popularity of Vico's ideas during the romantic period, there is every likelihood that Cole's highly original vision of ancient Rome was also influenced by the Neapolitan philosopher's work.

Like so many other American artists and writers of the romantic period, Cole studied abroad from 1829 until 1832, spending over a year and a half in Italy. And it was in Italy that he conceived *The Course of Empire*. The completed work included five separate canvases: *The Savage State*, *The Arcadian or Pastoral State*, *The Consummation of Empire*, *Destruction*, and *Desolation*.[1] As the catalog for a Washington exhibit in 1858 points out, the five separate paintings represent "a nation's rise, progress, greatness, decline, and fall, and the consequent changes in the same landscape. . . . the isolated rock crowning a precipitous hill in the distance identifies the scene in each of the series, but the observer's position varies in the several pictures."[2] The central canvas in the series, that devoted to the fulfillment of empire, dominates the five parts. The catalog description that accompanied the triumphant showing of *The Consummation of Empire* (figure 35) ten years earlier in New York seems copied almost directly from Gibbon's descriptions of the culmination of ancient Rome's imperial majesty: "It is a day of triumph: man has conquered man; nations have been subjugated. By wealth and power, knowledge, art, and taste, man has achieved the summit of human grandeur. The day is near the meridian."[3]

The shocking demise of this brilliant civilization immediately followed its historical apotheosis, and the images of *Destruction* (figure 36), as well as the reasons given for this historical cataclysm in the exhibit's catalog, are patterned upon the cycle Cole must have found in Montesquieu or Gibbon: "Ages have passed since the scene of glory. Luxury has enervated, vice has debased, and the strength of the mighty nation has consumed away. A barbarous enemy sacks the city. The heavens are darkened by a tempest, and the storm of war rages beneath, amid falling walls and colonnades, and the flames of temples and palaces."[4] With the final scene, *Desolation*, Cole leaves his viewer with the feeling that both historical evolution and the forces of Nature will combine to produce another cycle, one nevertheless compelled to follow the same pattern of rise, fulfillment, and decline.

There are elements in these five canvases—particularly the evocative, arcadian view of Nature—that are typical of the numerous romantic landscapes painted by European and American painters with a Roman

35. *Thomas Cole*, The Course of Empire:
The Consummation of Empire (*oil on canvas*).
New-York Historical Society, New York.

36. *Thomas Cole,* The Course of Empire:
Destruction *(oil on canvas).*
New-York Historical Society, New York.

setting. The original aspect of Cole's work resided in how cleverly he managed to use such traditional romantic landscapes to embody a thoroughly philosophical interpretation of the course of Roman history. And while his five canvases, like the prints of Piranesi, accentuated the philosophical or historical dimensions of Roman mythology rather than delivering a purely political message, the American painter may nevertheless have felt that his panoramic vision of the rise and fall of an entire civilization, modeled after that of ancient Rome, also contained an ominous warning for the American nation, which had been forged, only a few decades earlier, from a similar pastoral wilderness in a burst of republican energy. In his private journal for 21 August 1835, Cole wrote that he feared the union of the states which made up the United States of America might disintegrate and that "pure republican government" might end in the New World.[5] His *Course of Empire* thus served to alert his contemporaries and fellow citizens to the inevitable mutability of human history. It also warned them of the imminent danger to republican government set in motion by its success in moving westward. Just as republican Rome had been destroyed from within by its imperial conquests, so, too, in Cole's opinion, had America's energetic march toward the Pacific Ocean endangered its republican institutions and its civic consciousness. Cole's fears were prophetic, for even before the end of the century, American politics would be dominated by a quest for empire which rivaled that of the great European powers.

Thomas Cole was but one of countless European and American artists and writers during the romantic period who believed a sojourn in Italy (particularly in Rome, Venice, or Florence) was an absolute necessity. For Washington Irving, who arrived in Italy in 1804, Italy represented "enchanted ground." Besides the numerous Europeans (such as Goethe, Stendhal, George Eliot, Dostoyevsky, and Madame de Staël) whose visits to Italy became important influences upon their works, Americans were particularly intent upon polishing their culture and knowledge of the past. The list of visitors to Italy and Rome between the dawn of the romantic period and the late nineteenth century comprises almost anyone of any consequence: Benjamin West, Irving, Nathaniel Hawthorne, Horatio Greenough, George Ticknor, Henry Wadsworth Longfellow, James Fenimore Cooper, Margaret Fuller, Harriet Beecher Stowe, Charles Eliot Norton, Francis Parkman, William Dean Howells, Henry James, and Henry Adams are but a few of the most important names.[6]

In most cases, the experiences of these American writers or artists did not produce major contributions to Roman mythology, as in the case of

Thomas Cole's masterpiece. In fact, for these Americans Italy in general and Rome in particular often represented something quite far removed from the essentially secular or political thrust of the myth of Rome. For the majority of these writers and artists, Italy was a land which offered an entirely different kind of experience than they could encounter in the New World. It was a mysterious country full of beautiful art, a place boasting a landscape which reminded them of Arcadia or Eden before the Fall, but its customs, religious practices, and political institutions contrasted sharply to their own cultural values.

Since few of these visitors to the Eternal City actually associated with Italians of their own class, many never really learned to speak the language or appreciate the often startling events which were occurring around them as Italian intellectuals and patriots began the long struggle for national independence that is remembered as the Italian Risorgimento. In Rome, Americans usually associated with the decadent Roman aristocrats, not the emerging liberals who were actually closer to them in spirit and intellectual formation. A few, however, were quite sensitive to the plight of Italy and even contributed something to its improvement. Harriet Beecher Stowe, renowned all over Europe as the author of the antislavery novel, Uncle Tom's Cabin (1852), was almost unable to walk through the streets of the Eternal City unrecognized. And when she visited the shop of a Roman jeweler, she was given the head of an Egyptian slave carved in black onyx, as the goldsmith explained to her how her struggles to free the American slaves found a responsive chord in Italians, who remained slaves in their own country.[7] They were under the domination of foreigners, the moribund papal state, and the small principalities and duchies that had been reestablished in the wake of the restoration which followed the collapse of the Napoleonic empire. Margaret Fuller quite openly espoused the cause of the liberal revolutionaries who staged an unsuccessful revolt against the papacy in Rome in 1848–49, although the manuscript of her History of the Roman Republic, which she wrote to chronicle these stirring events, was lost in the shipwreck that claimed her life in 1850. Another American woman, Jesse White Mario, became an important force in the campaigns of the Risorgimento, becoming almost as famous in Italy as Florence Nightingale for service to the sick and wounded Italian patriots who fought with Giuseppe Garibaldi.

The most important event to shape Roman mythology in the entire nineteenth century was the Italian Risorgimento itself. During this multifaceted historical period, the geographical source of the myth of Rome—

the Eternal City itself—was the occasion for an entirely new dimension of Roman mythology. The city of Rome—until 1870, the capital of the Papal States—became the focal point for the energies of Italy's more radical republican patriots, who saw the city as the inevitable capital of a new Italian nation that, many hoped, was to be secular in nature and republican in design. Three men contributed the most to making a united Italy a reality. Count Camillo Cavour (1810–61), a Piemontese statesman and politician, created the foreign alliances that enabled the House of Savoy to effect Italy's freedom. Giuseppe Mazzini (1805–72), the most passionate spokesman for a *republican* united Italy, seemed frighteningly radical to Cavour, and Mazzini's insistence upon making Rome the capital of a united nation was always somewhat of an embarrassment to the northern Italian statesman. Giuseppe Garibaldi (1807–82), a fearless warrior and romantic revolutionary, provided the charismatic popular leadership that galvanized mass support around the Risorgimento's dream of a national state. By the time Italy actually achieved unification, his name had become synonymous with bravery and patriotism not only in Italy but all over the world.[8]

As Denis Mack Smith has noted, until the 1840s there were very few people in Italy who believed that Italian unification could or should be accomplished.[9] The peninsula was divided into ten separate states. Hapsburg Austria owned Lombardy and Venice and controlled the central duchies of Parma, Tuscany, and Modena through a network of family alliances. Austrian troops stood ready to suppress revolutionary uprisings in the kingdoms of Piedmont as well as in Naples, capital of the Kingdom of the Two Sicilies. At the same time, Rome and the Papal States were still controlled by the pope, who governed this territory as a secular ruler.

If few Italians or Europeans believed unification was possible or desirable, even fewer felt that such unification should take the form of a popular republic. Yet the memory of the days of the French Revolution and the momentous changes it caused Italy had not been forgotten. Mazzini emerged in the years before the European uprisings of 1848 as the most influential spokesman for *republican* nationalism, driving out French and Austrian influences, and returning the peninsula to its former glory with Rome as its necessary capital. On 15 November 1848, Count Pellegrino Rossi, the head of the papal government and an unpopular opponent of democratic rule, was assassinated by an angry crowd of Romans. His death and the pope's flight from the Eternal City set the stage for a republican revolution in Rome, in which both Mazzini and Garibaldi were to play important roles.

Giuseppe Garibaldi had already gained his well-deserved reputation as a charismatic leader of men in battles to the north of Rome against the Austrians and earlier in South America. Although his life was to be marked by a number of serious disagreements with both Mazzini and Cavour, there is no doubt that unlike the Pietmontese statesman, Garibaldi never wavered in supporting Mazzini's position that Rome must become the capital of a republican Italy. Mazzini saw a united Italy, with its capital in Rome, as the first in a series of peaceful popular republics: "Rome, by the design of Providence, and as the People have divined, is the *Eternal City* to which is entrusted the mission of disseminating the word that will unite the world. . . . Just as to the *Rome of the Caesars*, which through action united a great part of Europe, there succeeded the *Rome of the Popes*, which united Europe and America in the realm of the spirit, so the *Rome of the People* will succeed them both, to unite Europe, America and every part of the terrestrial globe in a faith that will make thought and action one. . . . The destiny of Rome and Italy is that of the world."[10] The executive power of the Roman revolutionary government was granted to a triumvirate, a title with obvious Roman republican overtones, which consisted of Mazzini, Count Aurelio Soffi (the leader of Liberals from Romagna), and Carlo Armellini, a Roman lawyer.

It was Garibaldi himself, elected to the Constituent Assembly from the city of Macerata, who proposed on 5 February 1849 the creation of a republican form of government, and he did so by invoking the tradition of ancient Rome: "I believe profoundly that, now the papal system of government is at an end, what we need in Rome is a republic. . . . Can it be that the descendants of the ancient Romans are not fit to constitute a Republic? As some people in this body evidently take offense at this word, I reiterate "Long live the republic!"[11] Years later, in his memoirs, Garibaldi even described the assassination of Rossi which provoked the revolt in Livian terms, praising the young Roman who had "recovered the steel of Marcus Brutus."[12] Garibaldi played a major role in organizing the city's defenses against armies allied with the pope and in galvanizing its citizen-soldiers into action. "Roma o morte!" ("Rome or death!") became the battle cry of his forces, and after their defeat it became the battle cry of the entire Italian Risorgimento until 1870, when unification finally was achieved. Even in defeat, the noble image of an embattled republic in the Eternal City did much to create a sense of unity and nationality among Italians who, until that date, had not even considered such revolutionary political changes possible.

Garibaldi's life represents one of the most remarkable stories in the entire nineteenth century, and his legend grew stronger and more attractive in both defeat and victory. When he led a ragtag group of survivors from the defense of Rome in a brilliant tactical retreat to Romagna, he declared: "Wherever we are shall be Rome."[13] In true Roman fashion, he offered only struggle and sacrifice to those who followed him. When he finally disbanded his followers, it was appropriate that he found temporary refuge from the forces of reaction in the last surviving city-state of the medieval republican tradition—the independent Republic of San Marino. For Garibaldi, the struggle had only begun. Later, when the international situation had changed to permit the possibility of offensive action, Garibaldi led his redshirts (a thousand volunteers, mostly from the North) in an incredible invasion of Sicily in 1860. Garibaldi liberated the island, then crossed the Straits of Messina, and after a brilliant campaign in Calabria, he captured Naples, the largest city in Italy, and proclaimed himself "Dictator of the Two Sicilies."

Garibaldi was always a fervent believer in the same "strong medicines" recommended by Machiavelli—in particular, the necessity of establishing a republican dictatorship to enable his forces to weather the kinds of emergencies constantly threatening them during the Risorgimento. But he was careful to recommend a dictatorship of the Livian type, not one which might degenerate into the tyranny of a Napoleon or a Caesar: "Dictatorship, like Machiavellianism, has been wrongly understood. Machiavelli, one of our greatest Italians, did but exhibit vice; he never counselled it. The fact that Sulla and Caesar were dictators, should but teach us to seek the more diligently for a Cincinnatus and a Washington. If a Bonaparte can corrupt, so much the worse for those who are corrupted. Ancient Rome, when republican and virtuous (which are but synonyms), finding herself in distress, sought out a man, and that man saved the republic."[14] Garibaldi remained absolutely true to the Livian republican tradition, never deriving any material benefit or ever allowing the power that passed through his hands to corrupt his ideals. Historians may still debate the wisdom of many of his actions or policies, but a century of intensive historical research has not turned up a single bit of credible evidence to discredit his patriotic idealism.

Intellectuals and military observers quite naturally compared Garibaldi to both Cincinnatus and to George Washington, even as Garibaldi's views on strong republican leaders in a time of troubles reveal that the soldier-hero saw himself in the Livian republican tradition. When Garibaldi handed over the entire southern peninsula to King Victor Emanuel in 1860 and proclaimed him king of an *almost* united Italy—Venice and the papal states were still outstanding—he immediately retired and returned to his small farm in Caprera (Sardinia), just as his classical and American counterparts had done. The connection linking ancient Roman republicanism, the "new Brutus" or "new Cincinnatus" of the New World, and this messianic Italian soldier found the perfect expression in a lithograph from that same year (figure 37). In it, Garibaldi receives a sword from Cincinnatus and a rifle from General Washington. But for the common people, the mostly illiterate masses who did not really understand the issues of the Risorgimento and who certainly did not appreciate the intricate diplomatic webs spun by Cavour in faraway Turin, Garibaldi seemed closer to Christ than any austere Roman hero, a Christ who had come to earth to bring a sword, not peace. Hundreds of eyewitness accounts of Garibaldi survive, and almost all of them speak of his simplicity, his natural eloquence, and his Christlike effect upon crowds. He became a saint of the Risorgimento long before his death, and none of his military setbacks sullied his reputation. A calendar for the year 1863 (figure 38) testifies to the religious awe in which he was held. Garibaldi's bust (with halo) stands on a republican altar; rifles replace the usual candles expected around an image of a Catholic saint. On the left are placed ex-votos in thanks for the liberation of Marsala, Palermo, and Naples, while on the right a plea is made for the liberation of both Venice and the Eternal City. A blatantly anticlerical series of verses accompanies the calendar: "Sons of Italy, if you wish / to dry / the lengthy tears of Venice and Rome / it matters very little if the priest doesn't chant, / for these are the candles and this is the saint."[15]

Garibaldi's appeal as the archetypical republican leader, fearless in battle and of extraordinary integrity, reached far beyond the borders of the Italian peninsula. Not only did Abraham Lincoln offer him a commission in the Union Army in July of 1861 (which he declined primarily because Lincoln was then unwilling to abolish slavery), but upon his visit to London as a private citizen in 1864, he was greeted by a completely spontaneous demonstration of an estimated 600,000 people in the streets of what was then the largest city in the world. As Denis Mack Smith quite rightly remarks, "no King, no Emperor, had ever been accorded such a triumph, anywhere."[16]

Garibaldi never abandoned his dream of a Roman capital in a united Italy, although his military campaigns were not directly responsible for bringing this event to pass. Many of his efforts, in fact, were unsuccessful. As early as 1862, he began to plan another march on Rome from Sicily, apparently with the covert support of King Victor Emanuel and his

37. Giuseppe Fochetti and Pietro Sindico,
The Most Worthy Triumvirate
(lithograph, 1860). Museo Centrale del
Risorgimento, Rome.
Soprintendenza per i beni artistici e storici della
provincia di Roma.

Figli d'Italia, se asciugar volete
Di Venezia e di Roma il lungo pianto ,

Poco v'importi se non canta il prete;
Queste son le candele e questo il Santo.

38. Garibaldi as the secular saint of the
Risorgimento, surrounded by rifles in place
of candles (lithograph calendar for 1863).
Milan: Civica Raccolta delle Stampe "A.
Bertarelli."
Soprintendenza per i beni artistici e storici della
provincia di Milano.

prime minister, but when his volunteers encountered regular Pietmontese forces at Aspromonte, Garibaldi was wounded and his men captured.
Pardoned by the king, he eventually led another group of volunteers in
1866 against the Austrians in the north. This campaign resulted in the
annexation of Venice. In 1867, he attempted yet another march on Rome
but was defeated at Mentana by French and papal forces. It would be the
defeat of the French protectors of the pope and the papal states in the
Franco-Prussian War of 1870 that finally permitted the annexation of the
Eternal City and the papal possessions and the creation of a united Italy.
When Italian troops breached the Porta Pia in Rome in 1870, bringing to
an end the thousand-year-old secular rule of the papacy in Italy, Garibaldi
was kept far away from what was represented as the triumph of the
House of Savoy and its constitutional monarch, Victor Emanuel. But Garibaldi's cry "Rome or death!" had provided the rallying point around
which the entire unification of Italy had taken place.

Garibaldi's charismatic personality and his fundamental goodness did
much to keep alive the ideals of Livian republicanism in an era which
would soon be characterized as an age of colonialism, an age with a
decidedly imperial, rather than republican, flavor. Perhaps the most interesting aspect of the race for empire from the last quarter of the nineteenth century until the outbreak of the First World War was that the
competition for overseas possessions was hotly contested not only by
governments which were organized as imperial dynasties (Russia, Germany, Japan, the French Second Empire), but also by states with republican institutions and parliamentary governments (the French Third Republic, the United States, Italy, and Great Britain). The justification for
such foreign adventures differed widely, as can be seen from an examination of Italian and American opinions on imperialistic policies. However,
colonial adventures seemed to promise additional natural resources or
foreign markets. Moreover, such ventures abroad could serve to divert
attention away from pressing social problems at home.

In post-Risorgimento Italy, the liberal regime which controlled the
country until the rise to power of the Fascists in 1922 often employed
Roman mythology to justify its foreign policies. When Francesco Crispi,
the Italian prime minister, brought Italy into a colonial war against Ethiopia which ended in a disastrous and humiliating defeat at Adowa in 1896,
the past colonial glories of ancient Rome were invoked to justify his
campaign. Again, in 1911–12, Prime Minister Giovanni Giolitti maneu-
vered the Italian government into the Italo-Turkish War (this time with
more success) in order to gain a "fourth shore" for the Italian people, the

North African coast held by the ancient Roman empire. Unlike the debacle in Ethiopia, this brief and successful war was extremely popular, and it resulted in the seizure of the Ottoman provinces of Tripolitania and Cyrenaica, making up what is today Libya. The link between Roman conquests in Africa and the victory of the modern Italian state can be seen quite clearly in a postcard of the period (figure 39). It celebrates the Italian sailors victorious in this brief conflict and pictures one of their number grasping the sword from the skeleton of a dead Roman legionnaire. Interestingly, the picture itself is reproduced from an English magazine of the period that had viewed Italy's imperial pretensions in North Africa in a far more tolerant light than it would later view Mussolini's African campaigns.

Such talk of modern Italy's ancient Roman heritage was not limited to propaganda supporting Italy's colonial wars abroad. With the victorious conclusion of the First World War, Prime Minister Vittorio Orlando addressed the Chamber of Deputies in Rome on 20 November 1918 in the following manner: "an altogether Roman breath of greatness pervades this latest epic; and certainly never as at this moment has Italy seemed a more worthy heir of Rome."[17]

Given the engrained republican traditions of the United States of America, American imperialism in the late nineteenth century could not be justified by invoking the once-proud Roman empire. American colonial adventures abroad and the creation of its empire as a result of the Spanish-American War required more subtle rationalizations. Unlike the Italians, who in fact counted the ancient dominion of Rome as part of their national heritage, the United States of America had been created in an anticolonial war by a culture steeped in Livian republican ideals. Thus, in order to justify the government's expansion southward (Cuba, Puerto Rico) as well as westward (the Philippines), American apologists for empire turned to a rationale typical of the epoch—that of progress and civilization. Even as the cannons cooled after Spain's defeat in the Spanish-American War, Muret Halstead—a war correspondent and the historian of the Philippine expedition—could thus write in 1898: "That the time was approaching when, with the irretrievable steps of the growth of a living Nation of free people, we would reach the point where it should be our duty to accept the responsibility of the dominant American power, and accomplish manifest Destiny by adding Cuba and Porto Rico to our dominion, has for half a century been the familiar understanding of American citizens."[18] With the sudden and almost unexpected addition of the Philippine Islands to the booty from the war, Halstead af-

39. "Italy brandishes the sword of ancient Rome" (postcard).
Private collection of Peter Bondanella.

firmed that the situation was "absolutely novel" but that it could not be said to be "out of the scope of reasonable American expansion and is in the right line of enlarging the area of enlightenment and stimulating the progress of civilization."[19] Furthermore, Halstead affirmed that "it was foreordained since the beginning when God created the earth, that we, the possessors of this imperial American zone, should be a great Asiatic Power."[20]

This attitude could be seen at international fairs held in the United States. Between 1879 and 1916, more than one hundred million people visited international expositions and fairs in Philadelphia, New Orleans, Chicago, Atlanta, Nashville, Buffalo, Portland, San Francisco, Seattle, and San Diego. One of the major attractions at most of these fairs was the anthropological exhibits devoted to the "uncivilized" natives of the newly conquered American possessions in the Far East. At the Trans-Mississippi and International Exposition (Omaha, 1898), a recreated native village boasting some sixteen "Manila warriors" confirmed the impression that the Philippines were populated by savage cannibals in dire need of civilizing. At the even more important Pan-American Exposition (Buffalo, 1901), the Philippine Islands' display was the focus of a planned exhibit of American overseas possessions. Director General William I. Buchanan wrote in 1899 to J. H. Brigham, the Chairman of the Exposition Board, that the fair represented "the first and best opportunity we have had to justify, by means of the most available object lessons we can produce, the acquisition of new territory; to demonstrate, as I am sure can be done, that the results to be obtained promise to be for us all ample compensation for the sacrifice already made, and for the burdens yet to be assumed."[21] The Philippine Islands' village, which was so popular a site for tourists at the Buffalo fair, was eleven acres in size and was guarded by a detachment of American soldiers. In President William McKinley's opening address at the fair, shortly before his assassination there by anarchist Leon Czolgosz, the link between material progress in America (the explicit theme of the fair) and imperialist expansion abroad (the fair's implicit theme) was made quite clear. As a brilliant recent study of the phenomenon puts it, the fair thus presented an "ideology of economic development, labeled 'progress'," and translated that imperialistic ideology into a "utopian statement about the future."[22]

Besides the various native villages erected as concrete proof of the need to spread American civilization around the globe, professional anthropologists were enlisted to support the vision of imperialism with theories of racial hierarchies. Social Darwinism was thus employed as a justification for colonies abroad, just as it had been earlier evoked as a rationale for the domination of one class over another at home.

Perhaps the most impressive sights at such expositions were the fairgrounds buildings themselves. At the Buffalo exposition (figure 40), McKinley's entrance—complete with a huge American flag—embodies the kind of fanciful pseudo-Roman imperial architecture typical of the period. It is gigantic, imposing, grandiloquent architecture clearly built to bolster the imperial vision of this era. Its style reminds the contemporary viewer more of the fanciful architectural structures in Thomas Cole's canvases or of the equally enormous movie sets soon to be employed in silent film epics about the Roman empire than it does the careful reconstructions of the actual buildings of ancient Rome. An equally interesting column, which recalled Roman imperial columns, was built at the Louisiana Purchase Exposition (St. Louis, 1904). On the Column of Progress (figure 41), the traditional figure of the Roman emperor, or the statue of a saint or martyr that replaced the emperors in Christian Rome, has given place to the new God—Progress. The sober, austere republican images typical of the greatest works inspired by the American Revolution have been replaced by massive celebrations of world domination.

40. McKinley's entrance to the Pan-
American Exposition, Buffalo, 1901.
Division of Prints and Photographs, Library of
Congress, Washington, D.C.

41. Opening day before the Column of
Progress at the Louisiana Purchase
Exposition, St. Louis, 1904.
Division of Prints and Photographs, Library of
Congress, Washington, D.C.

With the seizure of power in Italy by Benito Mussolini in 1922 and the establishment of a Fascist state, the myth of Rome was employed for the first time to manipulate an entire people's nationalistic sentiments.[1] Earlier expressions of the myth of Rome had been primarily the reflection of an elite culture. Petrarch never felt it necessary for the masses to possess the kind of classical erudition he enjoyed. It was sufficient that a man in power, Cola di Rienzo, shared his dream of a renewed Roman glory. Machiavelli's vision of a revitalized Roman republicanism was addressed primarily to his bookish circle of intellectuals and to the rulers of the period. And the art of the early modern period, either republican or imperial in spirit, was intended to reflect values and ideals shared by only a small and select group. Only during the revolutions of the late eighteenth century in France or America did the myth of Rome reach a relatively widespread audience, but even in these two countries, republican sentiment was predominantly an ideology used by the middle class to justify its political beliefs.

Mussolini, however, employed the imperial tradition of ancient Rome, expressed in a series of imposing architectural and engineering projects, to galvanize the masses behind his regime. Eventually, he used it to justify an expansionistic adventurism abroad, which not only destroyed the regime he created but its maker as well. Of course, Mussolini was not the first ruler to color his policies with imperial trappings. Napoleon had already done so, and the ruling houses of other European states often recalled the past glories of the Roman empire in the titles of their leaders—for example, the Kaiser of Germany or the Czar of Russia—which were derived from the name of Julius Caesar. Even the liberal regime which Mussolini overturned in 1922 had sporadically justified its colonial adventures by references to Rome's imperial past. But only Mussolini manipulated the myth of Rome in a *systematic* fashion to increase Italian nationalism, playing upon the sentiments of a people who had long suffered in their dealings with other great European powers. Italians, by virtue of their birthplace, could imagine themselves the *literal* descendants of republican or imperial Rome, and given the importance of the myth of Rome in the Italian Risorgimento, Mussolini had no need to invent the linkage, real or imagined, between ancient Roman glories and the "Roman spirit" (*romanità*) that found particular expression in Fascist propaganda. In Mussolini, the myth of Rome became the basis for a foreign policy, a program of imposing public works, and an imperialistic vision of the modern world.

Benito Mussolini remains today one of the most enigmatic figures of contemporary history. He was born on 29 July 1883 in the village of Predappio, a few kilometers from the larger town of Forlì in the Romagna, a province with a reputation for breeding revolutionaries. Mussolini was baptized with three Christian names, each of which recalled a famous left-wing leader: Benito (for Benito Juarez, the Mexican); Andrea and Amilcare (for two Italian leftists, Andrea Costa and Amilcare Cipriani). Yet, the Marxist leanings of his father were tempered by his mother's devout Catholicism. Even bearing three names sacred to Socialist popular culture, Mussolini was nevertheless baptized in the Catholic church. By disposition a bad-tempered and sometimes violent child, Mussolini combined something of the bohemian with the anarchist revolutionary. He began his career as a schoolteacher, but this calling proved too tame for his spirited disposition, and in 1902, he moved to Switzerland, where he began to exercise his newly discovered talent for public speaking among the largely illiterate population of expatriate Italian workers there. By 1904, he was acknowledged by all left-wing thinkers and activists in Switzerland and Italy as a promising young Marxist, and a Marxist he remained until 1914, in spite of subsequent attempts by Fascists, Communists, and Socialists to deny his ideological roots.

Mussolini's Socialist background had an important impact upon later Fascist doctrine, even though Mussolini and other Fascist ideologues would eventually present fascism as a novel ideology, owing little to traditional liberalism or Marxism.[2] From thinkers such as Georges Sorel, Gaetano Mosca, and Vilfredo Pareto (whose lectures Mussolini claimed to have attended in Switzerland), he learned to value the power of political mythology in order to arouse the inert and apolitical masses. Even while he professed himself a Marxist, Mussolini always remained fundamentally an elitist who believed that the masses required a strong leader to guide them. He had little patience for those Socialists who favored a social-democratic brand of Marxism and continued to admire Lenin even after he had turned away from the Socialists. Mussolini, however, embraced the doctrine of class struggle with the greatest of enthusiasm.

In fact, "Class Struggle" was the title of a four-page, weekly magazine (*La lotta di classe*) that he was asked to edit by the Socialist clubs of Forlì when he returned from Switzerland and the Austrian-held province of Trentino in 1910. So strong was Mussolini's original belief in the primacy of the class struggle that while in the Trentino, he ridiculed the aspirations of irredentists, who were committed to the annexation of the Italian-speaking province, because he felt patriotism and nationalism were bourgeois ideals, incompatible with a proletarian class unity transcending national frontiers. Even more interesting, considering his later foreign policy as dictator of Italy, was his strident opposition to the Italo-Turkish War, which Giolitti had declared largely to distract the country from major internal problems. Not only did Mussolini protest the war, but he actually advised open revolt in Forlì against the government to prevent the conflict. His subsequent arrest and five-month prison sentence first brought him to the attention of Socialists all over Italy.

In 1912, Mussolini was appointed to the editorship of the Socialist party newspaper, *Avanti!*, and his editorials championed an uncompromising campaign for revolution. This intransigent policy seemed to find favor with the electorate, and in the elections of 1913, the party gained fifty-three parliamentary seats with nearly a million votes. When the First World War broke out, Mussolini initially continued to follow a strictly Socialist internationalism, opposing Italian entrance into a war that he believed was only a squabble among capitalists. But it shortly became clear to him that the war would last for some time and that the working classes on opposing sides would not rebel against their governments. In short, the appeal of nationalism still far outweighed the sense of class identity among the workers. Mussolini then had a sudden change of heart that changed the course of his life. He declared in *Avanti!* on 18 October 1914 that he had been wrong and that neutrality or nonbelligerence was a mistaken policy for Socialists to follow. His abrupt shift resulted in his expulsion from the Socialist party. Soon thereafter, Mussolini founded quite a different kind of newspaper, its name alone—Il Popolo d'Italia ("The People of Italy")—symbolizing the long road he had traveled since his position on *La lotta di classe* in Forlì. Where once Mussolini had seen politics as a clash between different economic groups without regard to national boundaries, he now began to espouse highly nationalistic views that defined international politics as a struggle between plutocratic nations and proletarian nations—"haves" and "have-nots"— and he viewed Italy as a proletarian nation. Mussolini and many of his future Fascist colleagues, all of whom were radical interventionists, practiced what they preached: many, like Mussolini, volunteered for military service, and the majority served with relative distinction on the front lines.

Mussolini's conversion to a strident and patriotic nationalism would prevent any ideological compromise with his former Socialist comrades. Socialist opposition to the war, and the sometimes insensitive treatment of returning war veterans by Socialist officials and trade unionists, made it quite easy after the war to cast the Socialists in an unfavorable light with disgruntled veterans, the nucleus of the future Fascist party. Moreover, in the early days of the Fascist movement, the new political force retained much of its original leftist character and thus could appeal to the same constituency that the Socialists sought to win over. On 23 March 1919, near Milan's Piazza San Sepolcro, Mussolini met with some fifty like-minded revolutionaries and founded the *Fascio del combattimento*. The Italian word *fascio* refers both to the ancient Roman fasces and to a group or association (literally, a "bundle"). Clearly, the second meaning is that which Mussolini originally intended. His use of the term *fascio* for this purpose was not even original with him. In fact, both *fascio* and the term *duce* (from the Latin *dux*, "leader") were first employed not by Fascists but by left-wing activists. As Mussolini's political power and skill as a propagandist grew, however, the ancient Roman connotation of the word *fascio* would become increasingly useful to him. And the symbolic power of the word gave to the Fascist party its permanent identification and character—a revolutionary group with antecedents in ancient Rome.

Most of the first Fascists were ex-revolutionary interventionists. They included former socialists, anarchists, revolutionary syndicalists, army veterans, as well as republicans. Even members of the avant-garde artistic movement known as Futurism joined the party. While the middle class outnumbered representatives of either the upper or lower classes, all sectors of Italian society were represented, and unlike Hitler's later National Socialist movement in Germany, Mussolini's early fascism displayed no racial or religious prejudices. Jews were among the party's earliest supporters, and as late as the mid-1930s, Mussolini ridiculed the concept of racial "purity." Only after Nazi Germany began to dominate Italy's foreign affairs did Mussolini adopt the generally unpopular policy of separating Italy's relatively tiny Jewish community from the public life of the nation.[3] The party's original goals were "anticapitalist, antimonarchical, anticlerical, antisocialist, antiparliamentary, and, most especially, antibourgeois."[4]

Too often portrayed as a clownish figure whose only talent was his ability to strut and posture on palace balconies, Mussolini was in reality a masterful political tactician, skilled in the arts of popular journalism and in the manipulation of propaganda and political symbols. His Fascist movement obtained only 35 seats in the elections of 1921 (some 7 percent of the total), as opposed to 122 seats for the Socialists and 107 for the Catholic party, but the ballot box would be far less important in Mussolini's rise to power than the intimidation and violence directed against his opponents by the "punitive expeditions" of the Fascist *squadristi*, members of paramilitary groups that provided the party with its special brand of authority. And even though Mussolini's gangs provided more tangible support for his movement than Roman myth, the city of Rome, nevertheless, loomed large in his early plans to seize power. Rome had been the capital of the world under the empire, it had survived the Dark Ages as the center of Christianity, and the fledgling Italian republic had been founded by breaching its walls in 1870 behind the battlecry "Rome or death!" Mussolini was not slow to grasp the symbolic importance of seizing power in this special, mythical place. Seven months before the actual March on Rome (27–28 October 1922), which resulted in his taking the post of prime minister and precipitated the death of liberal, republican Italy, Mussolini underscored Rome's symbolic importance for Italian fascism in one of his speeches:

> We dream of a Roman Italy, that is to say wise, strong, disciplined, and imperial. Much of that which was the immortal spirit of Rome is reborn in Fascism: the Fasces are Roman; our organization of combat is Roman, our pride and our courage are Roman: Civis romanus sum. Now, it is necessary that the history of tomorrow, the history we fervently wish to create, not represent a contrast or a parody of the history of yesterday. . . . Italy has been Roman for the first time in fifteen centuries in the War and in the Victory: now Italy must be Roman in peacetime: and this renewed and revived romanità bears these names: Discipline and Work.[5]

Mussolini manipulated symbols consciously, being fully aware of the political potential they possessed. Just before the fateful March on Rome, he defined fascism in terms of mythmaking: "We have created our myth. The myth is a faith, a passion. It is not necessary that it be a reality. . . . Our myth is the Nation, our myth is the greatness of the Nation. And to this myth, to this greatness, which we desire to translate into a complete reality, we subordinate all the rest."[6]

Because of Mussolini's sensitivity to the power of political mythology as an integral component of a regime's domestic propaganda, he constantly linked Italian fascism with the glories of imperial, not republican, Rome. But Mussolini was equally aware of the need for fostering a strong, imperial image abroad. He arranged for what first passed as his autobiography to be published in English even before it appeared in Italy. This book, actually the collaboration of a pro-Fascist journalist, Luigi Barzini, Sr., and a former United States Ambassador to Italy, Richard Washburn Child, was employed by Mussolini to present his argument that Roman antecedents were in his mind when he planned the organization of the Fascist movement: "I made a scheme of military and political organization on the model of the old Roman legions. The Fascisti were divided by me into *principi* and *triari*."[7] Moreover, he gave the four men to whom he delegated the actual task of directing the details of the March on Rome (Italo Balbo, Michele Bianchi, Emilio De Bono, and Cesare Maria De Vecchi) the rather imperious title of quadrumvirs, recalling similar groupings under the Roman state. While Mussolini arrived in Rome in the comfort of a sleeping car, the regime encouraged the mythology of an imperial precedent for the March on Rome based upon Julius Caesar's earlier seizure of power, and eventually a popular legend grew up of Mussolini on horseback, leading his blackshirted legions across the Rubicon toward Rome.[8]

With the seizure of power by the Fascists in 1922 and their eventual transformation of the republican institutions of liberal Italy into a totalitarian state, Mussolini gained a wider range of propaganda possibilities for his unique version of imperial mythology. He gained, as well, the vast financial resources of the state to carry out whatever project he desired. The use of the myth of imperial Rome by his regime, implicit in his nationalistic views even before he came to power, developed slowly at first during the first decade of his rule, then increased dramatically as his regime turned toward foreign adventures in the second decade.

On 21 April 1924, Mussolini had himself proclaimed a "citizen of Rome" on the Capitoline Hill. The earlier example of Cola di Rienzo and his similar symbolic gestures were obviously in Mussolini's mind when he arranged this tribute to himself, and the dictator would have been well advised to recall, as well, Cola's eventually unhappy demise.

A mania for symbolic dates and anniversaries, also recalling Cola's policies six centuries earlier or those of the French revolutionaries, was typical of the regime's propaganda. The date of the ceremony, the day and month, according to legend that ancient Rome was founded in 753 B.C., was especially important to Mussolini. This symbolic association explains why 21 April replaced 1 May, which had Marxist connotations, as the Fascist Labor Day. And whenever possible, Mussolini arranged for important public ceremonies or events to take place on 21 April. The opening of Cinecittà ("Cinema City"), the vast studio complex that still serves as the backbone of the Italian film industry in Rome, or the inauguration of the many new towns Mussolini planned and constructed in the Pontine Marshes after that area had been drained and reclaimed, were usually celebrated on the day Rome was founded to encourage the feeling that the Fascist regime was continuing ancient Roman traditions. The year 1922 was proclaimed the Anno Primo ("Year One") of the new Fascist calendar and the new Fascist era, and soon public buildings and monuments were dated not only according to the Christian era (for example, 1926), but also with the second Fascist date: 1926 became Anno IV, E. F.—"Year Four of the Fascist Era."

In 1925, Mussolini founded the Institute for Roman Studies, an academic organization devoted to the study of the Eternal City. While the regime did not demand or always receive immediate propaganda benefits from such actions, it certainly looked favorably upon any scholarship that seemed to substantiate its own view of Italy's classical Roman heritage. In the following year, on 12 December, the official symbol of the Italian state became the lictors' fasces. The general tone of Mussolini's propaganda based upon imperial Roman themes is evident in two postcards from the period which were sold to young soldiers serving in the army or the highway patrol to send to their parents at home (figures 42 and 43). In the first card, a favorite historical theme of the regime is emphasized. The three figures—the Roman legionnaire, a redshirt from Garibaldi's nineteenth-century army of national liberation, and a Fascist blackshirt—graphically represent the historical continuity linking the most heroic moments in the national life of the Italian people as viewed by the regime. Mussolini obviously agreed with Garibaldi's views on the sometimes benevolent effects of a dictatorship (although Garibaldi would have surely considered him a tyrant, not a guardian of republican institutions), and he constantly underlined the continuity he felt existed between Garibaldi's march on Rome and his own seizure of power there. In May 1932, when dedicating a statue to Garibaldi's wife Anita on the Janiculan Hill, Mussolini declared: "The blackshirts who fought and died in those years of humiliation [immediately before the Fascist revolution of 1922] are legitimate descendants of the redshirts and their great condottiero. All his life long Garibaldi's heart was aflame with a single passion, as he fought for the unity and independence of the fatherland.

42. The Prince of Piemonte Legion (postcard).
Private collection of Peter Bondanella.

43. Highway militia (postcard).
Private collection of Peter Bondanella.

Never did he give way, never was he forced to surrender his high ideal—not by men, nor by the sects, not by parties or ideologies, nor by the declamation encountered in parliamentary assemblies. These assemblies Garibaldi despised, advocate as he was of an 'unlimited' dictatorship in difficult times."[9] The same sense of historical continuity and fulfillment in the Fascist victory can be seen in the second card, which pictures a Roman legionnaire showing the path to his Fascist descendant. Road building was obviously one of the major accomplishments of the Roman empire, and the many public-works projects undertaken by the Fascists—the draining of the Pontine Marshes (itself a project left unfinished by Julius Caesar), the construction of modern superhighways, numerous public buildings, power plants, stations, and stadia—were viewed not only as useful capital investments but were also seen as literally concrete embodiments of Fascist ideology and the imperial aspect of a newly revived Roman spirit in Fascist Italy.

During the second decade of the Fascist era (from 1932 until 1942), Mussolini's public speeches and writings showed a radical increase in the exploitation of the myth of Rome. Such speeches were usually linked to public spectacles and ceremonies orchestrated by the regime and depended as much upon the Duce's physical presence and the magic of his oratory as they did upon mythic content. A number of such public meetings were designed to celebrate major expositions or to inaugurate new buildings that physically embodied the various aspects of the Fascists' imperial vision of ancient Rome. Behind all the activity in this decade was the desire of the regime to justify a series of foreign adventures and the new, entangling alliance with Nazi Germany. Here, perhaps more than in any single component of Fascist ideology, the myth of Rome proved to be a crucial means of mobilizing mass support for the government's policies.

The year 1932 was important for the Fascist state because it marked the beginning of the second decade after the March on Rome. On 24 October 1932, Mussolini predicted in a speech in Milan that "within a decade, Europe will be Fascist or Fascistized" and that the dilemmas that plagued depression-stricken Western civilization could be resolved in only one manner—"with the doctrine and the wisdom of Rome."[10] An article Mussolini published in a party newspaper during the same month continued the theme of Rome's missionary role. In it Mussolini declared that Rome had been the birthplace of universal political ideals four times in its history—first under the Romans, then under the Apostle Paul, next during the Italian Renaissance, and finally under fascism.[11] A few days later, on

28 October, Mussolini inaugurated two grandiose projects aimed at the glorification of his regime. He opened the Via dell'Impero (now called the Via dei Fori Imperiali), a broad avenue formed by clearing away a huge space between the Colosseum and Piazza Venezia in the heart of Rome. As its name implied, this broad avenue allowed the Fascist government to stage impressive military parades beginning at the symbol of Rome's glorious imperial age, then past the Roman forums to the headquarters of Mussolini's government in the Palazzo Venezia. The symbolism was not lost on the cheering crowds of onlookers who were frequently massed in the square to listen to Mussolini's speeches.

An even more interesting, if less durable, exhibit was opened on the same day to commemorate the Fascist revolution of 1922—the Mostra della Rivoluzione Fascista ("Exhibit of the Fascist Revolution"). On Rome's Via Nazionale, a hall was decorated with a facade supporting three enormous metallic fasces twenty-five meters tall. The shape of these symbols of the regime, as well as much of the artwork inside the exhibit, avoided the kind of reactionary art usually associated with other totalitarian states, such as Hitler's Germany or Stalin's Russia, and was resolutely modernist in style. The regime intended the exhibit to function as a permanent shrine to its seizure of power, and it organized school trips and special visits to the show from all over Italy, encouraging mass participation with reduced rail fares and low group rates.[12]

The tone of Mussolini's Roman rhetoric became progressively more violent during the decade. It is rare, in fact, to find a photograph of Il Duce without a military uniform of some sort during this period. In an article written on 6 July 1933 in the *Popolo d'Italia* to celebrate the placement of a bronze statue of Julius Caesar on the Via dell'Impero, where it remains to this day, Mussolini linked the March on Rome with Caesar's crossing of the Rubicon: "This epoch, even this epoch, is one which can be called Caesarian, dominated as it is by exceptional personalities who take upon themselves the powers of the State for the good of the people against the Parliaments, just as Caesar marched against the Senatorial oligarchy in Rome without falling into the demagogic excesses of Marius."[13] In another brief essay, a preface to a book published in 1933 about Italian conquest and colonization of Libya, Mussolini stressed the Roman character of Italian accomplishments there: "Civilization, in fact, is what Italy is creating on the fourth shore of our ocean: Western civilization in general, Fascist civilization in particular. The Arabs who salute in the Roman manner recognize this new civilization, which restores well being and tranquility to their tribes and fertility to their lands."[14]

Mussolini's reference to the Roman salute raises an interesting problem concerning its origins. The outstretched arm with open palm, made even more famous after it was later adopted by Hitler's Nazis, was deemed by the regime as a proper Roman gesture and was made compulsory for all official greetings, although many Italians and even many Fascists avoided using it. However, as Luigi Barzini, Jr. has pointed out, we are by no means sure that the ancient Romans saluted each other by raising their right hands. In his opinion, the salute was "probably invented at the beginning of the century by the forgotten director of a silent movie version of *Quo Vadis?* or *Fabiola.*"[15] Denis Mack Smith has suggested that a possible explanation of the salute's adoption by the regime may be found in Mussolini's "morbid fear of physical contact" and in the salute's supposedly "more hygienic" character when compared to the traditional handshake.[16] An even more common explanation of the salute's origin traces it back to the occupation of the city of Fiume in 1919–20 by Gabriele D'Annunzio and his followers. The classicizing tendencies and strident nationalism of this poet-adventurer provided Mussolini with an early model and even a potential rival. D'Annunzio also had been involved in the scripting of a major silent film with an imperial Roman theme—Giovanni Pastrone's *Cabiria* (1914)—and it is quite possible that Luigi Barzini's suggestion is at least partially correct. If so, it is interesting to note that the most characteristic symbol of two major totalitarian movements in our century may derive ultimately from the cinema, the century's only new art form and a mass medium *par excellence.*

Another symbolic link to ancient Rome served to justify Italy's new and belligerent foreign policy. In 1934, the regime installed four large marble maps on the Basilica of Maxentius along the Via dell'Impero. These maps marked the various stages in the conquests that occurred during the early republic and the subsequent empire. The obvious message was that the Fascists intended to continue this imperialistic tradition, as indeed they did in Ethiopia in 1935–36, when a fifth map was added after the conquest of this African state to bring Roman imperial history "up to date." Today, the tourist to Rome may still examine the first four maps, although the fifth has been removed to avoid offense. With the Ethiopian war, Mussolini intended not only to blot out the shame caused by the memory of Italy's disastrous defeat at Adowa in 1896, but also to assert Italy's hegemony in the Mediterranean basin, "mare nostrum" as Mussolini preferred to call it, following the ancient Roman expression. Where *lebensraum* was used to justify the imperialism of Nazi Germany in eastern Europe, Mussolini's regime cited the history of imperial Rome as a precedent for its adventures in the Mediterranean and in Africa. The cost of the establishment of the Italian empire in Africa was enormous. It not only wasted precious resources and saddled the nation with future expenses that swallowed up more than a tenth of Italy's total foreign reserves, but it also had disastrous effects on Italy's foreign policy.[17] Isolated from the Western democracies, Mussolini was forced to move closer to an alliance with Hitler, ultimately bringing about the downfall of the regime. And yet, at the time of the fall of Addis Ababa on 5 May 1936, Mussolini enjoyed more prestige within Italy than during any other moment of his lengthy rule.[18]

The Ethiopian war gave Mussolini yet another opportunity to under-line the link between fascism and the Roman empire. While opponents of the war attacked his use of poison gas and air power, Mussolini's propaganda apparatus justified the invasion largely on the basis of Rome's universal mission of civilization. A period postcard (figure 44) is a good example of this perspective. Italian colonial troops are greeted as liberators by Ethiopian slaves, whose chains are broken by their gener-ous Italian saviors. Slavery was apparently still practiced in some parts of Ethiopia, and the Fascists made its abolition a rationale for the invasion. In the background of the postcard stands the *lupa*, the she-wolf who nourished Romulus and Remus, the founders of the Eternal City. The task of civilizing a barbarous continent, left incomplete by Italy's Roman ancestors, has thus been resumed by the Fascists. While the Western democracies decried Mussolini's policies in Ethiopia, few bothered to remember that only several decades earlier, a similar desire to "civilize" the barbarian natives of other lands had been employed by a number of European states and by the United States as a justification for imperialist conquest abroad.

The Fascist regime also sponsored a campaign to collect gold and jew-els from Italian citizens to help defray the costs of the African campaign. In so doing, they made conscious reference to a similar action under-taken centuries earlier by Roman matrons in defense of the Eternal City, an event also imitated by women during the French Revolution. Women from all social classes and walks of life participated in this vast outpour-ing of patriotic sentiment, the most important ceremony of them all being that which took place in Piazza Venezia at the Tomb of the Un-known Soldier in the center of Rome (figure 45).[19] While the typical offering was a woman's gold wedding band, other gifts were more sub-stantial. Luigi Pirandello, the dramatist, offered the gold medal he re-ceived at Stockholm for the Nobel Prize in Literature for 1936. Few play-

44. Italian colonialists free Ethiopian
slaves from bondage (postcard).
Private collection of Peter Bondanella.

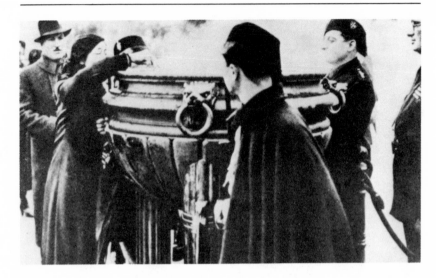

45. Italian women donate their wedding
rings and jewels to aid in the invasion of
Ethiopia.
Soprintendenza per i beni artistici e storici della
provincia di Roma.

wrights have produced works so totally antithetical to Fascist ideology, and Pirandello's gesture should be taken not only as a measure of the great writer's political naiveté but also as an indication of the depth of the patriotic feeling that greeted Mussolini's Ethiopian victory and the proclamation of the Italian empire.

With the fall of the Ethiopian capital, Mussolini was finally able to claim for his regime the place he demanded alongside the other Western imperial powers. On 9 May 1936, in one of his most famous and popular speeches from the balcony of the Palazzo Venezia, Il Duce announced to a cheering crowd the formation of the empire:

> Italy finally possesses its Empire. A Fascist Empire, because it bears the indestructible marks of the will and the power of the Roman fasces, and because this is the goal toward which for fourteen years the vital but disciplined energies of the young, vigorous Italian generations have been directed. . . . An Empire of civilization and of humanity for all the populations of Ethiopia. This is in the tradition of Rome which, after emerging victorious, joined the defeated peoples to its own destiny. The Italian people has created the Empire with its blood. It will nourish the Empire with its work and defend it against anyone with its arms. In this supreme certitude, oh legionnaires, raise high your standards, your blades, and your hearts to salute, after fifteen centuries, the reappearance of the Empire upon the fateful hills of Rome.[20]

On 18 March 1937 while inspecting the colony of Libya, Mussolini received the symbolic golden "Sword of Islam" and declared himself to be the protector of the Muslim population in that and other nearby countries. A photograph of Il Duce taken in this "fourth shore" of the revitalized Roman empire shows him escorted by black lictors carrying the fasces, the symbol of ancient Roman authority now reborn in the Fascist regime. It is most likely that Mussolini chose the black bodyguard to remind his followers of the Nubians, the legendary African troops from Rome's distant imperial past (figure 46).

Fascist foreign policy and Fascist internal propaganda were thus organized around the themes of *romanità* and the brutal concept, repeated often by both Mussolini and his followers, that "Rome dominates" ("Roma doma").[21] This increasingly bellicose attitude resonated through all the regime's public pronouncements. In the early years of his rule, Mussolini usually practiced what he himself called a "Scottish douche policy"—blowing hot and cold but normally never intending to back up

46. Mussolini is preceded by black Arabs
carrying the fasces.
Soprintendenza per i beni artistici e storici della
provincia di Roma.

his violent threats with equally violent actions. But as time passed, Mussolini began to view armed conflict as the only means of forging the new Italian character he felt was essential to the survival of a Fascist regime. As he put it in a speech echoing Machiavelli in Bologna on 25 October 1936, "anyone who possesses steel possesses bread; but when the steel is well tempered, he will probably also find gold."[22]

This emphasis upon *romanità* in propaganda worked best with imperial themes, but inside Italy, overenthusiastic acceptance of its premises could unwittingly produce comic effects. The photograph of the Casa del Fascio (the Fascist Party Headquarters) in the small Tuscan town of Signa shows the party faithful in Roman costumes assuming a somewhat uncomfortable pose that, at least to the contemporary observer, provides an unintentional parody of the regime's histrionic posturing and imperialistic ideology (figure 47). And an even more amusing story lies behind Mussolini's adoption of the Prussian goose step for military parades staged by the Italian armed forces. Mussolini did this during a period when he was increasingly under Hitler's influence, but he was unwilling to admit publicly that an Italian political movement that had earlier given the Nazis their famous Roman salute was now reduced to copying the gait of a non-Roman race. Consequently, the Fascists referred to the goose step as the *passo romano*, the "Roman step"! Moreover, Mussolini justified its adaptation with a specious Roman precedent. Centuries earlier during the first invasion of Rome by the Gauls, he reminded his faithful followers, the geese on the Capitoline Hill warned the city's inhabitants, giving them time to save the citadel.[23] Thus, the adoption of the goose step was presented as yet another reminder of ancient Roman tradition. The fact that Mussolini actually expected his countrymen to believe this incredible account reveals just how completely he had begun to confuse his own bellicose propaganda during the last few years before the outbreak of the Second World War with political realities.

Mussolini's policy of underscoring the links—real or imagined—between the imperial glories of ancient Rome and modern Fascist Italy's *romanità* reached its zenith with the inauguration of the Mostra Augustea della Romanità ("The Augustan Exhibit of Roman Spirit"). This celebration, which began in 1937 and ended in 1938, commemorated the two-thousandth anniversary of the birth of Augustus Caesar, ruler of most of the known world. This event left more of a lasting mark on today's Rome than others exclusively devoted to the Fascist revolution, because many of its exhibits are still on display at the Museo della Civiltà Romana ("The Museum of Roman Civilization") in the Esposizione Universale di Roma

47. Fascists in ancient Roman costumes in
the Tuscan town of Signa.
Soprintendenza per i beni artistici e storici per le
provincie de Firenze e Pistoia.

(E.U.R.) district of the city. Planned and organized by Professor Giulio Giglioili of the University of Rome, the exhibit contained an enormous number of plaster reproductions (over three thousand) of the major extant relics of the imperial period scattered throughout Europe, including a scale model of the city of ancient Rome which covered eighty square meters. Naturally, one of the rooms was devoted to the connection between fascism and *romanità*, underlining the parallel between the benevolent imperial rule of Augustus Caesar following a bloody succession of civil wars and that of the omnipotent and ominscient Duce, who had restored stability and tranquility to Italy and had finally given the country an empire to rival those of the other Western powers.[24]

Of all the possible manifestations of imperial Roman myth, those capable of being expressed in architecture and urban planning appealed most to Mussolini's taste. In an interview with Emil Ludwig, Il Duce declared that "to my mind, architecture is the greatest of all the arts, for it is the epitome of all the others."[25] When Ludwig commented that this was a very Roman sentiment, Mussolini replied: "I, likewise, am Roman above all."[26] Possessing an unparalleled grasp of the propaganda potential inherent in all public gestures, Mussolini realized that a vast program of public works would not only provide employment and visible proof that his regime was making progress, but it would also permit him to further certain ideological goals. It seems clear that Mussolini envisioned architecture and urban planning from the perspective of what a recent historian of Rome's urban planning has quite rightly called "urban scenography," where new Fascist buildings would provide an "open-air museum of live history" sympathetic to the regime's goals.[27]

Mussolini thus viewed architecture as a means of adding an "aura of respectability" to his regime, just as Augustus centuries earlier had done with his own newly formed state: like Augustus, Mussolini used architecture to associate his regime with great heros or heroic moments from the past and even to reinterpret history in the light of the achievements of his own regime.[28] In addition, between 1924 and 1938, the regime supported on a lavish scale all sorts of archaeological projects, and in the process of glorifying the Fascist state, Italian archaeology added more to our knowledge of the Rome of Augustus Caesar than had been learned in centuries.

However, Mussolini's concern for architectural embodiments of Italian *romanità* created a dilemma for the regime's architects. What style should such works reflect? On the one hand, Italian fascism presented itself as an

entirely new political and cultural phenomenon, transcending both classical nineteenth-century liberalism and individualism as well as Marxist
socialism and collectivism. In principle, therefore, fascism should embrace a new style of architecture embodying the most advanced modernist principles. On the other hand, Italian fascism, especially during the
decade between 1932 and 1942, was embarking on an increasingly imperialistic policy which stressed its connections with the ancient Roman
empire. Therefore, Italian Fascist architecture and urban planning also
aspired to reflect its Roman origins. In fact, the history of the Italian
Fascist regime itself is marked by vacillation between what an architectural historian has called "an apparently adventurous modernism and a
recalcitrant traditionalism."[29]

Mussolini personally favored a bold, inventive architecture that portrayed the modernity and novelty of fascism. After all, some of the original supporters of the Fascist revolution came from the Futurist movement. The Italian Movement for Rationalist Architecture (MIAR: Movi-
mento italiano per l'architettura razionale) was a powerful force during
the 1930s, and it represented an Italian branch of architectural modernism, modeling its design after the works of such foreigners as Le Cor-
busier, Wright, and others. The famous facade for the Mostra della Rivoluzione Fascista in 1932 had, in fact, been designed by one of the
organizers of the MIAR, Adalberto Libera, who also designed a com-
memorative room for the exposition. Another celebrated rationalist,
Giuseppe Terragni (1904–43), designed the Room of 1922 for the exhibit,
and between 1932 and 1936 constructed the even more famous Casa del
Fascio, the headquarters of the Fascist party in Como, which embodied
the most avant-garde style imaginable in such an authoritarian regime.
Rationalist architecture, like so much modernist work outside of Italy,
advocated an extensive use of glass for building surfaces, as well as a strict
correspondence between a building's shape and its function. It rejected
ornate decoration or anything which could be construed as a rhetorical
or declamatory architectural style. Thus, in its purest form, rationalist
architecture would oppose any revival of strictly imperial architecture,
especially an overgenerous use of columns and arches.

One of the most interesting of the major projects of the regime was
the Foro Mussolini ("Mussolini Forum"), now called the Foro Italico, in
Rome. The commission was given in 1927 to E. Del Debbio by the Opera
Nazionale Balilla, the Fascist youth organization designed to replace the
less militaristic Boy Scouts. The Forum was intended to celebrate sport

and strenuous physical exercise. Fascist leaders liked to picture their regime as a youthful one. After all, the Fascist hymn was "Giovinezza" ("Youth"), and not only Mussolini but a number of party leaders often had themselves photographed in various sporting poses. Some leaped over drawn bayonets or through burning hoops to demonstrate their physical fitness and personal courage. "Physical culture," as the Fascists liked to call it, was an important aspect of the regime's ideology. Italian achievements during the Fascist period in Olympic competitions and world athletic events were, indeed, remarkable. The Foro Mussolini, dedicated as it was to sports of all kinds, constituted an important showplace for meetings, athletic events, and governmental functions.

The major edifice at the Foro Mussolini was a stadium ringed with gigantic stone statues of athletes who also functioned as personifications of the cities of Italy. Nearby was constructed a walkway covered with Roman-style mosaics. In one section of the walkway (figure 48), youthful Fascists salute Il Duce. The word "Duce" is repeated in the mosaic, along with such often quoted Mussolinian slogans as "molti nemici, molto onore" ("many enemies, much honor"). Nearby, an inscription announces: "Duce, to you we dedicate our youth." Another mosaic celebrates the early *squadrista* epoch of nascent Fascism, 1919–22 (figure 49). In it, Fascist blackshirts go forth to do battle with the evil forces of bolshevism in a truck bearing the motto "Viva Mussolini!" and a flag with the slogan of the *squadristi*: "Me ne frego!" ("I don't give a damn!"). Above the truck is the Fascist battle cry "A Noi!" ("To Us!"). Below the truck lies a wounded martyr to the Fascist cause, supported by a comrade, while above it the bravery of the *squadristi* is compared to that of an ancient hero on horseback fighting an evil monster.

Elsewhere, the mosaics move from the theme of youth to that of Fascist empire. One impressive composition in the center of the walkway recalls Mussolini's famous speech announcing that Italy had finally created an empire with the conquest of Ethiopia: "9 May XIVth Year of the Fascist Era—Italy finally has its Empire" (figure 50). Nearby, a mosaic portrays the imperial Roman lion with its paw on a globe that shows Italy, Libya, and Ethiopia marked in sharp contrast to the rest of the world (figure 51). Near the Foro Mussolini stands one of the most interesting of the many statues scattered around the area—that of an idealized Fascist youth (figure 52). Part modern Roman warrior with gas mask and rifle, part athlete with muscular physique and gym shorts, this giant image embodied the warlike qualities of imperial Rome that Mussolini hoped

48. Roman-style Mussolini as the leader
of a renewed and youthful Fascist Italy
(mosaics in the Foro Italico, formerly Foro
Mussolini, Rome).
Soprintendenza per i beni artistici e storici della
provincia di Roma; photograph by Julia
Bondanella.

49. Roman-style celebration of the
squadrista epoch of fascism (1919–22)
(mosaics in the Foro Italico, formerly Foro
Mussolini, Rome).
Soprintendenza per i beni artistici e storici della
provincia di Roma; photograph by Julia
Bondanella.

50. Mussolini's famous proclamation of
the empire ("Finally Italy has its empire")
(mosaics in the Foro Italico, formerly Foro
Mussolini, Rome).
Soprintendenza per i beni artistici e storici della
provincia di Roma; photograph by Julia
Bondanella.

51. The imperial lion proclaims Italy's
imperial conquest of Libya and Ethiopia
(mosaic in the Foro Italico, formerly Foro
Mussolini, Rome).
Soprintendenza per i beni artistici e storici della
provincia di Roma; photograph by Julia
Bondanella.

52. The ideal Fascist youth (in the Foro
Italico, formerly Foro Mussolini, Rome).
Soprintendenza per i beni artistici e storici della
provincia di Roma; photograph by Julia
Bondanella.

to instill in Italy's young men. Today, these disintegrating and neglected images remain, an embarrassment to the democratic inheritors of Mussolini's regime who have done little to preserve them from gradual deterioration.

Mussolini apparently had even grander plans for the Foro Mussolini. The original design was to have the Foro Mussolini cover an area as large as the whole of Renaissance Rome. Moreover, the dictator initially intended that the Foro Mussolini should be dominated by a giant bronze statue, half-naked in the iconographical tradition of Hercules but bearing the familiar facial features of Il Duce. One hand would hold the Fascist *manganello* (the wooden club the *squadristi* employed to beat their leftist opponents senseless), while the other would be raised in a Roman salute. This enormous symbol of the regime's founder was supposed to stand eighty meters high, enabling it to look down upon the dome of St. Peter's Cathedral across the river! After some one hundred tons of metal were cast, money ran out. Only a foot and part of the face were completed, and the project was eventually abandoned with the outbreak of the war.[30]

While the Foro Mussolini project reflects the megalomania typical of most authoritarian rulers, Mussolini's taste in other projects is less stereotypical. Between 1932 and 1939, the Fascist state constructed five entirely new towns in the province of Lazio on land that had once been infested with malaria-carrying mosquitoes. Julius Caesar had left the reclamation of the Pontine Marsh incomplete, and it was important for the Fascist regime to demonstrate that it was capable of completing what the ancient Roman rulers had been unable to bring to fruition. Within a few years, the towns of Littoria (today called Latina to avoid reference to the fasces, the symbol of the regime), Sabaudia, Pontinia, Aprilia, and Pomezia arose. A number of buildings in these towns reflected modernist architectural principles, and they were constructed at approximately the same time as the Roman and Florentine train stations, also excellent examples of modernist architecture under fascism.

By 1934, architectural style had become the topic of some rather heated debate in both houses of parliament, with modernism coming under heavy attack by some Fascist ideologues who favored a more "Roman style" because of modernism's allegedly German or Bolshevik origin. Mussolini called together the architects of the town of Sabaudia and those who built the station of Florence, and in the presence of the Fascist party secretary, he made the following pronouncement:

I have summoned you because, after what has been said in the two houses of parliament, I would not wish you to believe that they were also my ideas. None of it: I wish to clarify in an unequivocal way that I am for modern architecture, for that of our time. . . . It would be absurd to think that we, today, were not able to have our own architectural thought; . . . even the monuments of Rome, that we are excavating today, responded to their function. . . . Tell the young architects who come out from the schools to make my motto theirs: "don't be afraid to have courage!" . . . It is not possible to remake the ancient, nor is it possible to copy it.[31]

In spite of Mussolini's general sympathy with the avant-garde architects of his time, the tendency toward a romanized style was perhaps inevitable, given the ideology underlying the regime's propensity for public display of *romanità*. Developments in archaeology, as well, were to increase the move toward a Fascist style indebted as much to ancient imperial Rome as to modernist principles. The image of Roman architecture that had come down to the twentieth century was largely that made popular by the writings of Vitruvius, which were indebted primarily to Greek models. However, the vast excavations of imperial Ostia, the seaport of ancient Rome, during the 1930s revealed an entirely different and much simpler imperial building style that soon was to find favor with the regime's urban planners. The excavations at Ostia had begun as early as 1909, but during the Fascist period they were considered a priority project. Carried out largely under the direction of Guido Calza, the work between 1938 and 1942 uncovered roughly half of the buildings now visible. The new and hitherto unsuspected imperial style revealed by these excavations was characterized by plain brickwork, unmolded window and door apertures, primary geometrical shapes, and very little adornment. Columns and capitals typical of the Vitruvian style were extremely rare, although simple arches played a major role in the overall design. Such a style was apparently the dominant style of imperial Rome as well as its foreign provinces, and the more familiar Vetruvian temple was apparently the only kind of public building in the ancient world that did not eventually give place to the appeal of this much simpler and more functional architecture.

Such a style reminds the contemporary viewer of the simple, yet mysterious architecture of Italian squares portrayed in the paintings of Giorgio De Chirico's "metaphysical" period. Although it could boast an ancient pedigree documented by the Ostian excavations, as well as other excavations in Libya, the simplicity of its style seemed to coincide, in many respects, with modernist architectural principles. Moreover, it could be reproduced relatively cheaply. It was therefore the perfect compromise style for a regime that straddled the twin fences of modernism and traditionalism and was employed in hundreds of public structures still standing all over Italy. An interesting example of the style is the Monument on the Janiculan Hill, by I. Jacobucci (1941), honoring the martyrs who died in the struggle for Rome from 1849 to the Fascist March on Rome in 1922. On the monument, Garibaldi's battle cry "Rome or Death!" underlines the regime's view that the Risorgimento had found its fulfillment in fascism. An even more obvious example of the style is the famous southwest flank of Rome's Stazione Termini, completed in the 1930s, which contains a series of simple and beautifully harmonious arches. The essence of this style was simplicity of design and simplicity of construction, as it utilized common materials easily available all over the peninsula—brick and travertine stone rather than the more expensive marble.[32]

Two extensive projects involving both architecture and urban renewal in Rome provide additional examples of the architectural legacy produced by Italian fascism's fascination with its imperial heritage: the Piazzale Augusto Imperatore in the center of Rome; and the entirely new quarter of the city known as the E.U.R. district. The first project involved the restoration of the Mausoleum of Caesar Augustus. Intent upon stressing the links between the Rome of the Caesars and the Rome of Il Duce, the man responsible for the final design of the new buildings, Vittorio Ballio Morpurgo, followed the plan used earlier in constructing the Via dell'Impero beside the Roman Forum, isolating the ancient Mausoleum and enclosing it within a new piazza. In addition, the Augustan Altar of Peace (the Ara Pacis) was reconstructed nearby. The project possessed some unique features, because the shell of the Mausoleum had been in constant use for centuries, serving as a concert hall and as a meeting place for civic gatherings. With its restoration, the shell was effectively reduced to the status of an "authentic" ruin, emptied of any civic function, and turned into an object of contemplation. The Forum of Augustus was also excavated. Originally, Augustus had set up statues of republican heroes in this forum in an attempt to stress the continuity of the old republic and his own regime. Augustus, like Mussolini, understood the use of architecture as propaganda, and it is therefore appropriate that so many Augustan monuments were excavated, studied, and restored during the Fascist period.

Implicit comparisons between Mussolini and Augustus had already been suggested at the Mostra Augustea della Romanità, the opening of which coincided with the construction of the Piazzale Augusto Imperatore. Indeed, a number of books by noted figures of the regime, including one entitled *L'Italia di Augusto e l'Italia di oggi* ("The Italy of Augustus and the Italy of Today"), by Giuseppe Bottai, then Minister of Education, made the parallels inherent in the regime's projects more explicit by drawing out the many affinities supposedly detectable in the lives of both "emperors."[33] The Piazzale project was sponsored by the Istituto Nazionale Fascista della Previdenza Sociale (the INFPS), a corporation responsible for a wide variety of social welfare and insurance programs, and the Istituto's offices were located in buildings around the Piazzale, which extend all the way to a central artery of downtown Rome, the Via del Corso. Two long facades, known as Fabbricato A and Fabbricato B, embodying the regime's imperial style, contain some interesting and extremely simple ornamentation.

On Fabbricato B along the Via dei Pontefici, imperial Roman arms and Fascist arms are juxtaposed around three windows. The Roman decorations include helmets, shields, bows and arrows, and musical instruments, while the corresponding Fascist decorations include rifles, gas masks, artillery pieces, and contemporary uniforms. A similar juxtaposition was made above the Via del Corso entrance into the Piazzale, where an imperial Roman eagle, shield, crown of victory, and a classical capital stand in contrast to a fasces and an open book crossed with a musket. This latter motif provides a visual expression of Mussolini's famous slogan, also placed over the entrances of the new, Fascist-style university buildings in Rome: "Libro e moschetto, fascista perfetto" ("Book and musket make the perfect Fascist"). The intermingling of the old and the new in a zone of the city identified with the Augustan age underlines quite clearly the parallel between Augustus and Mussolini, and the interested tourist in today's Rome may still visit these sites.

The Piazzale Augusto Imperiale and the Fascist regime's excavations and restorations of the Ara Pacis, the Augustan Mausoleum, and the Augustan Forum all invite the passerby to measure the accomplishments of Il Duce against those of the Emperor Caesar Augustus. In large measure, the impact of the projects is lessened precisely because Mussolini comes off second best in the comparison. As a recent assessment of the plan concluded, "our opinion of Augustus is not affected by his association with Mussolini, and our opinion of Mussolini is not enhanced. The Duce yields to the emperor and is lost."[34] But neither should it be forgotten that both men employed architecture to bolster the image of their regimes and both were masters at the art of architectural propaganda.

Another major project of the period involved an entirely new section of the city of Rome on the outskirts of its ancient boundaries. This area, the Esposizione Universale di Roma ("The Universal Exposition of Rome") is still known as the E.U.R. district. And here, even in the incomplete form in which the project was left when the war interrupted its construction, Mussolini's achievements are more durable and substantial. As early as 1936, Mussolini had arranged to hold a world's fair in Rome in 1942. It would not only bring thousands of foreign visitors to see the accomplishments of the Fascist regime but would also celebrate on a grandiose scale the second decade following the March on Rome in 1922. Accordingly, its opening was scheduled for 21 April 1942. The novelty of this project was that the fairground was conceived as an enduring monument, as a permanent quarter of a new urban center.[35] Mussolini, like the Americans who had organized the many expositions and fairs in the late nineteenth and early twentieth centuries, recognized the propaganda potential in such events.

In order to plan and organize this vast undertaking, an ENTE, an autonomous corporation possessing broad legal and economic powers, was formed under the guidance of Senator Vittorio Cini, an influential politician and philanthropist. In such a huge project, the question of architectural commissions and style arose quickly. On the planning commission, both academic, traditionalist architects and rationalists were represented. But since Cini appointed Marcello Piacentini (1881–1960) to the post of superintendent of architecture, parks, and gardens of the E.U.R., Piacentini's conservative views ultimately shaped the final plan and modified what might have otherwise been a completely modernist complex. The entire scheme was never actually completed under the regime, because Italy's entrance into the war blocked final construction. Thus, when work was suspended in 1942, during the twentieth anniversary of the March on Rome, the intended showcase for Italian fascism became, instead, an embarrassing monument to the emptiness of its imperial promises. Only after the war was the quarter completed, but with substantial changes in its original plan.

One building, however, was standing before the war brought work to a halt, and it still dominates the district as the visitor approaches it on the wide avenue leading from E.U.R. to Rome's ancient historical center (figure 53). Originally called the Palazzo della Civiltà Italiana ("The Palace of Italian Civilization"), it has now been renamed the Palazzo della Civiltà

53. Giovanni Guerrini, Ernesto Bruno La
Padula, and Mario Romano, architects,
Palazzo della Civiltà del Lavoro, formerly
called Palazzo della Civiltà Italiana;
E.U.R. district in Rome.
Soprintendenza per i beni artistici e storici della
provincia di Roma; photograph by Julia
Bondanella.

del Lavoro ("The Palace of the Civilization of Labor"). This undeniably ingenius and original work was designed by Giovanni Guerrini, Ernesto Bruno La Padula, and Mario Romano, and it was erected between 1938 and 1940. The history of its design also reflects the political struggle between the traditionalists and the rationalists. Original drawings reveal a perfect synthesis of rationalist architecture, calling for pure geometrical shapes. The building was to have consisted of a cube supported by a pedestal with squared openings. Little or no rhetorical decoration or ornamentation was to have been allowed. However, Piacentini found the original plans unsuitable. By this time he had become an advocate of *romanità* in all public buildings and monuments. For Piacentini, *romanità* meant either arches or columns, and given his crucial position on the planning commission, his suggestions to the young rationalist architects amounted to an ultimatum for a revision of the original design. Ernest La Padula's brother Attilio, and Giuseppe Perugini, then students at the School of Architecture at the University of Rome, noticed that the measurements for the apertures in the original plan were the same as the arches in Pompey's Theatre in the capital. As a result, and almost as a joke, the arches now visible in the final version of the completed building were added to the original proposal to provide the necessary touch of imperial Roman character. To the surprise of everyone, Piacentini enthusiastically approved the revisions and the building was completed on schedule.

In spite of the compromises involved in its construction, the Palazzo della Civiltà Italiana must be considered one of the most impressive architectural enterprises completed by the Fascist regime. In a very real sense, it did effect a workable marriage of modernist architecture and the ancient tradition of imperial Rome. And in so doing, it realized one of the long-standing dreams of Fascist ideology—the merger of ancient Roman imperial traditions and values with those of the new and modern Fascist state. Much as the ancient Colosseum still dominates the historical center of the Eternal City, this modern, "squared" Colosseum—its many arched apertures recalling those in the ancient structure—dominates the buildings in the E.U.R. district, even those built by Mussolini's democratic successors after the proclamation of the Italian republic in 1948. It is, of course, ironic, that Mussolini's Roman empire was beginning to crumble just at the moment this persuasive illustration of its guiding principle of *romanità* was nearing completion. There is an inscription on the four sides of the building, something which also violated the rationalists' desire for simple ornamentation and no rhetoric: "A nation of poets, artists, heroes, saints, thinkers, scientists, navigators, and emigrants." This was a famous and often-cited description of Italy by Mussolini, and it has yet to be erased. Perhaps it is only fitting that it should remain upon the regime's most original architectural achievement.

Few great artists or architects in the past questioned the ideologies or political motives of their patrons, and we should perhaps not expect Italian architects during the Fascist period to have acted any differently. Even the rationalists were generally supporters of the regime, at least until Italy entered the war.[36] Yet, it serves no useful purpose to reject everything connected with Mussolini and his regime, and our understanding of how the myth of Rome shaped not only Fascist architecture and urban planning but also its propaganda and foreign policy may still offer some useful lessons for those of us who prefer the republican tradition of Roman mythology. Mussolini's Roman empire collapsed with a series of military failures in Greece, the Axis defeats in North Africa and Russia, the Allied invasion of Sicily, and Mussolini's removal from power by a vote of the Fascist Grand Council in 1943.

The only other character in Italian history who seems to have expressed such a similar interest in Roman mythology and who also ended quite as badly as Mussolini was Cola di Rienzo, another would-be dictator of a revived Roman state. Luigi Barzini, Jr. reports an interesting anecdote about Mussolini during the apogee of his power. When an old Socialist friend came to Rome to pay him a visit at the Palazzo Venezia, he warned Mussolini: "This regime of yours, I am afraid, will end badly. Such things always do, Benito, you'll die like Cola di Rienzo." Mussolini expressed mock consternation, then laughed, and replied to his friend: "I wear no rings, you see. It will not happen to me."[37] But it did. An escaping Mussolini was recognized under a German soldier's uniform by partisans just as a fleeing Cola di Rienzo had been. Both men allowed their thirst for power to corrupt their dream of a revitalized Rome, and in a real sense, it might be said that the myth of Rome destroyed them both.

PERMUTATIONS OF THE

MYTH OF ROME IN MODERN

LITERATURE, CINEMA, AND

POPULAR CULTURE

I t is unlikely that another attempt to reestablish the imperial glory of the ancient Roman empire will be made in the foreseeable future as long as the memory of Mussolini's ill-fated venture remains fresh. Nor does it seem that the contemporary period is more hospitable to those political values that can be traced back to Livy's model of republican Rome. Even in the United States, developments since the Second World War have moved the nation closer to an "imperial" presidency and away from a system that could boast Cincinnatus as its symbol, as was the case during the time of George Washington. However, if the contemporary period has witnessed a general eclipse in political manifestations of Roman mythology, quite the opposite has occurred in popular culture (science fiction, cinema) and literature. In an era apparently dominated by scientific discovery and technology, the seemingly outmoded mythologies of republican or imperial Rome have surfaced in a number of very different artistic media. And the appearance of this mythology reflects a number of traditional preoccupations that have always characterized the development of the myth of Rome over the past six centuries.

The impact of Roman mythology upon the cinema, this century's only truly new art form, has been important enough to constitute a specific genre with recognizable stylistic traits and content. The vogue for Roman films first arose in Italy during the early days of the silent cinema. Giovanni Pastrone's *Cabiria* (1914) is the first feature-length film in the cinema's history that deserves to be called a masterpiece.[1] In this work, Pastrone (1883–1959) established many of the generic conventions that would characterize the Roman epic or spectacular throughout its long history in film. He exploited masterful special effects, among them the use of superimposed images for dream sequences. The convincing eruption of the volcano Etna and the destruction of a Roman fleet in the harbor at Syracuse were created with scale models and process shots. Even more impressive were his sumptuous sets, which became a required feature of every Roman film to follow. They were constructed in the Turin studios by Pastrone, reproducing with studious detail ancient Rome and its archrival for supremacy in the Mediterranean, Carthage. Massive crowd scenes, another feature of the Roman epic film, were filmed at great expense for *Cabiria*. In order to present an accurate image of Hannibal crossing the Alps, the film crew shot the scene on location where the event might have occurred—with real elephants! Pastrone invented the dolly for the film, in order to track in and out of the enormous sets, moving from extremely long shots to medium close-ups, thereby underscoring the heroic gestures and facial expressions of his actors.

Pastrone paid Gabriele D'Annunzio, then the world's most popular writer, a princely sum to compose the dialogue for the titles. And D'Annunzio followed Petrarch's example in his *Africa* by intertwining the narrative of the Second Punic War with a love story between Cabiria, a girl who is sold into slavery by Phoenician pirates to be sacrificed to the Carthaginian god Moloch, and Fulvio Axilla, a Roman patrician who, aided by his faithful slave Maciste, manages to rescue Cabiria in the nick of time. The premiere of the final version, a three-hour feature edited from some 20,000 meters of footage, took place to the accompaniment of a specially commissioned musical score by Ildebrando Pizzetti, which was performed by an orchestra of one hundred musicians.

The epic battle of two great classical civilizations—the virtuous, republican Rome and the evil Carthaginian empire—now came to life on the screen for the first time. Nowhere is the juxtaposition of two opposing ways of life more forcefully expressed in the film than in the celebrated scene (figure 54) in which Maciste interrupts the sacrifice of Cabiria to the cruel Carthaginian god Moloch. While republican Rome exercized a civilizing influence, establishing order and culture wherever it ruled, Carthage practiced human sacrifice and tyranny. The brutality of its culture ensured final Roman victory.

Nor was the motivation for this work merely entertainment on a lavish scale. The film appeared around the conclusion of the Italo-Turkish War, from which Italy emerged victorious, obtaining new colonies on the North African shore. There is no doubt that part of the unprecedented success of this work in Italy was due to the clear analogy between the past and the present that the film suggested. Republican Rome had conquered and "civilized" Northern Africa centuries earlier. Now history was

54. Giovanni Pastrone, Cabiria (1914):
Maciste (Bartolomeo Pagano) rescues
Cabiria from sacrifice to the Carthaginian
god Moloch.
Musuem of Modern Art, New York.

repeating itself, as the newly organized Italian republic born in the Risorgimento reclaimed its long-lost territories across the Mediterranean.

Pastrone's work would provide the model for the many silent Roman epics to follow. Maciste is the ancestor of hundreds of musclebound heroes who perform impossible feats. And the mixture of a love story— so crucial to the mythology of Rome since Petrarch—with more political themes continued in the Roman epic film from Pastrone to the present (figure 55). In fact, it was in a film with a similar setting that Theda Bara created the first "vamp" of the silent film era. This was in the 1917 American version of the story of Cleopatra (figure 56). Pastrone was the first of many directors who discovered that sex set in the ancient world would produce handsome profits at the box-office.

The silent cinema thus bequeathed a rich legacy of Roman subject matter to the screen. A large number of such works were made, and a recent survey of them reveals that for the most part, the cinema has been especially attracted to the period from the death of Julius Caesar to the fall of the Roman empire. This preference for a time of crisis, the birth of an empire, and its eventual destruction has provided the historical framework for dozens of films on tyrannical emperors (Nero, Tiberius, Caligula, Commodus), the love affairs of Cleopatra, Messalina, and other Roman wantons, and the like.[2] While providing a morally edifying illustration of the perils of overreaching power, such works also allowed a number of different directors to exploit the ever present prurient interest in Roman decadence and in the corruption produced by supreme power and unbridled sensuality.

The story of the Second Punic War and Rome's conquest of North Africa was a natural topic for Mussolini's regime to choose in its attempt to produce an Italian cinema that would express the more aggressive Fascist culture. Carmine Gallone's *Scipio Africanus* (1937) received an enormous subsidy from the regime—some twelve million prewar lire— which made it the most expensive film ever produced in Italy to that time. Before it was released at the Venice Film Festival, where it was not surprisingly awarded the Mussolini Cup, it became the subject of one of the most extensive advertising campaigns ever organized by the Italian industry. Furthermore, Mussolini himself visited the set in 1936 and was hailed by cries of "Duce, Duce!" from the cast of thousands of extras decked out in ancient Roman garb. Even the actors and crew understood one of the film's implicit themes: the reincarnation of the Roman imperial spirit in the man who would reestablish an Italian Fascist empire in Africa.

55. Giovanni Pastrone, Cabiria (1914):
Sophonisba (Italia Almirante Manzini)
dies by her own hand at the moment of
Rome's triumph, and Cabiria (Letizia
Quaranta) is finally reunited with Fulvia
Axilla (Umberto Mozzato), the Roman
hero.
Museum of Modern Art, New York.

56. Theda Bara in Cleopatra (1917).
Museum of Modern Art, New York.

Several elements in the film made clear reference to Mussolini's political movement. Scipio is pictured primarily as a prototypical mass leader, rather than as a Roman patrician general. His fustian rhetoric sometimes deadens the pace of the film and is hardly an accurate representation of the sober, disciplined speeches of senatorial politicians under the ancient Roman republic. The avid response of the enthusiastic Roman audiences, however, mirrored the response of the adoring crowds to Mussolini's skillful delivery of his spellbinding harangues. A more obvious link between Scipio and the modern Duce lies in the unintentionally humorous frequency with which characters give each other the "Roman" salute: they do so in the senate, in the street, in the privacy of their homes, and when the Roman fleet embarks for the invasion of Carthage (figure 57). Gallone's frequent use of the salute unmistakably insists on its ancient origins. If the impressive crowd and battle scenes with thousands of extras and herds of elephants obeyed the generic rules for the Roman epic film established twenty years earlier, the constant mention of battles in Spain and Africa were certainly not overly subtle analogies to current events: Mussolini's intervention in the Spanish Civil War and his imperialistic adventures in Ethiopia.

The essence of Scipio's embodiment of a Roman way of life—discipline, the defense of the family, the belief that war is a Roman's duty and highest calling—also implicitly supported Mussolini's campaigns to raise the birthrate in Italy and to instill a warlike prowess in his countrymen, better known for skill in art or music than for their military genius. Interviews with elementary school children in a 1939 issue of *Bianco e nero*, Italy's major film journal, revealed that the film had indeed achieved its desired effect. The children immediately grasped the implicit parallel between ancient Rome and Fascist Italy, between the earlier establishment of an empire in Africa and Il Duce's attempts to establish a "fourth shore" for his regime.[3]

The image of Rome in the early cinema could thus easily be adapted, as was the case in *Cabiria* or *Scipio Africanus*, to support political goals. However, in the majority of Roman epic films, the corrupt and decadent underside of Roman imperial history has more often served as a plausible excuse for torrid love affairs set in the distant, and therefore less offensive, Roman past. Rome as the center of sexual escapades in the ancient world has long been a far more popular theme in the cinema than the depiction of Rome as the source of imperial and republican political ideals. Two recent examples will demonstrate how this aspect of

57. Carmine Gallone, Scipio Africanus
(1937): ancient Romans giving the
Roman salute.
Museum of Modern Art, New York.

Roman mythology has been treated more recently in the cinema—Joseph Mankiewicz's *Cleopatra* (1963) and Tinto Brass's *Caligula* (1979).

Cleopatra set a record for extravagant sets that will probably never be surpassed.[4] Cleopatra's wigs, costumes, and jewelry cost the then-amazing sum of $130,000; extras for the battles of Pharsalia, Actium, and Phillipi cost over half a million dollars and required 26,000 costumes. Elizabeth Taylor's twenty-four-carat-gold dress for her spectacular entrance into the Roman Forum was valued at a mere $6,500, but the scene itself cost a half-million dollars to film. Perhaps even more important than the film's extravagance were the scandalous tales that accompanied the production of the movie. The ancient love affair of Cleopatra and Antony was reborn in film magazines, press conferences, and tabloids all over the world, as the much publicized liaison between Richard Burton (Antony) and Taylor (Cleopatra) became public knowledge and was then itself employed to publicize the film. After the shooting was transferred to Rome, the love affair almost obscured discussion of the film itself in the newspapers (figure 58), providing invaluable free advertising for what was the most expensive moving picture ever made to date ($62,000,000).[5]

Cleopatra was the most spectacular instance of the power of American cinema, which could afford to move production from Hollywood to Roman studios, which were dubbed "Hollywood on the Tiber" (figure 59). Although not a masterpiece, *Cleopatra* was not a poorly made film either. But its importance for Roman mythology lay not so much in its artistic merits as in its impact upon the popular imagination. For most of two years, the public throughout the entire world was bombarded with daily accounts of the torrid love affair between the two principal actors in the film, minutely described by newspapers and scandal sheets. In a real sense, the opulence of ancient Rome and the decadence of the late Roman republic—when men such as Caesar or Antony allowed themselves to be captivated and sometimes destroyed by their lust and love for Cleopatra—were repeated in the Rome of the Via Veneto. Life seemed to be copying art.

Another treatment of the decadent underside of Roman history is *Caligula*. The Emperor Caligula has always rivaled Nero in the popular imagination for the dubious honor of being the most corrupt and decadent of all Roman rulers. Thus, he was the obvious subject when the publisher of *Penthouse*, Bob Guccione, decided to produce a film that had as its express goal the depiction of *explicit* sexuality in the ancient world. Produced at a cost of over $17,000,000 and made in the same Roman

58. Joseph Mankiewicz, Cleopatra
(1963): Cleopatra (Elizabeth Taylor)
entertains Mark Antony (Richard Burton)
on her yacht.
Museum of Modern Art, New York.

59. Joseph Mankiewicz, Cleopatra
(1963): Hollywood on the Tiber—extras
in Roman garb prepare for the shooting of
the Battle of Actium.
Museum of Modern Art, New York.

studio in which *Cleopatra* had been filmed earlier, *Caligula* was lavishly costumed and boasted brilliant sets. But the film was controversial because its casting was unique: for the first time in cinematic history, major stars and very respectable actors (Peter O'Toole as Tiberius, Malcolm McDowell as Caligula, Sir John Gielgud as Nerva) performed in a work that quite effortlessly earned an X rating (figure 60). Despite numerous orgy scenes cluttered with nude *Penthouse* pin-up girls, unclad Italian extras, and the usually dressed but better known lead actors, the film director Tinto Brass made from Gore Vidal's script cannot in truth be called pornography. As Guccione put it in an interview, "an X rating would be demeaning and unfair to *Caligula*. The conventional connotation is still the $100,000 made-in-a-motel epic, and that, next to *Caligula*, is like comparing a street rumble to the Second World War."[6]

Guccione's *Caligula* expressed a simple but direct interpretation of the young Roman emperor: absolute power corrupts absolutely, leading inevitably to brutality and sexual excess. It is somewhat surprising that *Penthouse*, a periodical dedicated to hedonism and freedom of sexual expression, would sponsor a film which ultimately denigrated the total liberation of human sexuality as a destructive and insidious force in human history. Yet, Caligula's incest with his sister, his homosexual rape of a member of his own guard, his cruel and senseless murders, and his enforced prostitution of Roman patrician women and men were all cut from the same cloth: sexual depravity went hand and hand with unlimited cruelty and violence. There was no explanation, however, why this might have been the case in the specific instance of Caligula.

Perhaps the most interesting and unusual treatment of imperial Roman mythology in modern literature may be found in two masterful novels by Robert Graves: *I, Claudius* (1934) and *Claudius the God* (1935).[7] Besides being fine literary works in their own right, they have also inspired an equally distinguished film version for television by the British Broadcasting Company, which was shown very successfully in America. Graves examined the historical evolution of ancient Rome from a small but virtuous republic into a vast empire by focusing upon the private lives of the Emperor Augustus and the various members of his illustrious family. Claudius is, at first glance, a very unlikely candidate to be the protagonist of two imperial novels. Until he was proclaimed emperor by the palace guard after Caligula's assassination, many of his contemporaries and not a few ancient historians considered the awkward and stuttering Claudius to be an idiot. But Graves turned Claudius into a fascinating and infinitely complex individual, a figure who feigns stupidity in order to survive, not

60. Tinto Brass, Caligula (1979): a
degenerate Emperor Tiberius (Peter
O'Toole) embraces his terrified heir,
Caligula (Malcolm McDowell), who will
eventually murder him.
Museum of Modern Art, New York.

unlike the first Brutus. In Graves's fictional narrative, Claudius survives by using his wits and by confining all he knows concerning the dark history of the Claudian family to a journal that is destined, according to prophecy, to remain secret for a hundred generations (figure 61). Claudius is thus the fascinated observer not only of the numerous poisonings by his grandmother Livia, Augustus's last wife, but also of the terrifying reigns of terror under both Tiberius and Caligula.

Graves's imaginary recreation of Claudius made of this ancient ruler a distinctly contemporary figure. He possesses a particularly modern sense of history and irony, and he represents an historical anachronism, because Claudius reflects a sensibility that would have been impossible for a true Roman. His character is shaped by a prescience of things to come that could only have been grasped by a man familiar with the future course of Roman history—in short, a man of the twentieth century. With this type of ironic narrator, Graves was able to debunk much of the mythology of the ancient Roman republic and the empire that succeeded it.

Nowhere is his intention to demythologize Roman mythology clearer than in the imaginary encounter Graves fashioned between Claudius and the historian Livy, whom Claudius meets while working in the state archives. The two men have a fascinating discussion about the goals of historiography. Claudius was a staunch republican until his death, even though he was eventually forced to become emperor to save his life. Nevertheless, this character is convinced that Livy's brilliant narratives obscure the origins of the republic's decline: "Livy begins his history by lamenting modern wickedness and promising to trace the gradual decline of ancient virtue as conquests made Rome wealthy. He says that he will most enjoy writing the early chapters because he will be able, in so doing, to close his eyes to the wickedness of modern times. But in closing his eyes to modern wickedness hasn't he sometimes closed his eyes to ancient wickedness as well?" In fact, Graves employed his fictional Claudius to voice the many doubts and reservations modern scholars have expressed over the authenticity of the Livian legends. Claudius meekly points out to an enraged Livy that his treatment of the first Brutus, the exploits of Horatius at the bridge, or the amazing courage of Scaevola can all be disproved. Solid archaeological evidence, Claudius maintains, demonstrates that such Livian heroics were to no avail: Lars Porsenna actually captured Rome in spite of Horatio and Scaevola; Brutus and Collatinus, the first two consuls of the new republic, were merely entrusted after the death of Lucretia to collect the king's taxes!

61. Herbert Wise, I, Claudius (1977,
BBC Production), Part Two: "Waiting in
the Wings": Livia (Sian Phillips)
manipulates Augustus (Brian Blessed) for
her own political goals in the highly
successful adaptation of the novel by
Robert Graves.
BBC copyright.

The appeal of Graves's novels, as well as the excellent British adaptation of them for television, result from the reader's or viewer's empathy with this supposedly ineffectual stutterer, who survived not only the poisonings of his grandmother Livia but also the brutality of two emperors whose actions verged on the insane (figure 62). In Graves's recreation of ancient Rome, Claudius functions more as a modern antihero than as a powerful Roman emperor. And Claudius's narrative reflects the generic conventions of two popular forms of literature: the private memoir and the detective novel. The reader shares the amazement of the investigator-historian as the reluctant emperor finally unravels the truth about the skeletons in the Claudian family closet. And the version of the novels made for television quite consciously employs the conventions of another mass-audience television genre—the soap opera or family saga, such as Dallas, Dynasty, or the more highbrow English series, Upstairs, Downstairs.

The complex character of Claudius was developed further in Claudius the God, which treated the period of his reign as a recalcitrant emperor. Forced to choose between accepting the throne from the Praetorian Guards and instant death, Claudius once again concealed his desire to restore the ancient republic in order to save his life. Although he remains blind until almost too late to the machinations of his wife Messalina (whose deception of Claudius is worthy of his grandmother's manipulation of Augustus), Claudius eventually comes to realize that any republican restoration is doomed to failure. In a conversation with one of his most trusted advisers, Vitellius, he inquires why Vitellius always plays the role of courtier when, in a better time, he would have been one of the most virtuous men alive. Vitellius's response echoes Machiavelli's explanation for the disappearance of Roman virtue: "It was inevitable under a monarchy, however benevolent the monarch. The old virtues disappear. Independence and frankness are at a discount. Complacent anticipation of the monarch's wishes is then the greatest of all virtues. One must either be a good monarch like yourself, or a good courtier like myself—either an Emperor or an idiot." Of course, Claudius's newly acquired wisdom does not enable him to change the course of history: like so many others in his family, he is eventually poisoned to make way for Nero. Yet Claudius at least has the satisfaction of knowing that the Sibyl who informs him of this impending murder and of the brief rule of Nero afterward also prophesied that his "true" history of the transformation of the Roman republic into the Roman empire (that is,

62. Herbert *Wise*, I, Claudius (1977,
BBC Production), Part Seven: "Reign of
Terror": Claudius (Derek Jacobi) and
Caligula (John Hurt) must tread carefully
to survive during the reign of terror under
the Emperor Tiberius (George Baker).
BBC copyright.

the fictional narrative created by Graves) will be read in "nineteen hundred years or near."

Robert Graves treated Roman mythology with a completely ironic, modernist mistrust, using his narrator, in his humorous recreation of the private lives of Roman rulers, to debunk much of Livian mythology. Graves was less interested in historical accuracy than in creating an engaging and interesting character in the person of Claudius. Yet like so many other contributors to Roman mythology in Western culture, he was also fascinated by the vast panoramic saga of historical change, development, and decline which the Roman past embodied. Other works of popular culture betray the same interest. At least one excellent film— Anthony Mann's The Fall of the Roman Empire (1964)—attempts to examine the course of imperial history and to specify with as much accuracy as possible the precise moment when affairs in the widespread Roman empire began to slip into irremediable decline. While the film's opening voice-over informs the viewer that the so-called "fall" spread over three hundred years and was a long and complex process, the film nevertheless suggests that this process began with a crisis around A.D..180–193. At that time, the philosopher emperor Marcus Aurelius (played by Alec Guiness) died while leading his armies against the barbarian tribes along the Danube frontier. Commodus (Christopher Plummer), his successor, proved by his disastrous rule that ancient Roman virtues were no longer anything but a distant memory, valued only by ineffectual figures such as Livius Metellus (Stephen Boyd) and Lucilla (Sophia Loren), the dead emperor's daughter.

The Fall of the Roman Empire represents an interesting combination of patient attention to authenticity in costumes and sets with a certain freedom in developing the characters of the film's protagonists. The often spectacular battle scenes and uniforms reflect a thorough acquaintance with the friezes on Trajan's Column in Rome. The film also makes use of the ancient dress, weapons, and customs depicted in Mantegna's series, The Triumphs of Caesar, now preserved at Hampton Court Palace. And the shots of Rome are based on an impressive scale recreation of the Forum built on location in Spain. In addition, Edward Gibbon's history had a determining influence upon the script, and its credits boasted the historical expertise of one of the world's most popular historical writers—Will Durant. Appearing in the wake of Cleopatra, which produced audience resistance to costume epics, The Fall of the Roman Empire was a financial disaster for its makers, but undeservedly so. Nevertheless, the painstaking accuracy with which ancient Rome was reproduced in the costumes and the sets was so convincing that the *Encyclopedia Brittanica* purchased them from the producer and used them to make another film, *Memoirs of a Roman Boy*, which was designed for use in high school Latin courses.[8]

The most impressive aspect of Mann's film was his success in translating a kind of crepuscular, melancholic perspective on the fall of the Roman empire into striking images. Like Graves's novels, Mann's film is permeated by a contemporary sense of futility; as his characters struggle to prevent the dissolution of imperial order, they possess an anachronistic presentiment that all such attempts will be futile. They move within the film as if they had already read the conclusion of Gibbon's *Decline and Fall*. An air of foreboding is established by placing the first sequence of the film not in Rome but, rather, on the distant and snow-covered frontiers of the Danube, which are edged with dark, impenetrable forests filled with threatening, barbarian hordes. The forthcoming dissolution of Rome's vast dominions is captured perfectly by the eerie atmosphere: Roman soldiers warily advance through an ominous, shadowy wood, filled with misty and obscured paths. We are far removed from the usual sun-drenched locations so typical of the historical epic on Rome. While Roman civilization begins to decay on the frontiers, back in the capital, the evil Emperor Commodus amuses himself by entering the arena as a common gladiator, ignoring the impending disaster abroad.

The cremation of the noble Marcus Aurelius in the snow (figure 63) represents another excellent instance of how Mann established visual images expressing the general pessimism of the entire work. As the flames leap toward heaven and the camera pans up to follow the smoke from the funeral pyre, there is an abrupt and startling cut to the opulent metropolis of Rome with its decadent pastimes, its declining sense of citizenship, and its rotten splendor, which are all captured perfectly in the sumptuous reproduction of the Forum. Much of the dramatic force in the film is provided by the conflict between Commodus—made emperor against the wishes of Marcus Aurelius when the emperor's physician Cleander (Mel Ferrer) poisoned the old man—and Livius—the embodiment of the perfect Roman soldier, whose virtues would match not only those of Livy's republican heroes but also those positive traits of the most noble emperors. The very name of this foil to Commodus reminds us of the historian of the early republic and the republican mythology he created.

Livius possesses ancient Roman ideals and virtues that, during this period, exist only in memory. He is a character entirely out of step with his time, a throwback to an earlier and more virtuous epoch. Commodus

63. Anthony Mann, Fall of the
Roman Empire (1964): the somber
winter scene depicting the burial of the
Emperor Marcus Aurelius. Livius (Stephen
Boyd) and Lucilla (Sophia Loren) prove to
be no match for the evil Commodus
(Christopher Plummer).
Museum of Modern Art, New York.

reproduces the now typecast corrupt and cruel emperor of so many novels and films. His megalomania is captured neatly in a cinematic allusion to another equally fanatic leader, Hitler. Almost childlike in the delight derived from his unlimited power, Commodus does a little dance upon the mosaic map of the world in his palace, recalling not only the famous jig Hitler danced after the fall of France but also the well-known dance performed by Charlie Chaplin in *The Great Dictator*, where the ruler he parodies (obviously Hitler) waltzed with a globe of the world until it burst like a balloon (figure 64).

When Livius tries to overthrow Commodus and to reestablish the noble principles for which Marcus Aurelius fought, Commodus buys his army's fickle loyalty with bags of gold coin. For Mann, this particular scene (completely invented by him, however) explains the ultimate reason why Roman civilization was eventually overwhelmed. Its demise followed the death of an ideal, not the victories of the barbarian on the battlefield. The film concludes with another completely invented sequence. Commodus, a trained gladiator, challenges Livius to a battle to the death, and although already wounded, Livius manages to triumph. As the obsequious crowds now shout "Hail Caesar," Livius contemptuously turns away from this offer of supreme power. The last shot of the film reveals a squabbling band of army officers trying to buy the crown Livius has refused. In Mann's film, Livius emerges as a sort of imperial Cincinnatus, but his reason for refusing power differs markedly from that of the earlier republican hero. Livius has realized, as the moral of the film is delivered by a voice-over narrator, that a "great civilization is not conquered until it is destroyed from within." There no longer exists a Rome which corresponds to his outmoded ideals, and Livius therefore prefers a private life with his beloved Lucilla to court intrigue, corruption, and inevitable political decline. Such a surprising conclusion presented quite an original interpretation of the life of a Roman nobleman under the empire, and if the film's ending merely echoed Gibbon, it was nevertheless no less powerful a visual expression of his perspective on Rome.

The impact of Roman mythology has been even more important upon science fiction than upon the cinema. Since this vast literature arose from pulp magazines and mass-market novels, critics have long been reluctant to consider it a serious literary genre. But precisely because science fiction has captured a mass-market audience for decades, its preoccupations and its permutations of Roman mythology may tell us something useful about contemporary popular culture. One of the central themes or narrative structures in all of science fiction is the "galactic" or "inter-

64. Anthony Mann, Fall of the
Roman Empire (1964): the power-
mad evil Emperor Commodus prepares to
dance a jig over the map of his
possessions, watched by his obsequious
courtiers.
Museum of Modern Art, New York.

galactic" empire that, as an examination of three recent anthologies will reveal, has been employed by the best and most popular science fiction writers: Isaac Asimov, Poul Anderson, James Blish, A. E. van Vogt, Arthur C. Clarke, Cordwainer Smith, Clifford D. Simak, James White, and a host of others.[9] All serious students of science fiction are in general agreement that the author whose work established the popularity of this theme was Isaac Asimov, whose *Foundation* series has sold millions of copies and was voted a Hugo Award in 1966 by the World Science Fiction Convention for the best series ever published. Much of the trilogy originally appeared as short fiction in pulp magazines between 1942 and 1949 before its final publication as *Foundation* (1951), *Foundation and Empire* (1952), and *Second Foundation* (1953).[10]

There is no doubt that Asimov reconstructed the future in the Roman image. As he himself has admitted, "I modeled my 'Galactic Empire' (a phrase I think I was the first to use) quite consciously on the Roman Empire."[11] But Asimov's galactic empire also specifically reflects Edward Gibbon's view of the decline and fall of ancient imperial Rome and, as a result, the *Foundation* trilogy contains a complicated structure of historical evolution in the distant future that resembles, but modifies, Gibbon's well-known argument. And while Asimov's trilogy embraced a theory of history indebted to Gibbon's picture of the evolution of the Roman empire, it also invented a novel theory of "psychohistory" that enables his protagonists to predict the future. Asimov's science fiction is thus far more indebted to Roman mythology than to the so-called "hard" sciences or to modern notions of technology.

Few writers present quite as sweeping a perspective on the future as Asimov. His series opens with a description of a galactic empire that comprises some twenty-five million planets, all inhabited by humans who have colonized the universe from Earth. Their home planet, however, remains only a distant memory, its location lost in legend and time. Asimov's universe is an anthropocentric one, governed by scientifically verifiable laws of social history, not one filled with strange and frightening space monsters or robots. The empire, like its Roman counterpart, has kept the peace for centuries (some 12,000 years!), but a new social science capable of making predictions about mass behavior ("psychohistory," the invention of a genius named Hari Seldon), has revealed that the disintegration of the empire is imminent, to be followed by some 30,000 years of disorder and barbarian rule. Seldon therefore sets up two foundations—the First Foundation, composed of physical scientists at a place called Terminus; and the Second Foundation, made up of psychologists and social scientists, whose location and very existence remain hidden from the First Foundation. Asimov's trilogy charts the four centuries during which the First Foundation defends itself against the collapse of the galactic empire and enlists the assistance of the Second Foundation. These actions fulfill Seldon's aim of shortening the 30,000-year period of barbarian chaos and reestablishing universal order in a mere thousand years. Even this brief outline of the plot of the trilogy underscores how neatly Asimov has employed the general historical pattern of decline and fall from Gibbon, which he projects into the distant future of space.

In an initial crisis, Anacreon, one of the many planets ruled by local lords after the central power of the empire has weakened, attempts to conquer Terminus. But Mayor Salvor Hardin seizes power from the Foundation scientists and defeats Anacreon by a clever control of atomic power. Anacreon lacks atomic technology (one of the causes for the demise of the empire lies in a sudden decline of scientific knowledge around the empire's distant borders), but Terminus still retains this capacity. Hardin had given this source of energy to the barbarians within a framework of a mysterious religion complete with a cult of atomic priests, while never actually explaining how the technology worked to the less advanced Anacreons. When the ruler of Anacreon attempts to invade the home planet of this new religion, the priests of the attacking planet rebel and force their leader to spare Terminus, thereby saving the First Foundation.

Later, the Foundation evolves and employs atomic power rather than religion to retain its independence and increase its strength. The First Foundation scientists are transformed into merchant princes. In *Foundation and Empire*, events occurring some two centuries later are described. The Foundation, manipulating its monopoly on atomic power, now represents one of the most powerful forces in the galaxy, controlling all but the enormous portion of the universe still theoretically under the control of the now crumbling empire. One of the most capable imperial generals, Bel Riose—a figure patterned upon the Byzantine General Belisarius—now attacks the Foundation. But echoing many episodes in late imperial Roman history, this victorious general is eventually arrested by his incompetent emperor, since the emperor naturally considers the general's superior charisma a greater threat to his throne than the Foundation.

The Foundation eventually develops the same decadent vices practiced by the empire. When a mutant called the Mule, endowed with incredible psychological powers, begins to conquer the entire universe by mind control rather than by brute force, both the empire and the First Foundation on Terminus fall under his sway. Asimov apparently patterned the Mule's invasion, "coming from nowhere and conquering everything in sight," on the "notion of the Mongols."[12] The entire structure of the Foundation series employs the decline of the Roman empire, as interpreted by Gibbon, to construct an account of the future. The Mule's Sack of Trantor echoes that of Rome; the eventual failure of General Bel Riose to reconsolidate the empire parallels the failure of Belisarius to reinvigorate the heir of Rome, imperial Byzantium; the gradual dissolution of the empire's hold over its frontier planets and the establishment of barbarian kingdoms on its outer limits reflect the later imperial period when barbarian groups in Europe formed what were eventually to become feudal kingdoms on the far-flung marches of Rome's borders.

Second Foundation concludes the futuristic saga. Now aware of the Second Foundation's existence, the Mule combs the universe for this mysterious group but is lured into a trap and his mind changed by representatives of the Second Foundation. His memory of the group's existence erased, the Mule eventually dies a natural death, and his interplanetary rule disintegrates. Now, however, the First Foundation on Terminus begins to fear psychological manipulation from the Second Foundation. By a clever ruse, the Second Foundation convinces the First that it has been destroyed and that Seldon's plan has been restored. Thus, the members of the Second Foundation, the true guardians of the Seldon Plan, continue to work for the shortening of the interregnum between the demise of the old galactic order and a new, more vigorous order in a thousand years to come. The surprise ending of the series is provided by the startling discovery that the Second Foundation was located all the while on Trantor, the sacked planet that once served as the galactic empire's capital city. Asimov thus recreated ancient Rome's civilizing mission in the Trantor of his imaginary future. Out of the ruins of ancient Rome and future Trantor will spring the vital, invigorated shoots of new civilization.

Following Asimov's example, other science fiction writers have used the structure of the "galactic empire" to present a moral message about the gradual decay and corruption of future civilizations. The other works in this same genre, however, draw not only from Asimov but also from Gothic romance, myth, legend, and medieval history. They mix rocket ships or travel in hyper-space with pilots carrying broad swords who battle sorcerers and dragons! All of the many variants of the narrative structure introduced into science fiction by Asimov reflect a fascination with the ruins of former civilizations—an echo of Petrarch's nostalgia for the remains of ancient Rome, as well as a characteristic of the Gothic romance. The entire subgenre that concerns itself with the galactic or intergalactic empire manifests a deeply felt need for order, stability, and cohesion in the modern world as well as a general fear of impending doom.

Most of the best contemporary science fiction writers are Americans, and the seminal stories treating galactic empires were composed by Asimov and his followers between the mid-forties and the end of the fifties. The world had just emerged from the greatest confrontation of two rival power blocks in its history, and it had entered a period of Cold War.[13] It is no wonder that science fiction, always an excellent barometer of contemporary concerns, produced a subgenre that juxtaposed forces of republican or federated states with those of a tyrannical, decadent, and sometimes brutal imperial opponent.

It would be difficult to overestimate Asimov's influence upon science fiction in the years since the appearance of his trilogy. An entire subgenre evolved from his discovery that Gibbon's outline of Roman imperial history—combined with Asimov's matchless plotting and a few clever concepts such as psychohistory—could produce an extremely complicated narrative structure around which almost endless stories and novels could be built. Poul Anderson's immensely popular series of short stories and novels devoted to Dominic Flandry, a swashbuckling intelligence officer of an empire set in the thirtieth century, is one excellent instance of Asimov's direct influence. Yet, Anderson's work concentrates upon a single hero whose sexual exploits in the luxurious bedchamber of his rocket ship set on automatic hyper-glide for such occasions would be quite out of place in Asimov's more rational and philosophical narrative. Instead of a large group of individuals, such as the Foundation, battling to shorten the forthcoming Dark Ages, there is only one heroic figure in all the universe, Commander Flandry, who can postpone the destruction of Technic Civilization! While using a framework indebted to both Gibbon and Asimov, Anderson has created a James Bond character whose daring exploits seem extracted from legend or myth rather than from any credible human history. But the various stages marking the development, triumph, and eventual collapse of Technic Civilization remain so central to Flandry's narrative that the author supplies an appendix, "Chronology of Technic Civilization," to the concluding story in the series. This chronology spells out the rise and fall of this galactic empire until its collapse in the fortieth century. The end of Technic Civilization brings about a "Long Night" in the galaxy, a future "Dark Ages."[14] But unlike Asimov's optimistic conclusion that there will be a reestablishment of order after a time of troubles, there is nothing in Anderson's vision but emptiness and darkness.

Given its unparalleled popularity, it was inevitable that Asimov's trilogy would have an impact upon science fiction in the cinema. And in fact, its Gibbonian historical structure provided the nucleus around which the most successful film trilogy of all time was constructed, the *Star Wars* sagas of director and producer George Lucas: *Star Wars* (1977), *The Empire Strikes Back* (1980), and *The Return of the Jedi* (1983). Asimov was the first and almost only critic to point out this direct influence: "Galactic empires reached the cinema with this group of films, which here and there, offered more than a whiff of the Foundation. (No, I don't mind. Imitation is the sincerest form of flattery, and I certainly imitated Edward Gibbon, so I can scarcely object if someone imitates me)."[15] Lucas narrates his space epics in medias res, as all good poets have done since the time of Homer. In fact, the three films are actually episodes 4, 5, and 6 of a six-part story that will eventually explain the earlier history of the old republic. The three novels based upon the films clarify the relationship between the three Lucas films already produced and the Roman mythology filtered through Asimov that informs the entire story. In a prologue to *Star Wars*, history in future time and in the galaxies reads like a page from Gibbon or Asimov: "The Old Republic was the Republic of legend, greater than distance or time. . . . Once, under the wise rule of the Senate and the protection of the Jedi Knights, the republic throve and grew. But as often happens when wealth and power pass beyond the admirable and attain the awesome, then appear those evil ones who have greed to match."[16] Like the early Roman republic, Asimov's First Foundation, or a host of other galactic empires in science fiction literature, Lucas's intergalactic republic was destroyed from within. "Like the greatest of trees, able to withstand any external attack, the Republic rotted from within though the danger was not visible from outside."[17] The ambitious and cunning Senator Palpatine managed to have himself, in a crisis, elected President of the republic, promising to reunite the various peoples of the republic and to restore the glory of its rule. But soon after, he declared himself emperor, exterminated the Jedi Knights, the guardians of justice and stability in the universe, and proceeded to establish a reign of terror throughout the galaxy worthy of a Tiberius or a Caligula. The emperor's power exceeds even that of his ancient Roman models, however, for his means are far more awesome—a seemingly indestructible Death Star, which can disintegrate entire planets. Moreover, his second-in-command, Darth Vader, represents a worthy successor to Tiberius's Sejanus or Caligula's Macro.

The electronic gadgetry, the spectacular special effects, and the almost fairy-tale atmosphere surrounding Lucas's work cannot obscure the roots of these popular films in the political mythology and history of the ancient Roman republic and Roman empire. The Jedi Knights wield power thanks to a mysterious power called the "Force," an energy field apparently generated by all living beings in the universe. The "Force" can be turned to either good or evil purposes. In Lucas's films, this mysterious power may be viewed as a projection of republican idealism, fulfilling a similar narrative function but shaped to fit a new environment. The Jedi draw their strength from this mysterious source just as the Livian heroes of the past drew their virtue from the republican mythology that elevated duty, justice, and self-sacrifice above greed or ambition. But in the future, as in ancient Rome, moral principles degenerate into hollow myths, "lies" employed to obscure ignoble deeds and to conceal selfish political goals. Senator Palpatine realizes that much the same degradation of republican values has occurred and therefore uses the "dark side" of the Force—older republican values now corrupted— to advance his evil scheme of dominating the universe.

Lucas's three films create special characters who embody conflicting perspectives on government. Luke Skywalker represents the best of the surviving values of the old republic, now reorganized in a republican federation of rebel planets who oppose the evil emperor and his ally, Darth Vader. Vader is actually Luke's father, turned to the "dark side" by the emperor but once the greatest of Jedi warriors. The confrontation of Luke, the emperor, and Vader (figure 65) thus refers the viewer back to the conflict between the virtuous ideals of republican Rome and the corrupt, power-hungry policies of its decadent imperial successor. Darth Vader echoes the personal histories of several of the worst commanders of Rome's Praetorian Guard. The evil emperor certainly resembles a combination of all the despicable qualities of Caligula, Nero, and especially Tiberius. In fact, his very make-up and facial features at the conclusion of The Return of the Jedi suggest not only the figure of Tiberius in the BBC version of Graves's I, Claudius, but also that of Tiberius in Brass's film, Caligula (figure 66). And the unparalleled success of Lucas's films at the box office may be explained in part by the director's clever grafting of a swashbuckling adventure story set in future time and outer space onto a well-worked historical structure borrowed from one of Western civiliza-

65. *George Lucas*, The Empire Strikes
Back *(Irvin Kershner, director; 1980):
Luke Skywalker (Mark Hamill),
personifying the virtuous republic, and
Darth Vader (David Prowse), personifying
the evil empire, duel with light sabers.*
Museum of Modern Art, New York.

66. *George Lucas,* The Return of the Jedi
(Alan Levi, director; 1983): Luke Skywalker,
Darth Vader, and the evil emperor of
the Galactic Empire meet at last.
Lucasfilm, Ltd.; photograph by Albert Clarke.

tion's oldest and most creative mythologies—that of Rome. While modern political institutions or politicians may no longer turn to the myth of republican Rome for inspiration or for examples of virtuous actions to imitate, the moviegoing public, perhaps even less aware of the ultimate origins of the films' plots, nevertheless can be held spellbound by a tale which sets two ancient value systems into collision: Good, embodied in the new republic, eventually triumphs over Evil, Palpatine's empire.

By far the most original and most complex variation on the mythology of Rome in the contemporary world may be found in a group of films made by the Italian director Federico Fellini (b. 1922–): *La Dolce Vita* (1959); *Fellini Satyricon* (1969); and *Fellini's Roma* (1971).[18] Like Sigmund Freud, who viewed the Eternal City as a metaphor for the human psyche, Fellini sees Rome and its vast history as a storehouse of ideas, images, and suggestive starting points for his own personal and often quite fantastic artistic creations, mythologies of his own invention that provide disconcerting confrontations between the ancient world and our own times. His films not only offer original images derived from the venerable iconographical tradition of Roman mythology, but they also serve to demythologize aspects of the same tradition that represent, for Fellini, obstacles to the liberation of the human imagination.

While Fellini's *La Dolce Vita* cleverly captured the atmosphere of Rome as a Mecca for tourists or Hollywood directors in the 1950s, it also made an important statement about the very nature of Roman mythology itself. In the other parts of his Roman trilogy, Fellini expands this critique into a new and daring Roman mythology of his own, combining older and familiar elements with novel images. Fellini's obsession with a private fantasy world reflects his positive concern with combatting the outmoded, obsolescent ways of seeing or thinking. He seeks to reject dead mythologies that no longer sustain modern civilization, but, rather, impede human development. But the mythology of Rome represents for Fellini a positive force that still remains a vital element in Western culture. Rather than lamenting the process of decadence as do Petrarch, Gibbon, and other contributors to Roman mythology, Fellini sees a time of artistic, moral, political, and intellectual crisis as one offering new possibilities and a potential for rebirth: "I feel that decadence is indispensable to rebirth. I have already said that I love shipwrecks. So I am happy to be living at a time when everything is capsizing. It's a marvelous time, for the very reason that a whole series of ideologies, concepts and conventions is being wrecked. . . . This process of dissolution is quite natural, I think, I don't see it as a sign of the death of civilization but, on the contrary, as a sign of its life."[19]

For Fellini, the cinema exists solely for the purpose of individual self-expression, not merely for communication. Fantasy, rather than reality, is its proper domain, because only fantasy falls under the complete artistic control of the director. The essence of cinema is imagery and light, not the transmission of information. This explains why his later works, and especially those which express his personal Roman mythology, are produced almost entirely within the vast complex at Cinecittà, where Fellini's unique vision of life is reproduced by spectacular sets rather than by direct images from the outside world. Thus, the Via Veneto of *La Dolce Vita*, the subway or the freeway of *Fellini's Roma*, and even scenes that seem shot outside on location in *Fellini Satyricon* are often entirely a product of reconstructions inside a set. As a corollary of his view that cinema must reflect personal expression, Fellini opposes any social convention, institution, ideology, or mythology that inhibits the complete freedom of the individual: "What I care about most is the freedom of man, the liberation of the individual man from the network of moral and social convention in which he believes or rather in which he thinks he believes, and which encloses him and limits him and makes him narrower, smaller, sometimes even worse than he really is."[20]

Rome and its venerable mythology loom large in Fellini's films as a living metaphor for Western culture. Roman mythology contains not only a storehouse of outmoded images and ideals but is also a fertile source for new, contemporary permutations of traditional values. This view of Rome is especially important to *La Dolce Vita* and *Fellini Satyricon*. The first film presents a depressing picture of our own era, which has experienced not only the final disintegration of ancient Roman mythology but also that of Christian Rome as well. The second film provides further commentary on the present from the perspective of Rome's imperial past. The theme of *La Dolce Vita*—life defined as all facade and masquerade—reveals the ancient capital of the world and the successive seat of the universal Catholic church reduced to a city where life revolves around foolish public relations stunts, meaningless or shallow intellectual debates, and sterile love affairs. The noble ideals of the ancient Roman republic and even those less appealing ones of the Roman empire have vanished. Rome has now been captured by a new set of barbarians—the journalists who write for gossip sheets and the stars and starlets who have replaced the virtuous Roman heroes in the popular imagination. It is a moment of complete cultural confusion, finding its visual parallel in the most famous of the many remarkable images in the film—the shot of the helicopter carrying a statue of Christ with its ironic benediction over the ruins of an ancient Roman aqueduct (figure 67).

In *La Dolce Vita*, a number of images are juxtaposed to render the disparity between modern life and the cultural achievements of the Roman past. The animal energy of the sex goddess and starlet, Sylvia (Anita Ekberg), overwhelms the jaded and decadent sensuality of the Roman journalist, Marcello (Marcello Mastroianni), as she leads him on a whirlwind tour through the relics of past civilizations—ancient Rome (the Baths of Caracalla); Christian Rome (St. Peter's); the Rome of the papacy (the Trevi Fountain). The imposing Baths of Caracalla, now turned into a Roman nightclub by tasteless and uneducated exponents of mass culture, provide the setting for a frenzied dance by Sylvia (figure 68), and in the process, Fellini contrasts a magnificent ancient civilization with the superficial popular culture that has inherited Rome's values and ruins without understanding their significance or exploring their possible relevance.

Fellini's attitude toward these tableaux of spiritual poverty in our own times is nevertheless different from older, more embittered protests that pictured Rome as the Whore of Babylon, the source of all depravity (St. John, St. Augustine, Martin Luther). Fellini's perspective is not entirely that of the indignant moral reformer or the angry prophet. As he puts it, *La Dolce Vita* is "not a trial seen by a judge but rather by an accomplice."[21] Thus, the Italian director has set himself somewhat apart from the lengthy history of moralizing on Roman vice and virtue that extends as least as far back as Petrarch's revival of interest in Roman antiquity. Even in the midst of corruption all around him, Fellini sees hope for the evolution of a new Roman mythology for our times.

In *Fellini Satyricon*, Fellini employs an extremely personal adaptation of the classical narrative by Petronius to underline the extent of our alienation from the Roman past. The fragmentary, disjointed nature of Petronius's masterpiece appealed to Fellini, since its very incompleteness forced his film into the realm of fantasy. For Fellini, pre-Christian Rome is as unfamiliar to modern man as a distant planet or a dream world. Yet Fellini's vision of a dehumanized, chaotic, and disintegrating pagan world bears important analogies to our own world. And these analogies revolve around two themes—the status of the arts in ancient Rome, and the ancient myths of Roman antiquity. Like Petronius, Fellini builds on the picaresque but often disconnected adventures of Gitone (Max Born) and Encolpius (Martin Potter). As he follows these two male lovers

67. Federico Fellini, La Dolce Vita
(1959). Images from ancient Rome,
Christian Rome, and the present are
juxtaposed in a single shot.
Museum of Modern Art, New York.

68. Federico Fellini, La Dolce Vita
(1959). At a Roman nightclub located
among the ruins of the ancient Baths of
Caracalla, Silvia (Anita Ekberg) performs
an energetic and frenzied dance.
Museum of Modern Art, New York.

through Rome, Fellini reaches an evaluation of the status of ancient Roman culture that is far from favorable. The artist and his unique creations are rarely appreciated. When the poet Eumolpus (Salvo Randone) guides Encolpius through a museum dedicated to preimperial art, these ancient relics put contemporary imperial Roman art to shame, and in the scenes of the museum's superficial and hurried spectators, there is more than just a suggestion of the frantic tourists who today race through the Sistine Chapel or the Villa Borghese in order to return to the comfort of their air-conditioned American Express tour buses (figure 69). Ancient Roman theatre is equally decadent. If we take the scenes from Vernacchio's theatre as representative of the level reached by Roman drama, we find that acting has degenerated into breaking wind on stage and that the theatre of Sophocles and Plautus imitates the bloodletting in the Colosseum, with the hand of a slave actually cut off on the stage to titillate the audience (figure 70).

The episode of the Villa of the Suicides, placed in the middle of the film, illuminates the themes of decadence and corruption that precede and follow. The fate of the noble couple who kill themselves rather than fall into the hands of the emperor's cruel soldiers highlights the confusion, loss of values, and instability of a world stripped of structure and republican ideals. The values of the ancient republic are dead, and there is nowhere for a virtuous man or woman to escape the barbarity of the times except beyond the grave. Even pagan religion is dominated less by a sense of morality or a philosophical ideal than by magic, sorcery, superstition, witches, and hermaphrodites. The scenes from Trimalchio's banquet—almost the only part of the film directly inspired by passages from Petronius and not totally transformed by Fellini's surrealistic imagery—also reflect the only section of the film which follows the popular Hollywood image of ancient Rome in the cinema: feasting and dancing, gargantuan meals, and sexual excess (figure 71).

The twentieth-century spectator recognizes himself easily in the surrealistic images, the stylized makeup, the rhetorical flourishes, and the discontinuous, fragmented narrative of Fellini's portrait of the ancient world. Paradoxically, the frightening, nightmare vision conjured up by Fellini's imagination resembles far more closely our own times than the Rome of the imperial age. Yet once again, as in La Dolce Vita, Roman decadence offers the potential for rebirth and renewal. An age of crisis may well play the role of midwife for new and original mythologies. Eumolpus leaves his entire fortune to those of his friends and heirs who are willing to eat his flesh (an obvious parody of the Christian eucharist).

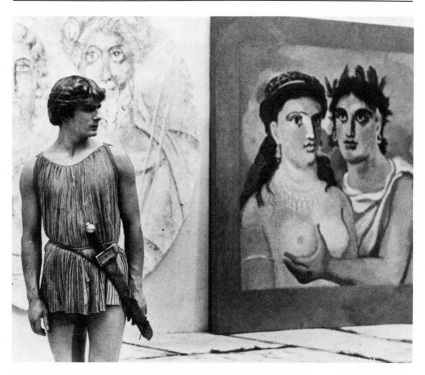

69. Federico Fellini, Fellini Satyricon
(1969). *Visiting an art gallery in ancient
Rome, Encolpius (Martin Potter) discovers
that he and his decadent age are as
estranged from the culture of their times
as Fellini believes modern man is today.*
Museum of Modern Art, New York.

70. Federico Fellini, Fellini Satyricon
(1969). *At the theatre, Vernacchio
(Fanfulla) reveals the depths to which the
once sublime classical theatre has sunken
under the empire of Petronius's times.*
Museum of Modern Art, New York.

71. Federico Fellini, Fellini Satyricon (1969).
Sensual revelry at Trimalchio's banquet.
Museum of Modern Art, New York.

While the old men chew uncomfortably on the poet's remains, the young reject this grisly sacrament, setting sail for new lands and taking with them still incompletely formulated values that will become the basis for an entirely new mythology in the future.

La Dolce Vita and Fellini Satyricon constitute an indictment, narrated by a director who admits his own complicity in the "crime" of modern values and those of the ancient Roman past. In the process, both the present and the past are revealed to have abandoned their dominant mythologies. The past is thus not so radically different from the present after all. If the culture visualized in Fellini Satyricon nevertheless served future generations as a source for new, reborn values, then even our own decadent era may well be fermenting and developing new, invigorating ideals and mythologies around which a new and more satisfying culture will be constructed in the future. And the films suggest that an authentic, deeply felt value system or mythology which elevates art and the process of artistic creation to its rightful status would cure the spiritual poverty of both epochs.

Fellini's Roma is a film not only about Rome but also about filmmaking—and therefore a work of art about the making of art itself. Fellini juxtaposes Rome's mythic past with a present-day Rome entirely of his own imagination and almost entirely constructed by his workmen inside the Cinecittà studios as if to emphasize its personal, unique status. Fellini also appears in the film as himself, shooting a documentary film about the city of Rome. Moreover, much of the film contains images from Fellini's childhood memories, his early encounter with the cinema, and his arrival in Rome in 1939 as a young provincial in the Eternal City. Fellini's Rome therefore combines a mixture of various perspectives and is primarily a city of myth and illusion—the center of Italian cinema, the home of the Catholic church, the headquarters of Benito Mussolini, Il Duce, and the seat of the new Italian republic. For Fellini, politics, religion, and cinema are all institutions relying upon the manipulation of images and myths, symbols and ideals. Rome emerges from the film not merely as a single cultural entity but as a combination of all these perspectives, each of which interpenetrates and enriches the connotations of the others.

Modern Rome possesses a mysterious link to its ancient past, yet the connection between these two distant worlds remains problematic, subject only to the power or the limitations of the imagination. When Fellini's film crew visits the site of an excavation for a new subway, work now halted by the discovery of an ancient Roman house with a complete set of frescoes, the impact of the modern air upon these ancient, yet strangely familiar works of art causes them to disappear before the director's very eyes (figure 72). A young boy, obviously an *alter ego* of Fellini himself, is horrified by his first visit to the cinema, where he witnesses one of the silent era's Roman spectaculars and confuses the murder of an ancient Roman senator at the Forum with reality. Mussolini's rhetoric advocating a Fascist empire patterned on the model of that of imperial Rome is satirized mercilessly. A pompous schoolmaster leads his class across the mythical Rubicon River, which both Caesar and Mussolini were reported to have crossed on their way to seize power in the Eternal City. But Fellini's Rubicon has been reduced to a tiny and ridiculous trickle of water, and the statue of Caesar the Fascists have erected in the town square serves only as a target for local pigeons!

In the village, the "Roman" Fascists resemble laughable circus clowns more than worthy successors to the purple mantle of ancient Rome's imperium. Yet the presence of ancient Rome can still be authentically felt through the artist's power of fantasy. A young woman parking with her boy friend in a car is suddenly transformed into the insatiable Messalina, wanton wife of the stuttering Emperor Claudius (figure 73). In the evening on a dark and deserted Roman street, the flickering light from an abandoned trolley car's electric cables throws the shadow of two stray dogs upon a wall, which are magically transformed into images of the she-wolf, the ancient symbol of republican Rome. Anna Magnani, the actress made famous by important roles in Italian and Hollywood films of the 1940s and the 1950s, appears in the Bohemian district of Trastevere, both vestal virgin and tramp, the perfect female embodiment of the Roman she-wolf or *lupa*. A glance at the sexually uninhibited hippies sunning themselves on the Spanish Steps causes Fellini to remember the furtive, guilt-ridden sex of his youth under the Fascist regime in the legalized Roman brothels. The implication that the sexuality of Fellini's youth is more perverse than the revelry of ancient Rome is created by the tolling of church bells in the Eternal City at the precise moment the young provincial enters the brothels (figure 74). A sense of Christian guilt renders sex more pleasurable for those of Fellini's generation.

The concluding scene from *Fellini's Roma* sets forth Fellini's modern version of the ancient barbarian hordes invading the Eternal City. A band of motorcyclists races about the city at night, illuminating most of the major monuments of the Capitoline Hill, the Forum, and the Colosseum, where they eventually converge. Previously Fellini and his crew had attempted to enter Rome by the *autostrada* but had been trapped at

72. Federico Fellini, Fellini's Roma
(1971). Ancient frescoes, discovered
during the excavations for the Roman
subway, disintegrate when they are
touched by the modern air.
Museum of Modern Art, New York.

73. Federico Fellini, Fellini's Roma
(1971). In Fellini's imagination, a young
woman parking in a motor car becomes
transformed into the nymphomaniac
Messalina, the wanton wife of Emperor
Claudius.
Museum of Modern Art, New York.

74. Federico Fellini, Fellini's Roma
(1971). Fellini returns to the more
inhibited days of his youth in the Roman
brothels.
Museum of Modern Art, New York.

the Colosseum by an enormous traffic jam filmed to recall Dante's *Inferno*. Yet now these barbarians pass by the spot with no difficulty whatsoever and roar out into the night along the Via Cristoforo Colombo toward a future which can only be imagined. A close examination of the final motorcycle ride through Rome reveals that it is not the cycles that speed down the center line of the road toward the Colosseum and beyond. It is, instead, Fellini's *camera*. Thus, the road is now free and unblocked for the director's *imagination*, because the camera's journey embodies the liberated and creative fantasy of the artistic mind behind the creation of the film. And the road upon which the camera, the symbol of the artist's liberated fantasy, travels is appropriately named after the discoverer of a New World (figure 75).

Fellini does not merely replace the older Roman mythology with another of his own making. His use of Roman mythology is unique. It makes manifest the concept that an artist's exhilaration in the act of creativity is the ultimate human freedom. In a real sense for Fellini, mythmaking and image making are the ultimate human activities, and it is fitting that he embodied this celebration of mythmaking in a film that explores the entire range of Roman mythology, perhaps the oldest and most influential mythology of our culture. In Fellini's films, Rome has once again become a fecund matrix, a willing midwife for new and contemporary permutations of its ancient heritage, an ever present depository of stories, myths, legends, and narratives that each individual may sack, like the ancient or modern barbarians, in order to construct future mythologies of his or her own. Thus, the way is cleared of all the baggage from the past, and all of the various expressions of Roman mythology are once again freed for the creative imagination to act upon. And Fellini's humanistic vision seems to promise the possibility of infinite transmutations of this complicated mythology. The future may well be renewed by its links to the presence of ancient Rome in the modern world, just as Fellini's poetic vision was liberated by its presence in his films.

75. Federico Fellini, Fellini's Roma
(1971). Fellini's vision of the liberation of
the artistic imagination is expressed in his
view of the new barbarians invading Rome
with motorcycles at the finale of the film.
Museum of Modern Art, New York.

I t would be quite impossible to predict the future development of Roman mythology. From the early Renaissance to the present, this multifaceted, long-lived cluster of heuristic ideas and striking images has enriched Western culture in countless ways. While its political relevance may be less than what it once was, this decline has been accompanied by a surprising expansion of Roman mythology into popular culture. And during its six centuries of development, the core myth—the image of Rome's virtuous republic juxtaposed against the decadent, tyrannical empire—has displayed a remarkable resilience and a tendency for survival that might not have been expected.

Consider the following photograph (figure 76) taken from an exclusive American magazine catering to the very elite class that, as recently as a century ago, viewed the republican myth of Rome as the basis for the creation of the American republic. We discover here a combination of cultural signifiers that play an important role in Roman mythology—ancient Roman ruins, the pose of a Roman aristocrat recalling a celebrated neoclassical marble statue by Canova, a palace evoking past dynastic glories connected with the Eternal City. Yet the photograph's message concerns a contemporary, consumer-oriented ideal from the world of fashion and advertising rather than the more traditional world of Roman political mythology. What the photograph conveys to us is quite simple: "Dress elegantly and consume the same luxury products as I do," as opposed to the far more demanding call of the older, heroic republican tradition, which exhorted the reader or the viewer to "Live virtuously and selflessly as I do." As a piece of photography, it is an excellent and evocative work. As a reflection of social history, the photograph seems at first glance to reveal a total lack of concern for the mythic tradition upon which it depends.

Before we rush to label such photography as a typical example of our contemporary lack of taste or brand it as an act of barbarism in the commercial use of visual images from the venerable tradition of Roman mythology, reducing these images to the status of "kitsch" art, it might be well to recall Fellini's final image from *Fellini's Roma* once again. In the conclusion to the film, the creative force of the liberated imagination is associated somewhat surprisingly with the new barbarians on the motor-

A rtfully recumbent beneath an evocative eighteenth-century landscape limning
Trajan's Column amid the ruins of ancient Rome, above, is Princess Benedetta
Boncompagni Ludovisi (nee Barberini Colonna di Sciarra). The history of the prin-
cess's own family, as well as that of her husband's, has been intertwined with the
papacy. One of the prince's ancestors is Gregory XIII, creator of the Gregorian
Calendar. Dress: Dior. Fragrance: Bal à Versailles by Jean Desprez. Necklace:
Bulgari. Papal history is a family affair, too, for Princess Maria Milagros del Drago
Colonna, right, photographed here in the magnificent 270-foot-long gallery of Palazzo
Colonna. Among the thirty-five noble titles that her husband, Don Aspreno, Prince
Colonna, holds is that of Hereditary Prince Assistant to the Holy See, a title that has
been in his family for 500 years. Fragrance: Miss Zadig by Pucci. Pearls: Bulgari.

76. Princess Benedetta Boncompagni Ludovisi in a pose reminiscent of Antonio
Canova's neoclassical statue of Venus seated underneath a painting in Palazzo
Colonna that presents a fantastic view of Roman ruins. Even the fragrance she is
wearing is mentioned. Rome has now become the backdrop for high-fashion photography.
Town and Country, Italian issue (September 1976); photograph by Larry Dale Gordon.

cycles who are racing out toward the future, supremely unconscious that they are bearing the seeds of new values and new mythologies. Let us also recall from the beginning of this book the image of the city of Rome which Sigmund Freud employed as a metaphor for the life of the mind. All of Roman history and all of the city's noble ideals lie in front of the modern spectator as if the various strata of the very different architectural expressions of each successive era are superimposed upon each other, all equally visible and all equally accessible to the imagination. Roman mythology thus represented for Freud, and still represents for artists of genius such as Fellini, a vast storehouse of precious images, values, and tales which each generation may accept, reject, or transform as its sees fit.

The ancient "barbarians" who pillaged these massive marble stones, or the even more important and valuable forms of Roman culture, were eventually civilized in the shadow of Rome's ancient monuments, taught language, literature, law, and philosophy through Rome's ancient example, and what they learned eventually constituted Rome's finest legacy to the future. Surely the true barbarians of our own times are those who have discarded with reckless abandon their cultural roots in Rome's ancient mythology and who ignore with indifference, rather than tear down to build anew, this magnificent intellectual structure.

NOTES

INTRODUCTION

1. See Roberto Weiss, *The Renaissance Discovery of Classical Antiquity* (Oxford: Basil Blackwell, 1969), p. 20; or Peter Burke, *The Renaissance Sense of the Past* (New York: St. Martin's, 1969), p. 29.

2. In *The Roman Stamp: Frame and Facade in Some Forms of Neo-Classicism* (Berkeley: University of California Press, 1974), pp. 9–10, Robert M. Adams asserts that the Roman myth was only an outlet for artistic urges that would have expressed themselves in some other manner without the existence of the myth: "The city is an occasion if not a downright pretext. . . . If Rome had not been handy, they would have found something else—or perished from exasperation at the lack of it." This declaration remains unsubstantiated by a convincing argument and is a curious remark in an otherwise provocative and engrossing account of several aspects of European neoclassicism.

3. Cited by Theodor E. Mommsen, "Petrarch's Conception of the Dark Ages," in *Medieval and Renaissance Studies*, ed. Eugene F. Rice (Ithaca: Cornell University Press, 1969), p. 122 (the citation is taken from the Latin work *Apologia contra cuiusdam anonymi Galli calumnias*).

4. This and future citations from Machiavelli are taken from *The Portable Machiavelli*, ed. Peter Bondanella and Mark Musa (New York: Penguin, 1979). The present letter, dated 10 December 1513, is found on pp. 66–71.

5. Cited by Henri Focillon in *G. B. Piranesi* (Paris: Laurens, 1928), p. 129.

6. *Civilization and Its Discontents*, trans. James Strachey (New York: Norton, 1961), p. 17.

CHAPTER 1

1. Weiss traces the exportation of much of the Eternal City's artistic patrimony throughout Europe. See *The Renaissance Discovery of Classical Antiquity* (Oxford: Basil Blackwell), p. 9.

2. Finley Hooper, *Roman Realities* (Detroit: Wayne State University Press, 1979), p. 540. In summarizing Roman history in this chapter, I follow Professor Hooper's invaluable presentation of the entire scope of Roman civilization, in addition to primary sources by the major Roman historians.

3. *The Early History of Rome*, trans. Aubrey De Selincourt (New York: Penguin, 1960), p. 34. The standard translation of Livy's history of Rome is contained in the four-volume Penguin edition. Besides *The Early History*, see *Rome and Italy*, trans. Betty Radice (New York: Penguin, 1982); *The War with Hannibal*, trans. Aubrey De Selincourt (New York: Penguin, 1965); and *Rome and the Mediterranean*, trans. Henry Bettenson (New York: Penguin, 1976).

4. Cited from Livy, *Rome and Italy*, p. 166.

5. For Cicero's discussion of Regulus, see the selection from *On Duties* in Cicero, *Selected Works*, trans. Michael Grant (New York: Penguin, 1971), pp. 198–204.

6. Hooper, *Roman Realities*, p. 479.

7. *The Portable Gibbon: The Decline and Fall of the Roman Empire*, ed. Dero A. Saunders (New York: Viking Penquin, 1952), p. 107.

8. For the details of this fascinating analysis of reading patterns in early modern

Europe, see Peter Burke, "A Survey of the Popularity of Ancient Historians, 1450–1700," *History and Theory* 5 (1966): 135–52.

CHAPTER 2

1. See Henry W. Litchfield, "National Exempla Virtutis in Roman Literature," *Harvard Studies in Classical Philology* 25 (1914): 1–72.

2. All references from St. Augustine come from *Concerning the City of God Against the Pagans*, trans. Henry Bettenson (New York: Penguin, 1972).

3. Cited by Mommsen in "Petrarch's Conception of the Dark Ages," in *Medieval and Renaissance Studies*, ed. Eugene F. Rice (Ithaca: Cornell University Press), p. 122.

4. *Letters on Familiar Matters* (6.2), cited from Morris Bishop, ed. and trans., *Letters from Petrarch* (Bloomington: Indiana University Press, 1966), p. 65.

5. See Agnes Heller's *Renaissance Man* (London: Routledge & Kegan Paul, 1978), p. 90.

6. For Petrarch's contributions to antiquarianism, see Weiss, *The Renaissance Discovery of Classical Antiquity* (Oxford: Basil Blackwell, 1969), pp. 30–47; Angelo Mazzocco, "Petrarca, Poggio, and Biondo: Humanism's Foremost Interpreters of Roman Ruins," in *Francis Petrarch, Six Centuries Later: A Symposium*, ed. Aldo Scaglione (Chapel Hill: University of North Carolina Press, 1975), pp. 353–63; or Angelo Mazzocco, "The Antiquarianism of Francesco Petrarca," *The Journal of Medieval and Renaissance Studies* 7 (1977): 203–24. For the impact of the ruins on the Renaissance imagination, see Thomas M. Greene, "Resurrecting Rome: The Double Task of the Humanist Imagination," in *Rome in the Renaissance: The City and the Myth*, ed. P. A. Ramsey (Binghamton, N.Y.: Center for Medieval & Early Renaissance Studies, 1982), pp. 41–54.

7. Cited from Bishop, ed., *Letters from Petrarch*, pp. 64–65.

8. For the complete history of Petrarch's Livian manuscripts, see Giuseppe Billanovich, "Petrarch and the Textual Tradition of Livy," *Journal of the Warburg and Courtauld Institutes* 14 (1951): 137–208.

9. For a discussion of this epic poem, see Aldo S. Bernardo, *Petrarch, Scipio and the "Africa": The Birth of Humanism's Dream* (Baltimore: The Johns Hopkins University Press, 1962); for a recent translation of the poem itself, see *Petrarch's "Africa"*, trans. Thomas G. Bergin and Alice S. Wilson (New Haven: Yale University Press, 1977).

10. A translation of these pastoral lyrics may be found in Thomas G. Bergin, ed. and trans., *Petrarch's "Bucolicum Carmen"* (New Haven: Yale University Press, 1974).

11. For a translation, see Ernest Hatch Wilkins, ed. and trans., *The Triumphs of Petrarch* (Chicago: University of Chicago Press, 1962).

12. For a discussion of Padua's *Sala virorum illustrium* and Petrarch's important role in its creation, see Mommsen, "Petrarch and the Decoration of the Sala Virorum Illustrium in Padua," in *Medieval and Renaissance Studies*, ed. Rice, pp. 130–74; for Petrarch's impact upon the plastic arts in general, see Victor Massena, Prince d'Essling and Eugene Muntz, *Pétrarque, ses études d'art, son influence sur les artistes, ses portraits, et ceux de Laure* (Paris: Gazette des beaux-arts, 1902).

13. Bishop, *Letters from Petrarch*, pp. 51–52, contains an English translation of this famous letter; for an interesting treatment of the tradition of poetic laureation, which was reborn with Petrarch, see J. B. Trapp, "The Poet Laureate: Rome, *Renovatio* and *Translatio Imperii*," in *Rome in the Renaissance: The City and the Myth*, ed. Ramsey, pp. 93–130.

14. For the English text of this oration, see Ernest Hatch Wilkins, *Studies in the Life and Works of Petrarch* (Cambridge, Mass.: The Medieval Academy of America, 1955), pp. 300–313, from which my citations are taken.

15. For a narrative of Arnold's life, see Ferdinand Gregorovius, *Rome and Medieval Cul-*

ture: *Selections from History of the City of Rome in the Middle Ages*, ed. K. F. Morrison (Chicago: University of Chicago Press, 1971); or George William Greenaway's *Arnold of Brescia* (Cambridge: Cambridge University Press, 1931), the most recent historical study of this figure.

16. *The Life of Cola di Rienzo*, trans. John Wright (Toronto: Pontifical Institute of Medieval Studies, 1975), provides an English translation of the chronicle, from which I cite here. Gregorovius, *Rome and Medieval Culture*, ed. Morrison, pp. 269–307, contains a good narrative of Cola's life. The most entertaining account of Cola is to be found in Luigi Barzini's *The Italians* (New York: Atheneum, 1964), pp. 122–38. For a detailed account of Petrarch's friendship with Cola, see Mario E. Cosenza's *Francesco Petrarca and the Revolution of Cola di Rienzo* (Chicago: University of Chicago Press, 1913), which also contains a number of the letters the two men wrote to each other. Other reliable accounts of this friendship may be found in Ernest Hatch Wilkins, *Life of Petrarch* (Chicago: University of Chicago Press, 1961), pp. 63–73; or Thomas G. Bergin, *Petrarch* (New York: Twayne, 1970), pp. 68–73.

17. See *Petrarch: A Humanist Among Princes*, ed. and trans. David Thompson (New York: Harper, 1971), pp. 65–81, for the citation of this entire letter.

18. For the narrative of Cola's deeds, I follow both Wilkins, *Life of Petrarch*, and Barzini, *The Italians*.

19. Cited from Barzini, *The Italians*, p. 138.

20. The classic discussion of "civic humanism" may be found in Hans Baron, *The Crisis of the Early Italian Renaissance: Civic Humanism and Republican Liberty in an Age of Classicism and Tyranny* (Princeton: Princeton University Press, 1966). Salutati's *On Tyranny* may be found in translation in Ephraim Emerton, ed., *Humanism and Tyranny: Studies in the Italian Trecento* (Cambridge, Mass.: Harvard University Press, 1925). For a perceptive critique and revision of Baron's thesis, see Quentin Skinner, *The Foundations of Modern Political Thought* (Cambridge: Cambridge University Press, 1978), vol. 1, *The Renaissance*, pp. 69–112.

21. For the English text of Bruni's *Panegyric to the City of Florence*, from which I cite, see Benjamin G. Kohl and Ronald G. Witt, eds., *The Earthly Republic: Italian Humanists on Government and Society* (Philadelphia: University of Pennsylvania Press, 1978), pp. 135–75. *Humanism & Liberty: Writings on Freedom from Fifteenth-Century Florence*, ed. Renée Neu Watkins (Columbia: University of South Carolina Press, 1978), pp. 27–96, contains an English selection from *The History of Florence*.

22. See Baron, *The Crisis of the Early Italian Renaissance*, pp. 58–60.

23. For the most complete recent studies of the frescoes in the Palazzo Pubblico, see Nicolai Rubinstein, "Political Ideas in Sienese Art: The Frescoes by Ambrogio Lorenzetti and Taddeo di Bartolo in the Palazzo Pubblico," *Journal of the Warburg and Courtauld Institutes* 21 (1958): 179–207; and Edna Carter Southard, *The Frescoes in Siena's Palazzo Pubblico 1289–1539: Studies in Imagery and Relations to Other Communal Palaces in Tuscany*, 2 vols. (New York: Garland, 1979), which contains English translations of the inscriptions.

CHAPTER 3

1. See H. W. Janson, *The Sculpture of Donatello* (Princeton: Princeton University Press, 1979), p. 198.

2. For detailed discussion of this tradition and the specific context of the painting in Boston attributed to Botticelli, see Herbert P. Horne, *Botticelli, Painter of Florence* (1908; reprint, Princeton: Princeton University Press, 1980), pp. 282–86; Guy Walton, "The Lucretia Panel in the Isabella Stewart Gardner Museum in Boston," in *Essays in Honor of Walter Friedlaender* (New York: Institute for Fine Arts, 1965), pp. 177–86; and Ronald

Lightbrown, *Sandro Botticelli* (London: Paul Elek, 1978), 1:141–45 and 2:101–6. For an excellent discussion of the Lucretia story, see Ian Donaldson, *The Rapes of Lucretia: A Myth and Its Transformations* (Oxford: The Clarendon Press, 1982).

3. The most complete discussion of Beccafumi's work is by Marianna Jenkins, "The Iconography of the Hall of the Consistory in the Palazzo Pubblico, Siena," *Art Bulletin* 54 (1972): 430–51. A fine overview of Beccafumi's *corpus* may be found in Bruce Cole, *Sienese Painting in the Age of the Renaissance* (Bloomington: Indiana University Press, 1985), pp. 156–82. For excellent detailed photographs of the entire cycle, see Giuliano Brignanti and Edi Baccheschi, *L'opera completa di Domenico Beccafumi* (Milan: Rizzoli, 1977). Beccafumi's use of Roman republican mythology was not limited to public commissions. Other important Livian subjects include the decoration of the Bindi-Sergardi Palace in Siena, containing *The Suicide of Cato of Utica, The Continence of Scipio, The Oath of Atilius Regulus,* and *The Punishment of Spurius Cassius; Lucretia's Suicide* (Siena); and another *Continence of Scipio* (Lucca). Clearly, the subject matter had popular appeal as well as the government's stamp of approval.

4. For an excellent brief history of Siena, see Judith Hook, *Siena, A City and Its History* (London: Hamish Hamilton, 1979).

5. Cited from D. J. Gordon, "Giannotti, Michelangelo and the Cult of Brutus," in *The Renaissance Imagination: Essays and Lectures by D. J. Gordon,* ed. Stephen Orgel (Berkeley: University of California Press, 1975), p. 235 (Gordon's translation). This article contains a detailed bibliography on the Florentine exiles and their many anti-Medici and pro-republican works.

6. A good account of the end of Florentine liberty and the capture of the city by imperial forces in 1530 is Cecil Roth, *The Last Florentine Republic* (1925; reprint, New York: Russell & Russell, 1968).

7. For excellent discussions of Brutus, see Howard Hibbard, *Michelangelo* (New York: Harper & Row, 1974); or the more recent *Michelangelo: A Psychoanalytic Study of His Life and Images* (New Haven: Yale University Press, 1983) by Robert S. Liebert.

8. For details on this problem, see Gordon, "Giannotti, Michelangelo and the Cult of Brutus," in *The Renaissance Imagination* or Liebert, *Michelangelo.*

9. For Machiavelli's intellectual background, see Roberto Ridolfi, *The Life of Niccolò Machiavelli,* trans. Cecil Grayson, (Chicago: University of Chicago Press, 1963); Felix Gilbert, *History: Choice and Commitment* (Cambridge, Mass.: Harvard University Press, 1977) or his *Machiavelli and Guicciardini: Politics and History in Sixteenth-Century Florence* (Princeton: Princeton University Press, 1965); J. G. A. Pocock, *The Machiavellian Moment: Florentine Republican Thought and the Atlantic Republican Tradition* (Princeton: Princeton University Press, 1975); or my own *Machiavelli and the Art of Renaissance History* (Detroit: Wayne State University Press, 1974).

10. Machiavelli makes a woman named Lucrezia (Lucretia in Italian) one of the main characters in his classic comedy, *The Mandrake Root.* Some readers of Machiavelli have seen a parallel between the seduction of Lucrezia in the play and the rape and suicide of Lucretia in Livy's history, thus making the comedy a political allegory of sorts. This argument can be traced in a number of recent works: Donaldson, *The Rapes of Lucretia;* Mark Hulliung, *Citizen Machiavelli* (Princeton: Princeton University Press, 1983); and Hanna Fenichel Pitkin, *Fortune Is a Woman: Gender and Politics in the Thought of Niccolò Machiavelli* (Berkeley: University of California Press, 1984).

11. For Tacitus and his European reputation, I rely upon two excellent sources: Kenneth C. Schellhase, *Tacitus in Renaissance Political Thought* (Chicago: University of Chicago Press, 1976); and Peter Burke, "Tacitism," in *Tacitus,* ed. T. A. Dorey (London: Routledge & Kegan Paul, 1969), pp. 149–71. For an older but still useful study, see Giuseppe Toffanin, *Machiavelli e il tacitismo* (1921; reprint, Naples: Guida Editore, 1972).

12. Cited from Schellhase, *Tacitus,* p. 33.

13. Cited from Leonard Forster, ed., *Selections from Conrad Celtis, 1459–1508* (Cambridge: Cambridge University Press, 1946), p. 53; for a general consideration of Germany's past in the Renaissance, see Frank Borchardt, *German Antiquity in Renaissance Myth* (Baltimore: The Johns Hopkins University Press, 1971).

14. Cited from Gerald Strauss, ed., *Manifestations of Discontent in Germany on the Eve of the Reformation* (Bloomington: Indiana University Press, 1971), p. 81.

15. For a discussion of these and other illustrations of the theme, see André Chastel, *The Sack of Rome, 1527* (Princeton: Princeton University Press, 1983), pp. 49–90; the best general historical treatment of the Sack of Rome in English may be found in Judith Hook, *The Sack of Rome, 1527* (London: Macmillan, 1972).

16. For discussions of both the Camera degli Sposi and the *Triumphs of Caesar*, see E. Tietze-Conrat, *Mantegna: Paintings, Drawings, Engravings* (London: Phaidon Press, 1955); and Maria Bellonci and Niny Garavaglia, *L'opera completa di Mantegna* (Milan: Rizzoli, 1967).

17. For Giulio Romano, I rely upon the excellent book by Frederick Hartt, *Giulio Romano*, 2 vols. (New Haven: Yale University Press, 1958).

18. Schellhase, *Tacitus*, p. 73; in the rest of this chapter, I rely upon this book for translations and for a guide to the major developments in Tacitean thought.

19. Translated by Schellhase, *Tacitus*, p. 87.

20. Translated in ibid., p. 91; the present illustration of the emblem comes from a later, 1614 edition.

21. For Guicciardini, see Roberto Ridolfi, *The Life of Francesco Guicciardini*, trans. Cecil Grayson, (New York: Knopf, 1968); Peter Bondanella, *Francesco Guicciardini* (Boston: Twayne, 1976); Mark Phillips, *Francesco Guicciardini: The Historian's Craft* (Toronto: University of Toronto Press, 1977); or Eric Cochrane, *Historians and Historiography in the Italian Renaissance* (Chicago: University of Chicago Press, 1981). Translations of Guicciardini's works may be found in *Selected Writings*, ed. Cecil Grayson (London: Oxford University Press, 1965), the edition I cite here.

22. See Burke, "Tacitism," in *Tacitus*, ed. T. A. Dory, p. 150, for these statistics.

23. Schellhase, *Tacitus*, p. 119.

24. Ibid., pp. 121–22 (*Oratio* 14, dated November 1580, although some scholars claim it to have been written in March of 1581).

25. Tacitus, *The Annals of Imperial Rome*, trans. Michael Grant (New York: Penguin, 1971), p. 334. For Ammirato, I am indebted to Eric Cochrane's engaging discussion in *Florence in the Forgotten Centuries: 1527–1800.* (Chicago: University of Chicago Press, 1973), pp. 95–161; see also Schellhase, pp. 142–45; and Rodolfo De Mattei, *Il pensiero politico di Scipione Ammirato con discorsi inediti* (Milan: Giuffré Editore, 1963).

26. Donaldson, *The Rapes of Lucretia*, p. 44. Hereafter, I cite Shakespeare's texts from Hardin Craig, ed., *The Complete Works of Shakespeare* (Glenview, Ill.: Scott, Foresman, 1961). Among the most useful treatments of Shakespeare's Roman tragedies may be included the following: Paul A. Cantor, *Shakespeare's Rome: Republic and Empire* (Ithaca: Cornell University Press, 1976); Allan Bloom and Harry Jaffa, *Shakespeare's Politics* (New York: Basic Books, 1964); Reuben A. Brower, *Hero & Saint: Shakespeare and the Graeco-Roman Heroic Tradition* (New York: Oxford University Press, 1971); Theodore Spencer, *Shakespeare and the Nature of Man* (New York: Collier, 1966) and *Shakespeare: The Roman Plays* (London: Longmans, Green, 1963); Derek Traversi, *Shakespeare: The Roman Plays* (Stanford: Stanford University Press, 1963); and J. L. Simmons, *Shakespeare's Pagan World: The Roman Tragedies* (Charlottesville: University Press of Virginia, 1973). An excellent treatment of the second Brutus may be found in M. L. Clarke, *The Noblest Roman: Marcus Brutus and His Reputation* (Ithaca: Cornell University Press, 1981).

CHAPTER 4

1. In addition to Donaldson, *The Rapes of Lucretia: A Myth and Its Transformations* (New York: Oxford University Press, 1982), I have found the following works useful in examining the Lucretia theme in art: Charles Hope, *Titian* (New York: Harper & Row, 1980); Harold E. Wethey, *The Paintings of Titian*, 3 vols. (London: Phaidon Press, 1975); Terisio Pignatti, *Veronese*, 2 vols. (Venice: Alfieri, 1976); Guido Piovene and Remigio Marini, *L'opera completa del Veronese* (Milan: Rizzoli, 1968); and Guido Piovene and Anna Pallucchini, *L'opera completa di Giambattista Tiepolo* (Milan: Rizzoli, 1968).

2. On Poussin, see Jacques Thullier, *L'opera completa di Nicolas Poussin* (Milan: Rizzoli, 1974); or Anthony Blunt, *Nicolas Poussin*, 2 vols. (Princeton: Princeton University Press, 1967).

3. Will G. Moore, *The Classical Drama of France* (London: Oxford University Press, 1971), p. 1.

4. Ibid., pp. 48–49.

5. For translations from Corneille, I cite from *Pierre Corneille: Seven Plays*, trans. Samuel Solomon (New York: Random House, 1969); for the original French texts, see Maurice Rat, ed., *Théâtre Complet de Corneille*, 3 vols. (Paris: Classiques Garnier, n.d.).

6. The best single treatment of the libretto in opera, including an assessment of Busenello, may be found in Patrick J. Smith, *The Tenth Muse: A Historical Study of the Opera Libretto* (New York: Schirmer, 1970); for the English translation of Busenello's libretto, I cite from the version provided with a recent recording (1981) of Nikolaus Harnoncourt directing the Monteverdi Ensemble of the Zurich Operahouse (Telefunken 6.35593 FK). This version was also broadcast as a television film over the American public television network.

7. For the English translation, I cite from *Three Plays of Racine*, trans. George Dillon (Chicago: University of Chicago Press, 1961); for the original French text, see Jean Racine, *Théâtre Complet de Racine*, ed. Maurice Rat (Paris: Classiques Garnier, 1960).

8. There probably exists no single source which includes every opera or libretto composed from the time opera was first developed until the present. However, *The Simon & Schuster Book of the Opera* (New York: Simon & Schuster, 1978), from which I have extracted this brief outline of Roman operas, lists over 800 operas which have achieved a certain measure of artistic success, historical importance, and public acclaim, and the impact of Roman themes during the baroque and neoclassical periods is remarkable.

9. Charles Rosen, *The Classical Style: Haydn, Mozart, Beethoven* (New York: Norton, 1972), p. 169.

10. I cite from the English translation of the libretto by Norman Clare, which was included in the only recording of the opera by the Berlin Chamber Orchestra under the direction of Vittorio Negri (Phillips 6769 004).

11. I cite from the libretto in English translation (no translator listed) supplied with the 1969 recording of *Lucio Silla* by the Angelicum Chamber Orchestra and Polyphonic Chorus of Milan, directed by Carlo Felice Cillario (RCA VICS-6117).

12. Wolfgang Hildesheimer, *Mozart*, trans. Marion Faber (New York: Vintage, 1983), p. 302. In addition to this excellent biography, I am also indebted to Charles Osborne's *The Complete Operas of Mozart: A Critical Guide* (New York: Da Capo Press, 1978) for information on Mozart's Roman operas.

13. Hildesheimer, *Mozart*, p. 303.

14. I cite from the libretto translated by Nicholas Granitto and Waldo Lyman included with a recent recording (Phillips 6703-079), directed by Colin Davis. A magnificent version of the opera, set amidst the ancient ruins of Rome, was recently presented on American public television. The original text of Metastasio's drama, the libretto's

ultimate source, is available in an eighteenth-century English translation: *The Works of Metastasio: Translated from the Italian by John Hoole*, 2 vols. (London: T. Davies, 1767).

15. Smith, *The Tenth Muse*, p. 95 (Hoole translation).

16. Vittorio Alfieri, *The Life of Vittorio Alfieri Written by Himself*, trans. Sir Henry McAnally (Lawrence: University of Kansas Press, 1953), p. 88.

CHAPTER 5

1. The best single introduction to Vico's *New Science* is the preface by the editors and translators of the standard English translation: *The New Science of Giambattista Vico*, trans. and ed. Thomas G. Bergin and Max H. Fisch (Ithaca: Cornell University Press, 1970). For a brilliant discussion of Vico's contribution to the rise of historicism, see Erich Auerbach, "Vico and Aesthethic Historicism," in his *Scenes from the Drama of European Literature: Six Essays* (New York: Meridian Books, 1959), pp. 183–98. Other recent studies of Vico include Isaiah Berlin, *Vico and Herder: Two Studies in the History of Ideas* (New York: Viking Press, 1976); and Leon Pompa, *Vico: A Study of the "New Science"* (London: Cambridge University Press, 1975). Arnaldo Momigliano, "Vico's Scienza Nuova: Roman 'Bestioni' and Roman 'Eroi'," *History and Theory* 5 (1966): 3–23, analyzes Vico's views on the class struggle between the Roman plebeians and aristocrats, so crucial a topic to all discussions of republican Rome from Machiavelli to Montesquieu.

2. *Considerations on the Causes of the Greatness of the Romans and Their Decline*, trans. David Lowenthal (Ithaca: Cornell University Press, 1968), pp. 25, 26. A thorough discussion of Montesquieu's political theory, accompanied by partial translations of his other major works, may be found in Melvin Richter, ed., *The Political Theory of Montesquieu* (Cambridge: Cambridge University Press, 1977). Robert Shackleton, "Montesquieu and Machiavelli: A Reappraisal," *Comparative Literature Studies* 1 (1964): 1–14; and Sheila M. Mason, "Livy and Montesquieu," in *Livy*, ed. T. A. Dorey (London: Routledge & Kegan Paul, 1971), pp. 118–58, are useful in tracing the influence of the classical historian and the Florentine political theorist upon Montesquieu's works.

3. Montesquieu, *Considerations*, p. 169.

4. Ibid., pp. 93–94.

5. For Rousseau's *Social Contract*, see Jean-Jacques Rousseau, *On the Social Contract*, ed. Roger D. Masters and trans. Judith R. Masters (New York: St. Martin's Press, 1978); and Roger D. Masters, *The Political Philosophy of Rousseau* (Princeton: Princeton University Press, 1968), which includes an ample bibliography.

6. *Social Contract*, p. 75 (Book 2, chapter 9).

7. Jean-Jacques Rousseau, *The First and Second Discourses*, ed. Roger D. Masters (New York: St. Martin's Press, 1964), p. 80.

8. Edward Gibbon, *The Portable Gibbon: The Decline and Fall of the Roman Empire*, ed. Dero A. Saunders (New York: Penguin, 1952), p. 106. For Gibbon, I have consulted G. M. Young, *Gibbon* (London: Peter Davies, 1932); D. M. Low, *Edward Gibbon 1737–1794* (London: Chatto and Windus, 1937); F. W. Bowerstock and Stephen K. Graubard, eds., *Edward Gibbon and the Fall of the Roman Empire* (Cambridge, Mass.: Harvard University Press, 1977); and Lionel Gossman, *The Empire Unpossess'd: An Essay on Gibbon's "Decline and Fall"* (Cambridge: Cambridge University Press, 1981).

9. Gibbon, *The Portable Gibbon*, ed. Saunders, p. 107.

10. Ibid., p. 81.

11. Ibid., p. 83.

12. Ibid., p. 84.

13. Carl L. Becker, *The Heavenly City of the Eighteenth-Century Philosophers* (New Haven: Yale University Press, 1932), p. 31.

14. Henri Foçillon, G. B. Piranesi (Paris: Laurens, 1928), p. 129. The best recent work on this artist is John Wilton-Ely, *The Mind and Art of G. B. Piranesi* (London: Thames & Hudson, 1978).

15. Robert Adams, *The Roman Stamp: Frame and Facade in Some Forms of Neo-Classicism* (Berkeley: University of California Press, 1974), p. 183.

16. See Luzius Keller, *Piranèse et les romantiques français: le myth des escaliers en spirale* (Paris: J. Corti, 1966).

17. The critical literature on this subject is vast and can only be mentioned here in passing. The older view of ideology's minimal impact upon the American Revolution may be found in such excellent histories as Daniel Boorstin's *The Genius of American Politics* (Chicago: University of Chicago Press, 1953), or Louis B. Hartz's *The Liberal Tradition in America: An Interpretation of American Political Thought Since the Revolution* (New York: Harcourt, 1955). In opposition to this school of thought, the reader may examine some of the following: Caroline Robbins, *The Eighteenth-Century Commonwealthman* (Cambridge, Mass.: Harvard University Press, 1959); Bernard Bailyn, *The Ideological Origins of the American Revolution* (Cambridge, Mass.: Harvard University Press, 1971); Gordon Wood, *The Creation of the American Republic 1776–1787* (Chapel Hill: University of North Carolina Press, 1969); and most importantly, from the Machiavellian perspective, J. G. A. Pocock's *The Machiavellian Moment: Florentine Political Thought and the Atlantic Republican Tradition* (Princeton: Princeton University Press, 1975). A remarkably readable history of republicanism has been written by William R. Everdell, *The End of Kings: A History of Republics and Republicans* (New York: The Free Press, 1983). For information on the cult of antiquity in revolutionary America and France, see Richard M. Gummere's excellent *The American Colonial Mind and the Classical Tradition: Essays in Comparative Culture* (Cambridge, Mass.: Harvard University Press, 1963); or Harold T. Parker's *The Cult of Antiquity and the French Revolutionaries: A Study in the Development of the Revolutionary Spirit* (Chicago: University of Chicago Press, 1937).

18. Pocock, *Machiavellian Moment*, p. 462.

19. Cited by Everdell, *End of Kings*, p. 151.

20. Gummere, *American Colonial Mind*, p. 59.

21. Ibid., pp. 13, 18.

22. Cited by Parker, *Cult of Antiquity*, p. 141. Christopher Hibbert, *The Days of the French Revolution* (New York: William Morrow, 1980), contains a highly readable account of the daily events which transpired between the fall of the Bastille and the rise of Napoleon.

23. Parker, *Cult of Antiquity*, pp. 148–49.

24. For the art of David, see Robert L. Herbert, *David, Voltaire, "Brutus," and the French Revolution: An Essay in Art and Politics* (New York: Viking, 1972); Robert Rosenblum, *Transformations in Late Eighteenth-Century Art* (Princeton: Princeton University Press, 1967); and Antoine Schnapper, *David: Temoin de son temps* (Paris: Bibliothèque des Arts, 1980).

25. Herbert, *David, Voltaire, "Brutus"*, p. 48.

26. Rosenblum, *Transformations*, p. 67.

27. Particulars about the commission may be found in H. H. Arnason, *The Sculptures of Houdon* (London: Phaidon Press, 1975); see also William H. Gerdts, *American Neo-Classic Sculpture: The Marble Resurrection* (New York: Viking, 1973). For an exhaustive consideration of the iconography of Washington in prints of the period, which also employ the image of Cincinnatus to depict the first American president, see Wendy C. Wick, *George Washington, An American Icon: The Eighteenth-Century Graphic Portraits* (Washington: Smithsonian Institution Traveling Exhibition Service, 1982). Washington's role as the Cincinnatus of the American Revolution has been examined by Garry Wills, *Cincinnatus: George Washington & the Enlightenment* (New York: Doubleday, 1984).

28. Vittorio Alfieri, *The Life of Vittorio Alfieri Written by Himself*, trans. Sir Henry McAnally (Lawrence: University of Kansas Press, 1953), p. 213.

29. Vittorio Alfieri, *The Tragedies of Vittorio Alfieri*, trans. E. A. Bowring (1876; reprint, Westport, Conn.: Greenwood Press, 1970), 2:265.

30. Ibid., 2:310.

31. Herbert, *David, Voltaire, "Brutus,"* p. 53. For an excellent discussion of the significance of the revolutionary oath and its classical antecedents, see Jean Starobinski, *1789: The Emblems of Reason*, trans. Barbara Bray (Charlottesville: University Press of Virginia, 1982), pp. 99–124.

32. For details about this revival and David's part in it, see Herbert, *David, Voltaire, "Brutus,"* pp. 67–93.

33. The best treatment of the theatre during the French Revolution may be found in Marvin Carlson, *The Theatre of the French Revolution* (Ithaca: Cornell University Press, 1966), from which I have taken most of my description of Roman themes in revolutionary theatrical performances.

34. For Ceracchi, see U. Desportes, "Giuseppe Ceracchi in America and his Busts of George Washington," *The Art Quarterly* 26 (1963): 140–79.

35. The best analysis of the background to Canova's commission is to be found in Philipp Fehl, "Thomas Appleton of Livorno and Canova's Statue of George Washington," in *Festschrift Ulrich Middeldorf*, ed. Antje Kosegarten and Peter Tigler (Berlin: De Gruyter, 1968), 1:523–52.

36. Ibid., 1:549.

37. The literature on Napoleon is voluminous. For simple, clear, and reliable accounts of the transition from republic to the Napoleonic empire, the reader will find the following useful: Felix Markham, *Napoleon* (New York: New American Library, 1963); Hibbert, *The French Revolution*; and Everdell, *End of Kings*.

38. Rosenblum, *Transformations*, p. 95. This study provides invaluable information concerning the transformation of older, iconographic traditions into subject matter suitable for the cult of Napoleon under the Empire.

CHAPTER 6

1. For my discussion of Thomas Cole, I am indebted to the following books: Richard J. Koke, ed., *American Landscape and Genre Paintings in the New-York Historical Society* (Boston: G. K. Hall, 1982), 1:199–203; Matthew Baigell, *Thomas Cole* (New York: Watson-Guptill, 1981); Abraham A. Davidson, *The Eccentrics and Other American Visionary Painters* (New York: Dutton, 1978); and Louis Lebrand Noble, *The Course of Empire, Voyage of Life, and Other Pictures of Thomas Cole, N. A.*, ed. Elliot S. Vessell (1853; reprint, Cambridge, Mass.: Harvard University Press, 1964).

2. Koke, *American Landscape*, 1:199.

3. Ibid., 1:201.

4. Ibid., 1:202.

5. Cited by Baigell, *Thomas Cole*, p. 52.

6. For a guide to these American visitors and a consideration of the impact of Italy or Rome upon their works, see Van Wyck Brooks, *The Dream of Arcadia: American Writers and Artists in Italy, 1760–1915* (New York: Dutton, 1958); Nathalia Wright, *American Novelists in Italy—The Discoverers: Allston to James* (Philadelphia: University of Pennsylvania Press, 1965); or Erik Amfitheatrof, *The Enchanted Ground: Americans in Italy, 1760–1980* (Boston: Little, Brown, 1980).

7. Cited in Brooks, *Dream of Arcadia*, p. 129.

8. The critical literature on the Italian Risorgimento resembles that on Italian fascism

in that it is voluminous and full of polemical controversies. No better guide through the complex events and personalities that make this period so fascinating can be found than a number of books by Denis Mack Smith: *Cavour: A Biography* (New York: Knopf, 1985); *Cavour and Garibaldi 1860: A Study in Political Conflict* (1954; reprint, Cambridge: Cambridge University Press, 1985); *Victor Emanuel, Cavour, and the Risorgimento* (London: Oxford University Press, 1971); and *Garibaldi*, ed. Denis Mack Smith (Englewood Cliffs, N.J.: Prentice-Hall, 1969). I have found much useful information on the various schools of thought concerning the Risorgimento in A. William Salomone, ed., *Italy from the Risorgimento to Fascism: An Inquiry into the Origins of the Totalitarian State* (New York: Doubleday, 1970); in Luigi Salvatorelli, *The Risorgimento: Thought & Action* (New York: Harper, 1970); and in Derek Beales, ed., *The Risorgimento and the Unification of Italy* (London: George Allen & Unwin, 1971). Christopher Hibbert, *Garibaldi and His Enemies: The Clash of Arms and Personalities in the Making of Italy* (Boston: Little, Brown, 1966), provides a superbly told account of this epoch, and his more recent *Rome: The Biography of a City* (New York: Norton, 1985), contains an excellent description of life in Rome during the Risorgimento. Garibaldi's memoirs may be consulted in *Memorie* (Milan: Rizzoli, 1982). Elizabeth Daniels's *Jesse White Mario: Risorgimento Revolutionary* (Athens: Ohio University Press, 1972) will be of great interest to American students of the Risorgimento. Even though written decades ago, three superb works by George Macaulay Trevelyan are still worth consulting: *Garibaldi and the Making of Italy* (London: Longmans, Green, 1948); *Garibaldi and the Thousand* (London: Longmans, Green, 1948); and *Garibaldi's Defense of the Roman Republic* (London: Longmans, Green, 1948).

9. Mack Smith, *Victor Emanuel*, p. 1.

10. Cited by Hibbert in *Garibaldi and His Enemies*, p. 42.

11. Cited in Mack Smith, *Garibaldi*, p. 19.

12. Garibaldi, *Memorie*, p. 157 (author's translation).

13. Cited by Hibbert in *Garibaldi and His Enemies*, p. 94.

14. Cited in Mack Smith, *Garibaldi*, p. 85.

15. Garibaldi's impact upon the art and popular culture of the Risorgimento is documented in Alberto M. Arpino et al., eds., *Garibaldi: arte e storia*, 2 vols. (Florence: Centro Di, 1982).

16. Cited in Mack Smith, *Garibaldi*, p. 73.

17. Cited by Edward R. Tennenbaum, *The Fascist Experience: Italian Society and Culture, 1922–1940* (New York: Basic Books, 1972), p. 24.

18. Muret Halstead, *The Story of the Philippines: The Eldorado of the Orient* (Chicago: Our Possessions Publishing Co., 1898), p. 13.

19. Ibid., p. 14.

20. Ibid., pp. 14–15.

21. Robert W. Rydell, *All the World's a Fair: Visions of Empire at American International Expositions, 1876–1916* (Chicago: University of Chicago Press, 1984), p. 139. In my discussion of the role of the international expositions in providing ideological justifications for American imperialism, I am deeply indebted to this highly original and stimulating work.

22. Ibid., p. 3.

CHAPTER 7

1. It is impossible to separate the history of Italian fascism from the biography of its founder, and the literature on Mussolini is voluminous. Early literature, either apologies for the regime or polemical attacks on it by contemporaries, are still worth examining, although with caution. In English, see Benito Mussolini, *My Autobiography*, rev. ed.

(London: Hutchinson, 1939); and Benito Mussolini, *My Diary 1915–17*, trans. Rita Wellman (Boston: Small, Maynard, 1925). For negative views of Mussolini published during his lifetime, see John Bond, *Mussolini: The Wild Man of Europe* (Washington: Independent Publishing Co., 1929); and George Seldes, *Sawdust Caesar: The Untold History of Mussolini and Fascism* (New York: Harper, 1935). A fascinating series of interviews with Mussolini is contained in Emil Ludwig, *Talks With Mussolini* (Boston: Little, Brown, 1933). Postwar biographies of Mussolini are more reliable: see Ivone Kirkpatrick, *Mussolini: A Study in Power* (New York: Hawthorn Books, 1964); Roy MacGregor-Hastle, *The Day of the Lion: The Life and Death of Fascist Italy 1922–1945* (New York: Coward-McCann, 1964); and F. W. Deakin, *The Last Days of Mussolini* (London: Penguin, 1962). The definitive biography of Mussolini in Italian is the five-volume work (a sixth is still in progress) by Renzo De Felice: *Mussolini il duce: gli anni del consenso 1929–1936* (Turin: Einaudi, 1974); *Mussolini il duce: lo stato totalitario 1936–1940* (Turin: Einaudi, 1981); *Mussolini il fascista: la conquista del potere 1921–1925* (Turin: Einaudi, 1966) *Mussolini il fascista: l'organizzazione dello stato fascista 1925–1929* (Turin: Einaudi, 1968); and *Mussolini il rivoluzionario* (Turin: Einaudi, 1965). In English, the now definitive treatment is the superb biography by Denis Mack Smith, *Mussolini* (New York: Knopf, 1982). I am greatly indebted to the studies of De Felice and Mack Smith in my treatment of Mussolini and Italian fascism.

2. For Fascist ideology, the basic source remains the many volumes of Mussolini's own writings: *Opera omnia di Benito Mussolini*, ed. Edoardo and Diulio Susmel, 35 vols. (Florence: La Fenice, 1951–62). For selections in English, see *Italian Fascisms: From Pareto to Gentile*, ed. Adrian Lyttleton (London: Jonathan Cape, 1973). Two works by A. James Gregor are fine introductions to the origins and development of Fascist ideology: *The Ideology of Fascism: The Rationale of Totalitarianism* (New York: The Free Press, 1969); and *Young Mussolini and the Intellectual Origins of Fascism* (Berkeley: University of California Press. 1979).

3. For studies of Italy's Jews under Fascism, see Renzo De Felice, *Storia degli ebrei italiani sotto il fascismo*, 3d ed. (Turin: Einaudi, 1972); and Meir Michaelis, *Mussolini and the Jews: German-Italian Relations and the Jewish Question in Italy 1922–45* (Oxford: Institute for Jewish Affairs, 1978).

4. Edward R. Tennenbaum, *The Fascist Experience: Italian Society and Culture, 1922–1940* (New York: Basic Books, 1972), p. 25. The various explanations for the rise of fascism, its success in Italy, the social background of its followers, and the like are still hotly debated. For a convenient guide to the various issues involved, see A. James Gregor, *Interpretations of Fascism* (Morristown, N.J.: General Learning Press, 1974); and Renzo De Felice, *Interpretations of Fascism* (Cambridge, Mass.: Harvard University Press, 1977).

5. Cited by Renzo De Felice and Luigi Goglia in *Mussolini: il mito* (Rome: Laterza, 1983), p. 158 (author's translation).

6. Ibid. (author's translation).

7. Mussolini, *My Autobiography*, p. 160.

8. Mack Smith, *Mussolini*, p. 54.

9. Cited by Denis Mack Smith, ed., in *Garibaldi* (Englewood Cliffs, N.J.: Prentice-Hall, 1969), p. 166. The impact of fascism upon Italian popular culture was enormous. For postcards, see Mario Donadei, *L'Italia delle cartoline 1919–1945* (Cuneo: Edizioni L'Arciere, 1978); and Giuliano Vittori, *C'era una volta il duce: il regime in cartolina* (Rome: Savelli, 1975). For the comic strip, see Claudio Carabba, *Il fascismo a fumetti* (Rimini: Guaraldi Editore, 1973). For Italian cinema under fascism, see Massimo Cardillo, *Il Duce in moviola: politica e divismo nei cinegiornali e documentari "Luce"* (Bari: Edizioni Dedalo, 1983); Jean A. Gili, *Stato fascista e cinematografia: repressione e promozione* (Rome: Bulzoni Editore, 1981); a briefer discussion in English may be found in Peter Bondanella, *Italian Cinema: From Neorealism to the Present* (New York: Frederick Ungar Publishing, 1983). For two general treatments of popular culture under fascism, see Plinio Ciani, *Graffiti del*

Ventennio: guida al curioso, al comico, all'aneddotico nell'architettura e nell'arte mussoliniane (Milan: Sugar Edizioni, 1975); and Philip V. Cannistraro, La fabbrica del consenso: fascismo e mass media (Rome: Laterza, 1975). A fascinating study of how the regime tried to organize the leisure time of its subjects may be found in Victoria De Grazia, The Culture of Consent: Mass Organization of Leisure in Fascist Italy (Cambridge: Cambridge University Press, 1981). For recordings of popular music during the Fascist era, including the texts of the songs, see several recent reprintings of older recordings issued by Editrice Fonit-Cetra in Italy: Alla guerra per faccetta nera (Number FC3649, Series 4, Number 9); or Quel motivetto che fa: Duce (Number FC3644, Series 4, Number 4).

10. Mussolini, Opere, 25:148 (author's translation).

11. Ibid., 25:52.

12. Although this exhibit is no longer in existence, an excellent reproduction of its program, including color illustrations, gives some idea of its ambitious scope: Dino Alfieri and Luigi Freddi, eds., Mostra della rivoluzione fascista: guida storica (Rome: Partito Nazionale Fascista, 1933; Milan: Edizioni del Candido Nuovo, 1982).

13. Mussolini, Opere, 26:21 (author's translation).

14. Ibid., 26:30 (author's translation).

15. Luigi Barzini, The Europeans (New York: Penguin, 1984), p. 88.

16. Mack Smith, Mussolini, p. 110.

17. Mack Smith, Mussolini's Roman Empire (New York: Viking, 1976), p. 121.

18. De Felice, Gli anni del consenso, p. 758.

19. For a description of this ceremony at the Piazza Venezia, see Glorney Bolton, Roman Century: A Portrait of Rome as the Capital of Italy, 1870–1970 (New York: Viking, 1970), p. 226.

20. Mussolini, Opere, 27.268–69 (author's translation).

21. Ibid., 27.243 (author's translation).

22. Ibid., 28.60 (author's translation).

23. Mack Smith, Mussolini's Roman Empire, p. 134; or Mussolini, p. 218.

24. For a history of this exhibit and its impact upon the present museum in Rome, see Renato Niccolini, ed., Roma capitale 1870–1911: Dalla mostra al museo (Venice: Marsilio Editori, 1983), pp. 77–90.

25. Ludwig, Talks With Mussolini, p. 211.

26. Ibid.

27. Spiro Kostof, "The Emperor and the Duce: The Planning of the Piazzale Augusto Imperatore in Rome," in Henry A. Millon and Linda Nochlin, eds., Art and Architecture in the Service of Politics (Cambridge, Mass.: MIT Press, 1978), p. 287. See also Kostof's The Third Rome 1870–1950: Traffic and Glory (Berkeley: University of California Press, 1973).

28. Paul MacKendrick, The Mute Stones Speak: The Story of Archaeology in Italy (New York: St. Martin's Press, 1960), p. 141. MacKendrick's excellent book contains a useful outline of Fascist archaeology, discussing its successes and its role in glorifying Rome's imperial past.

29. Diane Yvonne Ghirardo, "Italian Architects and Fascist Politics: An Evaluation of the Rationalist's Role in Regime Building," Journal of the Society of Architectural Historians 39 (1980): 114. For the best recent book on Fascist architecture containing numerous photographs, see Carlo Cresti, Architettura e fascismo (Florence: Vallecchi Editore, 1986).

30. Mack Smith, Mussolini, pp. 136–37. For more detailed photographs of the Foro Mussolini, see Sculpture italienne à Rome au temps du fascisme, ed. Yve-Alain Bois (Paris: Jacques Damase Éditeur, 1978).

31. Cited by Henry A. Millon, "Some New Towns in Italy of the 1930s," in Art and Architecture, ed. Millon and Nochlin, p. 332.

32. For the story of how this Fascist period style emerged in part from the excavations of the period, see William L. MacDonald, "Excavation, Restoration, and Italian

Architecture of the 1930s," in Helen Searing, ed., In Search of Modern Architecture: A Tribute to Henry-Russell Hitchcock (Cambridge, Mass.: MIT Press, 1982), pp. 298–320; or Mac-Kendrick, The Mute Stones Speak, pp. 145–71.

33. For details of this project, including excellent illustrations, see Kostof, "The Emperor and the Duce."

34. Ibid., p. 322.

35. For details on the construction of the E.U.R., including many photographs of the various stages of the buildings under construction, see Achille M. Ippolito, Roma— E.U.R. 83: storia ed analisi critica dell'architettura del quartiere E.U.R. dal piano per l'E42 ai giorni nostri (Rome: Fratelli Palombi Editori, 1983); and Joanne B. Funigiello and Philip J. Funigiello, "EUR, 1936–1942: Town Planning, Architecture, and Fascist Ideology," Canadian Journal of Italian Studies 4 (1980–81): 83–103. For a more detailed account of how architectural historians generally supported the regime's imperialist claims with their scholarship, see Henry A. Millon, "The Role of History of Architecture in Fascist Italy," Journal of the Society of Architectural Historians 24 (1965): 53–59.

36. This thesis is persuasively argued by Ghirardo, "Italian Architects and Fascist Politics."

37. Luigi Barzini, The Italians (New York: Atheneum, 1964), pp. 139–40, recounts this anecdote.

CHAPTER 8

1. For treatments of the Italian silent cinema, see Gian Piero Brunetta, Storia del cinema italiano 1895–1945 (Rome: Editori Riuniti, 1979); Aldo Bernardini, Cinema muto italiano: arte, divismo e mercato 1910–1914 (Rome: Laterza, 1982); and chapter 1 of Peter Bondanella, Italian Cinema: From Neorealism to the Present (New York: Frederick Ungar Publishing, 1983). A frame-by-frame breakdown of Cabiria is provided in Giovanni Pastrone, Cabiria: visione storica del III secolo a.c., ed. Roberto Radicati and Ruggero Rossi (Turin: Museo Nazionale del Cinema, 1977). The best general treatments of Rome's impact upon world cinema are Jon Solomon's The Ancient World in the Cinema (Cranbury, N.J.: A. S. Barnes, 1978); and John Cary's Spectacular!: The Story of Epic Films (Secaucus, N.J.: Castle Books, 1974).

2. An almost complete listing of these Roman films arranged by historical periods in the development of ancient Rome may be found in Solomon, The Ancient World, pp. 62–64.

3. For the impact of Fascism upon the Italian cinema, see Brunetta, Storia del cinema, and Bondanella, Italian Cinema; in addition, see Adriano Aprà and Patrizia Pistagnesi, eds., The Fabulous Thirties: Italian Cinema 1929–1944 (Milan: Electra, 1979); Claudio Carabba, Il cinema del ventennio nero (Florence: Vallecchi, 1974); Marcia Landy's excellent Fascism in Film: The Italian Commercial Cinema, 1931–1943 (Princeton: Princeton University Press, 1986); and a fascinating study by James H. Hay, Popular Film Culture in Fascist Italy (Bloomington: Indiana University Press, 1987), which I have been able to consult in manuscript form. Carabba (pp. 52–54) reprints the reactions of Italian schoolchildren to Scipio Africanus, and Hay contains some English translations of these interviews.

4. For particulars on Cleopatra, see Solomon, The Ancient World, pp. 45–52; or Hank Kaufman and Gene Lerner, Hollywood sul Tevere (Milan: Sperling & Kupfer, 1982).

5. For details, see Solomon, The Ancient World, pp. 46–47.

6. Cited in "Penthouse Interview," p. 114, in a special Caligula issue of Penthouse 11, no. 9, which contains numerous color photographs of the elaborate sets and, of course, the players in various states of undress and sexual arousal. For a fictional version of the

film that is faithful to the script, see William Howard's *Gore Vidal's "Caligula"* (New York: Warner, 1979), a novel based upon Vidal's original screenplay.

7. See Robert Graves, *I, Claudius* (New York: Vintage, 1961); and *Claudius the God* (New York: Vintage, 1962), from which my citations are taken.

8. For details on the production of this film, I am indebted to Solomon, *The Ancient World*; Cary, *Spectacular*; and to a public lecture delivered at Indiana University in 1984 by Professor Timothy Long, "The Roman Empire in the Movies."

9. Brian Aldiss, ed., *Galactic Empires: Volume One* (New York: St. Martin's Press, 1976), and *Galactic Empires: Volume Two* (New York: St. Martin's Press, 1976); Isaac Asimov, Martin H. Greenberg, and Charles G. Waugh, eds., *Intergalactic Empires* (New York: New American Library, 1983).

10. I have consulted the following editions: *Foundation* (New York: Avon, 1966); *Foundation and Empire* (New York: Avon, 1966); and *Second Foundation* (New York: Avon, 1964). Citations in the text are taken from these editions. For a collection of essays by Asimov himself, including a discussion of the *Foundation* trilogy, see *Asimov on Science Fiction* (New York: Avon, 1981). I have omitted any discussion of the more recent *Foundation's Edge* or *Foundation and Earth*, since these two novels appeared long after Asimov's concept of galactic empires from the trilogy had permeated the entire field of science fiction literature.

11. Asimov, *Intergalactic Empires*, p. 9. In a private letter to me in response to several questions about the genesis of his series (28 February 1984), Asimov stated: "When I first wrote the Foundation trilogy, I did indeed have Gibbon in mind."

12. Asimov, private letter to author, ibid.

13. I owe these observations to Brian Aldiss, ed., *Galactic Empires: Volume One*, pp. xiv, xv, 6; and *Galactic Empires: Volume Two*, pp. vi, viii. However, in the same private letter cited in note 11, Asimov asserts he did *not* have contemporary history in mind when he completed his trilogy.

14. See Poul Anderson, *A Stone in Heaven* (New York: Ace, 1979); the appendix can be located on pp. 237–55.

15. Asimov, *Intergalactic Empires*, p. 10. For prose versions of the Star Wars trilogy, see George Lucas, *Star Wars* (New York: Ballantine, 1976); Donald F. Glut, *The Empire Strikes Back* (New York: Ballantine, 1980); and James Kahn, *The Return of the Jedi* (New York: Ballantine, 1983).

16. Lucas, *Star Wars*, p. 1.

17. Ibid.

18. For a guide to Fellini criticism, see John C. Stubbs, *Federico Fellini: A Guide to References and Resources* (Boston: G. K. Hall, 1978). A cross section of interviews and essays on Fellini are collected in Peter Bondanella, ed., *Federico Fellini: Essays in Criticism* (New York: Oxford University Press, 1978); Fellini's place in Italian cinematic history may be traced in Bondanella, *Italian Cinema*. The best recent discussion of *La Dolce Vita* is in Frank Burke, *Federico Fellini: "Variety Lights" to "La Dolce Vita"* (Boston, Twayne, 1984), pp. 85–99. An especially important interpretation of *Fellini's Roma* may be found in Walter C. Foreman, "Fellini's Cinematic City: *Roma* and the Myths of Foundation," *Forum Italicum* 14 (1980): 78–98. Statements by Fellini on the art of the cinema are collected in several recent books: Federico Fellini, *Fare un film* (Turin: Einaudi, 1980); Federico Fellini, *Intervista sul cinema* (Rome: Laterza, 1983); and *Fellini on Fellini* (London: Eyre Methuen, 1976). For scripts of the films discussed in this chapter, see *La Dolce Vita* (New York: Ballantine, 1961); *Fellini Satyricon*, ed. Dario Zanelli (New York: Dell, 1970); and *Roma di Federico Fellini*, ed. Bernardino Zapponi (Bologna: Cappelli, 1972).

19. *Fellini on Fellini*, p. 157.

20. Ibid., pp. 157–58.

21. Cited by Suzanne Budgen in *Fellini* (London: British Film Institute, 1966), p. 99.

BIBLIOGRAPHY

Adams, Robert M. *The Roman Stamp: Frame and Facade in Some Forms of Neo-Classicism.* Berkeley: University of California Press, 1974.

Aldiss, Brian, ed. *Galactic Empires: Volume One.* New York: St. Martin's Press, 1976.

——, ed. *Galactic Empires: Volume Two.* New York: St. Martin's Press, 1976.

Alfieri, Dino and Luigi Freddi, eds. *Mostra della rivoluzione fascista: guida storica.* Rome: Partito Nazionale Fascista, 1933; Milan: Edizioni del Candido Nuovo, 1982.

Alfieri, Vittorio. *The Life of Vittorio Alfieri Written by Himself.* Translated by Sir Henry McAnally. Lawrence: University of Kansas Press, 1953.

——. *The Tragedies of Vittorio Alfieri.* 2 vols. Translated by E. A. Bowring. 1876. Reprint. Westport, Conn.: Greenwood Press, 1970.

Alla guerra per faccetta nera. With Daniele Serra. Editrice Fonit–Cetra, Number FC3649, Series 4, Number 9, n.d.

Amfitheatrof, Erik. *The Enchanted Ground: Americans in Italy, 1760–1980.* Boston: Little, Brown, 1980.

Anderson, Poul. *A Stone in Heaven.* New York: Ace, 1979.

Aprà, Adriano and Patrizia Pistagnesi, eds. *The Fabulous Thirties: Italian Cinema 1929–44.* Milan: Electra, 1979.

Arnason, H. H. *The Sculptures of Houdon.* London: Phaidon Press, 1975.

Arpino, Alberto M., et. al., eds. *Garibaldi: arte e storia.* 2 vols. Florence: Centro Di, 1982.

Asimov, Isaac. *Asimov on Science Fiction.* New York: Avon, 1981.

——. *Foundation.* New York: Avon, 1966.

——. *Foundation and Earth.* New York: Doubleday, 1986.

——. *Foundation and Empire.* New York: Avon, 1966.

——. *Foundation's Edge.* New York: Doubleday, 1982.

——. Letter to the author, 28 February 1984.

——. *Second Foundation.* New York: Avon, 1964.

——, Martin H. Greenberg, and Charles G. Waugh, eds. *Intergalactic Empires.* New York: New American Library, 1983.

Auerbach, Erich. *Scenes from the Drama of European Literature: Six Essays.* New York: Meridian Books, 1959.

Augustine, Saint. *Concerning the City of God Against the Pagans.* Trans. Henry Bettenson. New York: Penguin, 1972.

Baigel, Matthew. *Thomas Cole.* New York: Watson-Guptill, 1981.

Bailyn, Bernard. *The Ideological Origins of the American Revolution.* Cambridge, Mass.: Harvard University Press, 1971.

Baron, Hans. *The Crisis of the Early Italian Renaissance: Civic Humanism and Republican Liberty in an Age of Classicism and Tyranny.* Princeton: Princeton University Press, 1966.

Barzini, Luigi. *The Europeans.* New York: Penguin, 1984.

——. *The Italians.* New York: Atheneum, 1964.

Beales, Derek, ed. *The Risorgimento and the Unification of Italy.* London: George Allen & Unwin, 1971.

Becker, Carl L. *The Heavenly City of the Eighteenth-Century Philosophers.* New Haven: Yale University Press, 1932.

Bellonci, Maria and Niny Garavaglia. *L'opera completa di Mantegna.* Milan: Rizzoli, 1967.

Bergin, Thomas G. *Petrarch.* New York: Twayne, 1970.

Berlin, Isaiah. *Vico and Herder: Two Studies in the History of Ideas.* New York: Viking Press, 1976.

Bernardini, Aldo. *Cinema muto italiano: arte, divismo e mercato 1910–1914.* Rome: Laterza, 1982.

Bernardo, Aldo S. *Petrarch, Scipio, and the "Africa": The Birth of Humanism's Dream.* Baltimore: The Johns Hopkins University Press, 1962.

Billanovich, Giuseppe. "Petrarch and the Textual Tradition of Livy." *Journal of the Warburg and Courtauld Institutes* 14 (1951): 137–208.

Bloom, Allan and Harry Jaffa. *Shakespeare's Politics.* New York: Basic Books, 1964.

Blunt, Anthony. *Nicolas Poussin.* 2 vols. Princeton: Princeton University Press, 1967.

Bois, Yve-Alain, ed. *Sculpture italienne à Rome au temps du fascisme.* Paris: Jacques Damase Éditeur, 1978.

Bolton, Glorney. *Roman Century: A Portrait of Rome as the Capital of Italy, 1870–1970.* New York: Viking, 1970.

Bond, John. *Mussolini: The Wild Man of Europe.* Washington: Independent Publishing Co., 1929.

Bondanella, Peter. *Francesco Guicciardini.* Boston: Twayne, 1976.

————. *Italian Cinema: From Neorealism to the Present.* New York: Frederick Ungar Publishing, 1983.

————. *Machiavelli and the Art of Renaissance History.* Detroit: Wayne State University Press, 1974.

————, ed. *Federico Fellini: Essays in Criticism.* New York: Oxford University Press, 1978.

Boorstin, Daniel. *The Genius of American Politics.* Chicago: University of Chicago Press, 1953.

Borchardt, Frank. *German Antiquity in Renaissance Myth.* Baltimore: The Johns Hopkins University Press, 1971.

Bowerstock, F. W. and Stephen K. Graubard, eds. *Edward Gibbon and the Fall of the Roman Empire.* Cambridge, Mass.: Harvard University Press, 1977.

Brignanti, Giuliano and Edi Baccheschi. *L'opera completa di Domenico Beccafumi.* Milan: Rizzoli, 1977.

Brooks, Van Wyck. *The Dream of Arcadia: American Writers and Artists in Italy, 1760–1915.* New York: Dutton, 1958.

Brower, Reuben A. *Hero & Saint: Shakespeare and the Graeco-Roman Heroic Tradition.* New York: Oxford University Press, 1971.

Brunetta, Gian Piero. *Storia del cinema italiano 1895–1945.* Rome: Editori Riuniti, 1979.

Bruni, Leonardo. "The History of Florence." In *Humanism & Liberty: Writings on Freedom from Fifteenth-Century Florence,* edited and translated by Renée Neu Watkins, pp. 27–96. Columbia: University of South Carolina Press, 1978.

————. "Panegyric to the City of Florence." In *The Earthly Republic: Italian Humanists on Government and Society,* edited and translated by Benjamin G. Kohl and Ronald G. Witt, pp. 135–75. Philadelphia: University of Pennsylvania Press, 1978.

Budgen, Suzanne. *Fellini.* London: British Film Institute, 1966.

Burke, Frank. *Federico Fellini: "Variety Lights" to "La Dolce Vita."* Boston: Twayne, 1984.

Burke, Peter. *The Renaissance Sense of the Past.* New York: St. Martin's Press, 1969.

————. "A Survey of the Popularity of Ancient Historians 1450–1700." *History and Theory* 5 (1966): 135–52.

————. "Tacitism." In *Tacitus,* edited by T. A. Dorey, pp. 149–71. London: Routledge & Kegan Paul, 1969.

Cannistraro, Philip V. *La fabbrica del consenso: fascismo e mass media.* Rome: Laterza, 1975.

Cantor, Paul A. *Shakespeare's Rome: Republic and Empire.* Ithaca: Cornell University Press, 1976.

Carabba, Claudio. *Il cinema del ventennio nero.* Florence: Vallecchi, 1974.

————. *Il fascismo a fumetti.* Rimini: Guaraldi Editore, 1973.

Cardillo, Massimo. *Il Duce in moviola: politica e divismo nei cinegiornali e documentari "Luce."* Bari: Edizioni Dedalo, 1983.

Carlson, Marvin. *The Theatre of the French Revolution.* Ithaca: Cornell University Press, 1966.

Cary, John. *Spectacular!: The Story of Epic Films.* Secaucus, N.J.: Castle Books, 1974.

Celtis, Conrad. *Selections from Conrad Celtis, 1459–1508.* Edited by Leonard Forster. Cambridge: Cambridge University Press, 1946.

Chastel, André. *The Sack of Rome, 1527.* Princeton: Princeton University Press, 1983.

Ciani, Plinio. *Graffitti del Ventennio: guida al curioso, al comico, all'aneddotico nell'architettura e nell'arte mussoliniane.* Milan: Sugar Edizioni, 1975.

Cicero. *Selected Works.* Translated by Michael Grant. New York: Penguin, 1971.

Clarke, M. L. *The Noblest Roman: Marcus Brutus and His Reputation.* Ithaca: Cornell University Press, 1981.

Cochrane, Eric. *Florence in the Forgotten Centuries: 1527–1800.* Chicago: University of Chicago Press, 1973.

———. *Historians and Historiography in the Italian Renaissance.* Chicago: University of Chicago Press, 1981.

Cole, Bruce. *Sienese Painting in the Age of the Renaissance.* Bloomington: Indiana University Press, 1985.

Corneille, Pierre. *Pierre Corneille: Seven Plays.* Translated by Samuel Soloman. New York: Random House, 1969.

———, *Théâtre Complet de Corneille.* Edited by Maurice Rat. 3 vols. Paris: Classiques Garnier, n.d.

Cosenza, Mario E. *Francesco Petrarca and the Revolution of Cola di Rienzo.* Chicago: University of Chicago Press, 1913.

Cresti, Carlo. *Architettura e fascismo.* Florence: Vallecchi Editore, 1986.

Daniels, Elizabeth. *Jesse White Mario: Risorgimento Revolutionary.* Athens: Ohio University Press, 1972.

Davidson, Abraham A. *The Eccentrics and Other American Visionary Painters.* New York: Dutton, 1978.

Deakin, F. W. *The Last Days of Mussolini.* London: Penguin, 1962.

De Felice, Renzo. *Interpretations of Fascism.* Cambridge, Mass.: Harvard University Press, 1977.

———. *Mussolini il duce: gli anni del consenso 1929–1936.* Turin: Einaudi, 1974.

———. *Mussolini il duce: lo stato totalitario 1936–1940.* Turin: Einaudi, 1981.

———. *Mussolini il fascista: la conquista del potere 1921–1925.* Turin: Einaudi, 1966.

———. *Mussolini il fascista: l'organizzazione dello stato fascista 1925–1929.* Turin: Einaudi, 1968.

———. *Mussolini il rivoluzionario.* Turin: Einaudi, 1965.

———. *Storia degli ebrei italiani sotto il fascismo.* 3d ed. Turin: Einaudi, 1972.

De Felice, Renzo and Luigi Goglia. *Mussolini: il mito.* Rome: Laterza, 1983.

De Grazia, Victoria. *The Culture of Consent: Mass Organization of Leisure in Fascist Italy.* Cambridge: Cambridge University Press, 1981.

De Mattei, Rodolfo. *Il pensiero politico di Scipione Ammirato con discorsi inediti.* Milan: Giuffré Editore, 1963.

Desportes, U. "Giuseppe Ceracchi in America and his Busts of George Washington." *The Art Quarterly* 26 (1963): 140–79.

Donadei, Mario. *L'Italia delle cartoline 1919–1945.* Cuneo: Edizioni L'Arciere, 1978.

Donaldson, Ian. *The Rapes of Lucretia: A Myth and Its Transformations.* Oxford: The Clarendon Press, 1982.

Dorey, T. A., ed. *Livy.* London: Routledge & Kegan Paul, 1971.

———. ed. *Tacitus.* London: Routledge & Kegan Paul, 1969.

Emerton, Ephraim, ed. and trans. *Humanism and Tyranny: Studies in the Italian Trecento.*

Cambridge, Mass.: Harvard University Press, 1925.

Everdell, William R. *The End of Kings: A History of Republics and Republicans*. New York: The Free Press, 1983.

Fehl, Philipp. "Thomas Appleton of Livorno and Canova's Statue of George Washington." In *Festschrift Ulrich Middeldorf*, 2 vols., edited by Antje Kosegarten and Peter Tigler, 1:523–52. Berlin: Walter De Gruyter, 1963.

Fellini, Federico. *Fare un film*. Turin: Einaudi, 1980.

———. *Fellini on Fellini*. London: Eyre Methuen, 1976.

———. *Fellini Satyricon*. Edited by Dario Zanelli. New York: Dell, 1970.

———. *Intervista sul cinema*. Edited by Giovanni Grazzini. Rome: Laterza, 1983.

———. *La Dolce Vita*. New York: Ballantine, 1961.

———. *Roma di Federico Fellini*. Edited by Bernardino Zapponi. Bologna: Cappelli, 1972.

Foçillon, Henri. *G. B. Piranesi*. Paris: Laurens, 1928.

Foreman, Walter C. "Fellini's Cinematic City: *Roma* and the Myths of Foundation." *Forum Italicum* 14 (1980): 78–98.

Freud, Sigmund. *Civilization and Its Discontents*. Translated by James Strachey. New York: Norton, 1961.

Funigiello, Joanne B. and Philip J. "EUR, 1936–1942: Town Planning, Architecture, and Fascist Ideology." *Canadian Journal of Italian Studies* 4 (1980–81): 83–103.

Garibaldi, Giuseppe. *Memorie*. Milan: Rizzoli, 1982.

Gerdts, William H. *American Neo-Classic Sculpture: The Marble Resurrection*. New York: Viking, 1973.

Ghirardo, Diane Yvonne. "Italian Architects and Fascist Politics: An Evaluation of the Rationalist's Role in Regime Building." *Journal of the Society of Architectural Historians* 39 (1980): 109–27.

Gibbon, Edward. *The Portable Gibbon: The Decline and Fall of the Roman Empire*. Edited by Dero A. Saunders. New York: Penguin, 1952.

Gilbert, Felix. *History: Choice and Commitment*. Cambridge, Mass.: Harvard University Press, 1977.

———. *Machiavelli and Guicciardini: Politics and History in Sixteenth-Century Florence*. Princeton: Princeton University Press, 1965.

Gili, Jean A. *Stato fascista e cinematografia: repressione e promozione*. Rome: Bulzoni Editore, 1981.

Glut, Donald F. *The Empire Strikes Back*. New York: Ballantine, 1980.

Gordon, D. J. "Giannotti, Michelangelo and the Cult of Brutus." In *The Renaissance Imagination: Essays and Lectures by D.J. Gordon*, edited by Stephen Orgel, pp. 234–45. Berkeley: University of California Press, 1975.

Gossman, Lionel. *The Empire Unpossess'd: An Essay on Gibbon's "Decline and Fall."* Cambridge: Cambridge University Press, 1981.

Graves, Robert. *Claudius the God*. New York: Vintage, 1962.

———. *I, Claudius*. New York: Vintage, 1961.

Greenaway, George William. *Arnold of Brescia*. Cambridge: Cambridge University Press, 1931.

Greene, Thomas M. "Resurrecting Rome: The Double Task of the Humanist Imagination." In *Rome in the Renaissance: The City and the Myth*, edited by P. A. Ramsey, pp. 41–54. Binghamton, N.Y.: Center for Medieval & Early Renaissance Studies, 1982.

Gregor, A. James. *The Ideology of Fascism: The Rationale of Totalitarianism*. New York: The Free Press, 1969.

———. *Interpretations of Fascism*. Morristown, N.J.: General Learning Press, 1974.

———. *Young Mussolini and the Intellectual Origins of Fascism*. Berkeley: University of California Press, 1979.

Gregorovius, Ferdinand. *Rome and Medieval Culture: Selections from History of the City of Rome* in the Middle Ages. Edited by K. F. Morrison. Chicago: University of Chicago Press, 1971.

Guicciardini, Francesco. *Selected Writings*. Edited and translated by Cecil Grayson. London: Oxford University Press, 1965.

Gummere, Richard M. *The American Colonial Mind and the Classical Tradition: Essays in Comparative Culture*. Cambridge, Mass.: Harvard University Press, 1963.

Halstead, Muret. *The Story of the Philippines: The Eldorado of the Orient*. Chicago: Our Possessions Publishing Co., 1898.

Hartt, Frederick. *Giulio Romano*. 2 vols. New Haven: Yale University Press, 1958.

Hartz, Louis B. *The Liberal Tradition in America: An Interpretation of American Political Thought Since the Revolution*. New York: Harcourt, 1955.

Hay, James H. *Popular Film Culture in Fascist Italy*. Bloomington: Indiana University Press, 1987.

Heller, Agnes. *Renaissance Man*. London: Routledge & Kegan Paul, 1978.

Herbert, Robert L. *David, Voltaire, "Brutus," and the French Revolution: An Essay in Art and Politics*. New York: Viking, 1972.

Hibbard, Howard. *Michelangelo*. New York: Harper & Row, 1974.

Hibbert, Christopher. *The Days of the French Revolution*. New York: William Morrow, 1980.

_____. *Garibaldi and His Enemies: The Clash of Arms and Personalities in the Making of Italy*. Boston: Little, Brown, 1966.

_____. *Rome: The Biography of a City*. New York: Norton, 1985.

Hildesheimer, Wolfgang. *Mozart*. Translated by Marion Faber. New York: Vintage, 1983.

Hook, Judith. *The Sack of Rome*. London: Macmillan, 1972.

_____. *Siena: A City and Its History*. London: Hamish Hamilton, 1979.

Hooper, Finley. *Roman Realities*. Detroit: Wayne State University Press, 1979.

Hope, Charles. *Titian*. New York: Harper & Row, 1980.

Horne, Herbert P. *Botticelli: Painter of Florence*. 1908. Reprint. Princeton: Princeton University Press, 1980.

Howard, William. *Gore Vidal's "Caligula."* New York: Warner, 1979.

Hulliung, Mark. *Citizen Machiavelli*. Princeton: Princeton University Press, 1983.

Ippolito, Achille M. *Roma—E.U.R. 83: storia ed analisi critica dell'architettura del quartiere E.U.R. dal piano per l'E42 ai giorni nostri*. Rome: Fratelli Palombi Editori, 1983.

Janson, H. W. *The Sculpture of Donatello*. Princeton: Princeton University Press, 1979.

Jenkins, Marianna. "The Iconography of the Hall of the Consistory in the Palazzo Pubblico, Siena." *Art Bulletin* 54 (1972): 430–51.

Kahn, James. *Return of the Jedi*. New York: Ballantine, 1983.

Kaufman, Hank and Gene Lerner. *Hollywood sul Tevere*. Milan: Sperling & Kupfer, 1982.

Keller, Luzius. *Piranèse et les romantiques français: le myth des escaliers en spirale*. Paris: J. Corti, 1966.

Kirkpatrick, Ivone. *Mussolini: A Study in Power*. New York: Hawthorn Books, 1964.

Koke, Richard J., ed. *American Landscape and Genre Paintings in the New-York Historical Society*. 2 vols. Boston: G. K. Hall, 1982.

Kostof, Spiro. "The Emperor and the Duce: The Planning of the Piazzale Augusto Imperatore in Rome." In *Art and Architecture in the Service of Politics*, edited by Henry A. Millon and Linda Nochlin, pp. 271–325. Cambridge, Mass.: MIT Press, 1978.

_____. *The Third Rome 1870–1950: Traffic and Glory*. Berkeley: University of California Press, 1973.

Landy, Marcia. *Fascism in Film: The Italian Commercial Cinema, 1931–1943*. Princeton: Princeton University Press, 1986.

Liebert, Robert S. *Michelangelo: A Psychoanalytic Study of His Life and Images*. New Haven: Yale University Press, 1983.

The Life of Cola di Rienzo. Translated by John Wright. Toronto: Pontifical Institute of Medieval Studies, 1975.

Lightbrown, Ronald. *Sandro Botticelli.* 2 vols. London: Paul Elek, 1978.

Litchfield, Henry W. "National Exempla Virtutis in Roman Literature." *Harvard Studies in Classical Philology* 25 (1914): 1–72.

Livy. *The Early History of Rome.* Translated by Aubrey De Selincourt. New York: Penguin, 1960.

————. *Rome and Italy.* Translated by Betty Radice. New York: Penguin, 1982.

————. *Rome and the Mediterranean.* Translated by Henry Bettenson. New York: Penguin, 1976.

————. *The War with Hannibal.* Translated by Aubrey De Selincourt. New York: Penguin, 1965.

Low, D. M. *Edward Gibbon 1737–1794.* London: Chatto and Windus, 1937.

Lucas, George. *Star Wars.* New York: Ballantine, 1976.

Ludwig, Emil. *Talks With Mussolini.* Boston: Little, Brown, 1933.

Lyttleton, Adrian, ed. *Italian Fascisms: From Pareto to Gentile.* London: Jonathan Cape, 1973.

MacDonald, William L. "Excavation, Restoration, and Italian Architecture of the 1930s." In *In Search of Modern Architecture: A Tribute to Henry-Russell Hitchcock,* edited by Helen Searing, pp. 298–320. Cambridge, Mass.: MIT Press, 1982.

MacGregor-Hastle, Roy. *The Day of the Lion: The Life and Death of Fascist Italy 1922–1945.* New York: Coward-McCann, 1964.

Machiavelli, Niccolò. *The Portable Machiavelli.* Edited and translated by Peter Bondanella and Mark Musa. New York: Penguin, 1979.

MacKendrick, Paul. *The Mute Stones Speak: The Story of Archaeology in Italy.* New York: St. Martin's Press, 1960.

Mack Smith, Denis. *Cavour: A Biography.* New York: Knopf, 1985.

————. *Cavour and Garibaldi 1860: A Study in Political Conflict.* 1954. Reprint. Cambridge: Cambridge University Press, 1985.

————. *Mussolini.* New York: Knopf, 1982.

————. *Mussolini's Roman Empire.* New York: Viking, 1976.

————. *Victor Emanuel, Cavour, and the Risorgimento.* London: Oxford University Press, 1971.

————, ed. *Garibaldi.* Englewood Cliffs, N.J.: Prentice-Hall, 1969.

Markham, Felix. *Napoleon.* New York: New American Library, 1963.

Mason, Sheila M. "Livy and Montesquieu." In *Livy,* edited by T. A. Dorey, pp. 118–58. London: Routledge & Kegan Paul, 1971.

Massena, Victor, Prince d'Essling and Eugene Muntz. *Pétrarque, ses études d'art, son influence sur les artistes, ses portraits, et ceux de Laure.* Paris: Gazette des beaux-arts, 1902.

Masters, Roger D. *The Political Philosophy of Rousseau.* Princeton: Princeton University Press, 1968.

Mazzocco, Angelo. "The Antiquarianism of Francesco Petrarca." *The Journal of Medieval and Renaissance Studies* 7 (1977): 203–24.

————. "Petrarca, Poggio, and Biondo: Humanism's Foremost Interpreters of Roman Ruins." In *Francis Petrarch, Six Centuries Later: A Symposium,* edited by Aldo Scaglione, pp. 353–63. Chapel Hill: University of North Carolina Press, 1975.

Metastasio, Pietro. *The Works of Metastasio: Translated from the Italian by John Hoole.* 2 vols. London: T. Davies, 1767.

Michaelis, Meir. *Mussolini and the Jews: German-Italian Relations and the Jewish Question in Italy 1922–45.* Oxford: Institute for Jewish Affairs, 1978.

Millon, Henry A. "The Role of History of Architecture in Fascist Italy." *Journal of the Society of Architectural Historians* 24 (1965): 53–59.

————. "Some New Towns in Italy in the 1930's." In *Art and Architecture in the Service of*

Politics, edited by Henry A. Millon and Linda Nochlin, pp. 326–41. Cambridge, Mass.: MIT Press, 1978.

Momigliano, Arnaldo. "Vico's *Scienza Nuova*: Roman 'Bestioni' and Roman 'Eroi'." *History and Theory* 5 (1966): 3–23.

Mommsen, Theodor E. "Petrarch and the Decoration of the Sala Virorum Illustrium in Padua." In *Medieval and Renaissance Studies*, edited by Eugene F. Rice, pp. 130–74. Ithaca: Cornell University Press, 1959.

————. "Petrarch's Conception of the Dark Ages." In *Medieval and Renaissance Studies*, edited by Eugene F. Rice, pp. 106–29. Ithaca: Cornell University Press, 1959.

Montesquieu, Charles Louis de Secondat. *Considerations on the Causes of the Greatness of the Romans and Their Decline.* Translated by David Lowenthal. Ithaca: Cornell University Press, 1968.

Monteverdi, Claudio. *L'incoronazione di Poppea.* With Rachel Yakar, Eric Tappy, and Trudeliese Schmitd. Cond. Nikolaus Harnoncourt. Monteverdi Ensemble of the Zurich Operahouse. Telefunken 6.35593 FK, 1981.

Moore, Will G. *The Classical Drama of France.* London: Oxford University Press, 1971.

Mozart, Wolfgang A. *La clemenza di Tito.* With Janet Baker, Yvonne Minton, and Stuart Burrows. Cond. Colin Davis. Chorus and Orchestra of the Royal Opera House, Covent Garden. Phillips 6703–079, 1976.

————. *Lucio Silla.* With Ferrando Ferrari, Fiorenza Cossotto, Dora Gatta, and Anna Maria Rota. Cond. Carlo Felice Cillario. Angelicum Chamber Orchestra and Polyphonic Chorus of Milan. RCA VICS-6117, 1969.

Mussolini, Benito. *My Autobiography.* Rev. ed. London: Hutchinson, 1939.

————. *My Diary 1915–17.* Translated by Rita Wellman. Boston: Small, Maynard, 1925.

————. *Opera omnia di Benito Mussolini.* 35 vols. Edited by Edoardo and Diulio Susmel. Florence: La Fenice, 1951–62.

Niccolini, Renato, ed. *Roma capitale 1870–1911: Dalla mostra al museo.* Venice: Marsilio Editori, 1983.

Noble, Louis Lebrand. *The Course of Empire, Voyage of Life, and Other Pictures of Thomas Cole, N. A..* Edited by Elliot S. Vessell. 1853. Reprint. Cambridge, Mass.: Harvard University Press, 1964.

Osborne, Charles. *The Complete Operas of Mozart: A Critical Guide.* New York: Da Capo Press, 1978.

Parker, Harold T. *The Cult of Antiquity and the French Revolutionaries: A Study in the Development of the Revolutionary Spirit.* Chicago: University of Chicago Press, 1937.

Pastrone, Giovanni. *Cabiria: visione storica del III secolo a. c..* Edited by Roberto Radicati and Ruggero Rossi. Turin: Museo Nazionale del Cinema, 1977.

Penthouse. 11, no. 9.

Petrarca, Francesco. *Letters from Petrarch.* Translated by Morris Bishop. Bloomington: Indiana University Press, 1966.

————. *Petrarch: A Humanist Among Princes.* Edited and translated by David Thompson. New York: Harper, 1971.

————. *Petrarch's "Africa."* Translated by Thomas G. Bergin and Alice S. Wilson. New Haven: Yale University Press, 1977.

————. *Petrarch's "Bucolicum Carmen."* Edited and translated by Thomas G. Bergin. New Haven: Yale University Press, 1974.

————. *The Triumphs of Petrarch.* Edited and translated by Ernest Hatch Wilkins. Chicago: University of Chicago Press, 1962.

Phillips, Mark. *Francesco Guicciardini: The Historian's Craft.* Toronto: University of Toronto Press, 1977.

Pignatti, Terisio. *Veronese.* 2 vols. Venice: Alfieri, 1976.

Piovene, Guido and Remigio Marini. *L'opera completa del Veronese*. Milan: Rizzoli, 1968.
———— and Anna Pallucchini. *L'opera completa di Giambattista Tiepolo*. Milan: Rizzoli, 1968.
Pitkin, Hanna Fenichel. *Fortune Is a Woman: Gender and Politics in the Thought of Niccolò Machiavelli*. Berkeley: University of California Press, 1984.
Pocock, J. G. A. *The Machiavellian Moment: Florentine Political Thought and the Atlantic Republican Tradition*. Princeton: Princeton University Press, 1975.
Pompa, Leon. *Vico: A Study of the "New Science"*. London: Cambridge University Press, 1975.
Quel motivetto che fa: Duce. With Daniele Serra, Carlo Buti, and Alfredo Del Pelo. Editrice Fonit–Cetra, Number FC3644, Series 4, Number 4, n.d.
Racine, Jean. *Théâtre Complet de Racine*. Edited by Maurice Rat. Paris: Classiques Garnier, 1960.
————. *Three Plays of Racine*. Translated by George Dillon. Chicago: University of Chicago Press, 1961.
Ramsey, P. A., ed. *Rome in the Renaissance: The City and the Myth*. Binghamton, N.Y.: Center for Medieval & Early Renaissance Studies, 1982.
Richter, Melvin, ed. *The Political Theory of Montesquieu*. Cambridge: Cambridge University Press, 1977.
Ridolfi, Roberto. *The Life of Francesco Guicciardini*. Translated by Cecil Grayson. New York: Knopf, 1968.
————. *The Life of Niccolò Machiavelli*. Translated by Cecil Grayson. Chicago: University of Chicago Press, 1963.
Robbins, Caroline. *The Eighteenth-Century Commonwealthman*. Cambridge, Mass.: Harvard University Press, 1959.
Rosen, Charles. *The Classical Style: Haydn, Mozart, Beethoven*. New York: Norton, 1972.
Rosenblum, Robert. *Transformations in Late Eighteenth-Century Art*. Princeton: Princeton University Press, 1967.
Roth, Cecil. *The Last Florentine Republic*. 1925. Reprint. New York: Russell & Russell, 1968.
Rousseau, Jean-Jacques. *The First and Second Discourses*. Translated by Roger D. Masters. New York: St. Martin's Press, 1964.
————. *On the Social Contract*. Edited by Roger D. Masters and translated by Judith R. Masters. New York: St. Martin's Press, 1978.
Rubinstein, Nicolai. "Political Ideas in Sienese Art: The Frescoes by Ambrogio Lorenzetti and Taddeo di Bartolo in the Palazzo Pubblico." *Journal of the Warburg and Courtauld Institutes* 21 (1958): 179–207.
Rydell, Robert W. *All the World's a Fair: Visions of Empire at American International Expositions, 1876–1916*. Chicago: University of Chicago Press, 1984.
Salomone, A. William, ed. *Italy from the Risorgimento to Fascism: An Inquiry into the Origins of the Totalitarian State*. New York: Doubleday, 1970.
Salutati, Coluccio. "De Tyranno." In *Humanism and Tyranny: Studies in the Italian Trecento*, edited and translated by Ephraim Emerton, pp. 70–116. Cambridge, Mass.: Harvard University Press, 1925.
Salvatorelli, Luigi. *The Risorgimento: Thought & Action*. New York: Harper, 1970.
Schellhase, Kenneth C. *Tacitus in Renaissance Political Thought*. Chicago: University of Chicago Press, 1976.
Schnapper, Antoine. *David: Temoin de son temps*. Paris: Bibliothèque des Arts, 1980.
Searing, Helen, ed. *In Search of Modern Architecture: A Tribute to Henry-Russell Hitchcock*. Cambridge, Mass.: MIT Press, 1982.
Seldes, George. *Sawdust Caesar: The Untold History of Mussolini and Fascism*. New York: Harper, 1935.
Shackleton, Robert. "Montesquieu and Machiavelli: A Reappraisal." *Comparative Literature*

Studies 1 (1964): 1–14.
Shakespeare, William. The Complete Works of Shakespeare. Edited by Hardin Craig. Glenview, Ill.: Scott, Foresman, 1961.
Simmons, J. L. Shakespeare's Pagan World: The Roman Tragedies. Charlottesville: University Press of Virginia, 1973.
The Simon & Schuster Book of the Opera. New York: Simon & Schuster, 1978.
Skinner, Quentin. The Foundations of Modern Political Thought. Vol. 1, The Renaissance. Cambridge: Cambridge University Press, 1978.
Smith, Patrick J. The Tenth Muse: A Historical Study of the Opera Libretto. New York: Schirmer, 1970.
Solomon, Jon. The Ancient World in the Cinema. Cranbury, N.J.: A. S. Barnes, 1978.
Southard, Edna Carter. The Frescoes in Siena's Palazzo Pubblico, 1289–1539: Studies in Imagery and Relations to Other Communal Palaces in Tuscany. 2 vols. New York: Garland, 1979.
Spencer, Theodore. Shakespeare and the Nature of Man. New York: Collier, 1966.
———. Shakespeare: The Roman Plays. London: Longmans, Green, 1963.
Starobinski, Jean. 1789: The Emblems of Reason. Translated by Barbara Bray. Charlottesville: University Press of Virginia, 1982.
Strauss, Gerald, ed. and trans. Manifestations of Discontent in Germany on the Eve of the Reformation. Bloomington: Indiana University Press, 1971.
Stubbs, John C. Federico Fellini: A Guide to References and Resources. Boston: G. K. Hall, 1978.
Tacitus. The Annals of Imperial Rome. Translated by Michael Grant. New York: Penguin, 1971.
Tennenbaum, Edward R. The Fascist Experience: Italian Society and Culture, 1922–1940. New York: Basic Books, 1972.
Thullier, Jacques. L"opera completa di Nicolas Poussin. Milan: Rizzoli, 1974.
Tietze-Conrat, E. Mantegna: Paintings, Drawings, Engravings. London: Phaidon Press, 1955.
Toffanin, Giuseppe. Machiavelli e il tacitismo. 1921. Reprint. Naples: Guida Editori, 1972.
Trapp, J. B. "The Poet Laureate: Rome, Renovatio and Translatio Imperii." In Rome in the Renaissance: The City and the Myth, edited by P. A. Ramsey, pp. 93–130. Binghamton, N.Y.: Center for Medieval and Early Renaissance Studies, 1982.
Traversi, Derek. Shakespeare: The Roman Plays. Stanford: Stanford University Press, 1963.
Trevelyan, George Macaulay. Garibaldi and the Making of Italy. London: Longmans, Green, 1948.
———. Garibaldi and the Thousand. London: Longmans, Green, 1948.
———. Garibaldi's Defense of the Roman Republic. London: Longmans, Green, 1949.
Vico, Giambattista. The New Science of Giambattista Vico. Translated and edited by Thomas G. Bergin and Max H. Fisch. Ithaca: Cornell University Press, 1970.
Vittori, Giuliano, ed. C'era una volta il duce: il regime in cartolina. Rome: Savelli, 1975.
Vivaldi, Antonio. Tito Manlio. With Giancarlo Luccardi, Rose Wagemann, Julia Hamari, and Margaret Marshall. Cond. Vittorio Negri. Berlin Chamber Orchestra. Phillips 6769 004, n.d.
Walton, Guy. "The Lucretia Panel in the Isabella Stewart Gardner Museum in Boston." In Essays in Honor of Walter Friedlaender, pp. 177–86. New York: Institute for Fine Arts, 1965.
Weiss, Roberto. The Renaissance Discovery of Classical Antiquity. Oxford: Basil Blackwell, 1969.
Wethey, Harold E. The Paintings of Titian. 3 vols. London: Phaidon Press, 1975.
Wick, Wendy C. George Washington, An American Icon: The Eighteenth-Century Graphic Portraits. Washington: Smithsonian Institution Traveling Exhibition Service, 1982.
Wilkins, Ernest Hatch. Life of Petrarch. Chicago: University of Chicago Press, 1961.
———. Studies in the Life and Works of Petrarch. Cambridge, Mass.: The Medieval Academy

of America, 1955.

Wills, Garry. *Cincinnatus: George Washington & the Enlightenment*. New York: Doubleday, 1984.

Wilton-Ely, John. *The Mind and Art of G. B. Piranesi*. London: Thames & Hudson, 1978.

Wood, Gordon. *The Creation of the American Republic 1776–1787*. Chapel Hill: University of North Carolina Press, 1969.

Wright, Nathalia. *American Novelists in Italy—The Discoverers: Allston to James*. Philadelphia: University of Pennsylvania Press, 1965.

Young, G. M. *Gibbon*. London: Peter Davies, 1932.

INDEX

Page numbers in boldface refer to illustrations.

Adams, John, 128, 129, 130; *Defense of the Constitutions of America*, 130
Adrian IV (pope), 31
Agrippa, 6
Agrippina the Younger, 19
Alciati, Andrea, 78–80; *Annotationes in Cornelium Tacitum*, 78–79, 81; *Emblemata*, 79, **80**, 81
Alfieri, Vittorio, 113–14; *Bruto primo*, 137; *Bruto secondo*, 137
Allori, Alessandro, 76–78; *The Consul Flaminius in Council with the Achaeans*, 76; *Julius Caesar Receives Tribute from Egypt*, 76; *Syphax of Numidia Receives Scipio, Victor Over Hasdrubal in Spain*, 76; *The Return of Cicero from Exile*, 76, **77**
Ammirato, Scipione, 83; *Discourses on Cornelius Tacitus*, 83
Anderson, Poul, 232–33
Antiquity, cult of: in "civic" humanism, 37–46; in the American Revolution, 129–30, 136–37; in the French Revolution, 130–36, 138–39, 141–43; in the Italian Risorgimento, 160–65; as justification for imperialism, 165–66; in Italian fascism, 172–206
Antoninus Pius (emperor), 20
Antony, Mark, 87–89, 215, **216**
Appleton, Thomas, 144
Aquinas, St. Thomas, 30
Arcimbaldo, Angelo, 66
Aristotle, 41–42
Armellini, Carlo, 160
Arminius, 68–69, **70–71**
Arnold of Brescia, 31
Asimov, Isaac: invention of "galactic empire" theme by, 229; link to Gibbon in, 229; influence on science fiction cinema of, 233; *Foundation* trilogy by, 229–33
Aude, Joseph, 143
Augustine, St., 23–25, 84; *The City of God*, 23, 31

Augustus (emperor), 8, 18, 150; in Corneille, 106–7; in Montesquieu, 119; compared to Napoleon, 189; compared to Mussolini, 191, 201–3; in Graves, 220, **221**, 222
Aurelius, Marcus (emperor), 20, 61, 224, 225, **226**, 227
Autocracy, 8

Bara, Theda, 210, **212**
Barzini, Luigi, Jr., 35, 183, 206
Barzini, Luigi, Sr., 177
"Battle of the Books," 21
Beccafumi, Domenico, 52–55, 73, 79; *Decapitation of Spurius Cassius*, **54**; *Execution of Marcus Manlius "Capitolinus,"* **55**
Berthélemy, Jean-Simon, 133; *Manlius Torquatus Condemning His Son to Death*, **134**
Biondo, Flavio, 2
Boccaccio, Giovanni, 66
Boccalini, Traiano, 83–84; *Advertisements from Parnassus*, 83; *Commentaries on Cornelius Tacitus*, 83
Boiston, Joseph, 141
Bonaparte, Napoleon. *See* Napoleon
Borgia, Cesare, 60
Boscoli, Paolo, 56, 59
Bottai, Giuseppe, 202
Botticelli, Sandro, 48–52, 91; *The Tragedy of Lucretia*, **50–51**
Bracciolini, Poggio, 37, 60
Brass, Tinto, 215, 218, 234; *Caligula*, **219**, 234
Brenet, Nicholas Guy, 133
Brigham, J. H., 168
Bruni, Leonardo, 38–39, 60, 66; *History of Florence*, 38; *Panegyric to the City of Florence*, 38
Brutus, Lucius Junius ("First" Brutus): in Livy, 11, 47; in Di Bartolo, 23, 42; in Machiavelli, 61; in von Hutten, 69–70; in Shakespeare, 84–85; cult of during French Revolution, 130–31, 143; in David, 132, 141, **142**, 143; in Alfieri, 137–38, 141; compared to Mirabeau, 143; in Graves, 220